OCR
DRAMA
FOR GCSE

DAVID CROSS AND
CHRISTOPHER REYNOLDS

Official Publisher Partnership

HODDER
EDUCATION
AN HACHETTE UK COMPANY

Hachette UK's policy is to use papers that are natural, renewable and recyclable products and made from wood grown in sustainable forests. The logging and manufacturing processes are expected to conform to the environmental regulations of the country of origin.

Orders: please contact Bookpoint Ltd, 130 Milton Park, Abingdon, Oxon OX14 4SB. Telephone: (44) 01235 827720. Fax: (44) 01235 400454. Lines are open 9.00–5.00, Monday to Saturday, with a 24-hour message answering service. Visit our website at www.hoddereducation.co.uk

First published in 2009 by
Hodder Education,
an Hachette UK company
338 Euston Road
London NW1 3BH

Impression number	5	4	3	2	1	
Year	2014	2013	2012	2011	2010	2009

Cover image © Donald Cooper/Photostage

Typeset in Palatino and Helvetica Neue
Diagrams on pages 36 & 37 by Tony Wilkins
Editorial and production by Topics – The Creative Partnership Ltd, Exeter
Printed in Italy

A catalogue record for this title is available from the British Library

ISBN: 978 0340 983 409

Contents

Introduction

The aim of this book is to help you develop a wide range of drama skills as you work towards your assessed units for GCSE. You will also gain a good understanding of the course itself and what examiners will need to see if you are to gain high marks for your GCSE Drama.

The book is divided into three sections.

Section 1: Introducing Key Course Concepts

- The basic requirements of the course are explained.

- The concepts of 'tools' and 'drama language' are introduced.

- Each of the Areas of Study is explored:
    - Its meaning is defined.

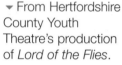

▼ From Hertfordshire County Youth Theatre's production of *Lord of the Flies*.

- Activities are suggested that you might carry out to aid your understanding.

- There is direct advice from experienced examiners in the form of hints and tips to give you an idea of what they will be looking for.

- For those of you who work really fast, there are sections giving you an opportunity to stretch your skills through extension activities.

Section 2: Creating Drama and Developing Skills

- A series of self-contained drama projects are offered for you to work through, focusing on different aspects of the Areas of Study.

- These projects can be used to develop your skills in drama but might also become the starting points for *Unit 1 From Page to Stage, Unit 2 Drama in the Making* and *Unit 3 From Concept to Creation*.

Section 3: Preparing for Assessment

- This is where you will find vital practical tips and suggestions about each unit of the course. There is advice about:

  - how to record what you do for your Working Record
  - presenting the best of your work
  - preparing for the practical examination
  - undertaking the practical examination
  - choosing from four Context Briefs for the final assessment.

At the end of the book you will also find a **Resources** list and a **Glossary**. All terms highlighted in blue in the text are explained in the **Glossary**.

We hope that this book will help you to get the best from your course and from working as a team with your class or group.

David Cross and Christopher Reynolds

SECTION 1
Introducing Key Course Concepts

The Purpose of the Course

This is how the course is summarised:

By following the course candidates will gather knowledge and understanding of drama and theatre and related skills, and of the social, historical and cultural influences that inform the way drama is devised and structured.

This tells you two things:

- There will be a range of skills to learn about and draw together in your work.
- There will always be a context, and whatever that context might be, it will have an impact on what you produce.

The work you do will never be an accident or haphazard: it will be structured, carefully put together by you, deliberately and for a purpose.

The course *'emphasises and assesses drama process as well as the final product'*. So, whilst the final outcome of any work you do in drama is of course important, it is not the only thing of importance. *How* and *why* you have reached that point is equally important.

◄ New writing for young actors often explores challenging contemporary issues. Mark Ravenhill's *Citizenship*, one of the plays commissioned recently by the National Theatre for the NT Connections project, explores the difficulty and loneliness of growing up.

Any study you make of texts or of different periods or aspects of drama is intended to help you create better drama. During the course you will use the content and knowledge of drama process to interpret text and to devise your own drama. You will learn to evaluate your work as part of the process as you devise material and define performance.

Very often, evaluation is seen as writing about something after it has happened in order to express opinions about what has been produced and to recommend how it could be improved. In this course, evaluation is partly about this, but mostly it is linked with the process – what you're doing, as you're doing it. So you will need to consider what you are doing at all times. This will involve:

- reviewing
- redesigning
- being honest about what you are creating
- considering whether you have selected the right tools for the job
- then building the results of your evaluation into the next stage.

The course actively encourages you to bring your own cultural experiences to your work, whatever they may be. You will be introduced to a wide range of 'texts' in different modes – spoken, written, aural or visual (moving or still images). You will be challenged to look at the world around you and what happens in it. You may be asked to view the world through history, or to explore different cultures and customs and consider how they might affect your work. You will need to keep a very open mind and to expect to look at things from different perspectives, some of which might seem strange to you at first.

Understanding and knowing how to use the 'language of drama' is also important in any work you create and comment upon. You *'will acquire the ability to develop drama outcomes using a variety of appropriate terminology, utilising the knowledge and understanding developed through the course of study'*.

And now for probably the most exciting part of the introduction, summarising what is expected at the end of your course:

> *Through candidates' understanding of the processes involved in drama they will improve their performance skills, by creating work themselves, and preparing existing text(s) for performance. They will develop: qualities of imagination; the ability to create drama; ways of communicating intention; skills in working with others to a common purpose; and the beginnings of artistic evaluation.*

By absorbing and understanding what it is that makes drama work, by knowing the tools of drama and which to select and when to use them, you should be able to work successfully with others in creating drama. Your imagination will have developed so that you can do this in an exciting way, and you will be able to start having an opinion about what you have created and be able to explain why it works or perhaps why some aspects don't work.

The Tools and the Language of Drama

Electricians, hair stylists and beauticians, plumbers and mechanics have a set of tools so that they can complete their tasks to a high standard and satisfy their customers. Architects, doctors and computer experts have their tools too, specialised to meet the demands of their roles.

In the same way, drama has its 'tools'. Aspects of the GCSE Drama course introduce you to tools you can use to achieve high-quality drama and satisfy the examiner. If you think about the different ideas you are introduced to as a set of tools, you can 'select' the right one to achieve your purpose. As you practise your drama, you will become more expert at selecting and using the right tool.

Technicians or builders, teachers or lawyers use a common 'language' for the skills needed for their work. This acts as a sort of shorthand and ensures that everyone is talking about things using the same terms, so that there is shared meaning, and everyone understands each other.

By becoming competent in using the 'language of drama', you will become more confident in your drama. You will be able to express ideas clearly, and others will know what you are talking about without you needing to give lots of explanation.

Most of the tools and the language of drama will be introduced to you in the discussion of the four Contexts below and the units on the six Areas of Study on pages 8–79.

Terms highlighted in blue in this book are explained in the Glossary on page 260.

The Contexts

There are four Contexts that cover the different ways you will be working. These are:

■ Deviser   ■ Designer   ■ Director   ■ **Performer**.

Deviser

In the Context of Deviser, you can create the drama, or it can be work created by another person (by a playwright and published as a play, for example).

The course requires two things of you:

■ that you are able to create script yourself using the appropriate Areas of Study

■ that you have some understanding of how playwrights have created a script, and the particular skills they have used to do so.

So, for example, when you are working on structure, you will be thinking about how to structure and shape your own work and will also look at how and why a playwright has structured and shaped a play. This applies to any of the Areas of Study that you might use as part of learning about devising.

Designer

Students taking GCSE Drama used to look at aspects like make-up or costume design as separate elements. This is not the approach of this course, which directs you to view design as something that influences all aspects of a piece of drama.

Once an idea is being used to devise drama, there will be suggestions about how it will be presented, how its message will be put across, or what sort of experience the audience will have. The elements of design are linked to each other, and rely on one another, so should be considered together, not in isolation. This means that set design, costume design, lighting design, make-up, sound design, properties and furniture will all be part of the process of creating a piece of drama.

The course also requires each student to experience and develop understanding of design, to test out their ideas by planning, creating mock-ups or scale models and design sheets. Every area of design may make its own contribution to creating a piece of drama, but in some cases all elements may not be necessary, depending on the genre or style of the piece.

It is important in this Context to have a crystal-clear understanding of the language of drama.

Director

The Context of Director does not mean bossing everyone else around. A good Director will listen to the ideas of others, and will use them. Sometimes direction will take place as a combined action with several of you taking on the role jointly.

Two key elements are:
- reviewing what has gone on so far
- making decisions to improve the drama.

In this book we use the terms **edit**, **adapt** and **add** to refer to steps in the process of reviewing and improving your longer pieces of work during their development. Some pieces of drama produced will be work in progress but the effect of the Director will still be evident.

Performer

The Context of Performer probably seems the most obvious. It relates to the 'doing' of the drama – communicating the drama to an audience through varied performance styles and conventions.

It is not just about acting though. The course requirements make it clear that as well as communicating through role and character, you should also consider communicating through symbol in this Context.

Integration of the Contexts

The four Contexts should be understood separately along with the language of drama that is associated with each. However, as the course progresses you will learn to combine them. So, if you are working in a group, you may begin in the role of Deviser, then switch to Designer, followed by Director, back to Deviser, then become Director again, and finally Performer. The roles will interlink so that effective drama is created.

The course encourages you to develop skills and understanding in using all four approaches when it is appropriate to do so, and for these approaches to work together.

The Areas of Study

The six Areas of Study are the foundations of the course and will underpin all your work during the course. They are:

1 Character, Context and Plot
2 Structure
3 Audience and Performance Space
4 Improvisation
5 Genre, Performance Style and Convention
6 The Semiotics of Drama and Theatre.

Having a clear understanding of these elements of the course is the best starting point for interpreting scripts or creating your own. So let's take a closer look at each Area of Study.

1.1 Character, Context and Plot

What the course demands

The minimum requirement for Area of Study 1 is that character, context and plot must be studied, analysed and applied practically throughout the course.

Your aims

Character: You are going to learn not only how a character is created by an actor or writer, but also how character is communicated to an audience, defined by ideas within the play and informed by the character's motivations.

Context: You will explore the context of drama scenarios using the questions: 'What?', 'Who?', 'Why?', 'Where?', 'When?' You will begin to understand how the situation or circumstances in which a piece of drama is set or devised, including historical, cultural or social influences, help to shape it.

Plot: You will learn about the different ways the action of a play can be plotted, looking at how a character responds to a situation and how other characters, in turn, respond.

The examiner will need evidence that you know what each of the three main terms means. So let's have a look at character, context and plot in more detail.

Character

This term will probably be quite easy to grasp. You will have heard people say things like 'She's a funny character ...', or 'Look out, he's a tough character ...'.

Usually this means they are recognising one or more features about the person. The feature may be about how they look, or how they sound. It might be about the way the person laughs, or the way they speak. Perhaps it is about the way they walk, or is it about the way they behave? Are they funny or sad, jolly or grumpy?

Action

On your own, choose someone you think other people in your class might know or recognise. Choose an adult, perhaps a teacher or someone else who works in the school, or a television or film star. Do **not** choose another student.

How would you recognise your person? Make a list of features by which you might recognise them. Take just **5 minutes** to do this. Then share your list with another student and see if you can guess each other's person.

Sometimes, the features about another person may have something to do with what they do, or their position in society. It might be that they have power, or that they have none. It might be that they are a criminal, or someone very kind.

Action

In small groups, agree on a person with a particular position in society that you all know or might recognise. Then make a list of the features by which you might recognise them.

One of you can act as notetaker or scribe. Have two columns in your list: one for personal features like being happy or kind, the other for things to do with the person's position in society.

Do this again for a second example, picking someone different.

For example, you might choose:

- someone with a position in society such as a police officer, school caretaker, lollipop woman/man, refuse collector, bank manager, farmer, member of a pop group
- a real person such as your teacher, your postman/woman, the person who services the car of someone you know
- a famous person such as the prime minister, a film star or a sportsperson.

The features you have listed are some of the things that might define the person.

In a play, the actor will be representing a character or creating a role. To be successful, the role must come to life, must have

INTRODUCING KEY COURSE CONCEPTS

SECTION 1

9

meaning. The features on your lists are the kinds of things that an actor or director will have to explore and use in developing the role.

Here are some features that might define a role:

- *Status:* The character's power or position in society
- *Class:* Are they poor or well off, working class or middle class?
- *Beliefs:* Are there things they feel strongly about that drive them?
- *Personality:* Individual features about the person
- *History:* Their background, how they grew up, what makes them what they are
- *Job:* What they do, their occupation
- *Attitudes:* How they see life or other people, or themselves.

There may be some aspects that are not defined for you. Can you think of any possible reasons for this?

Action

Turn to page 80 and read Scenario A.

In small groups, build up the profile for the character of the street man. Use the list above to help you. You will have to use the information provided to build up your character. Some things will be obvious, there may be clues for other aspects, but for some there will be no information at all.

Sometimes characters are described as 'flat', or 'one-dimensional'. This means that they have no depth, that an audience watching them is not able to discover much about them, or does not know why they are behaving in the way they are. There are just the obvious characteristics on show.

Action

One of your group should stand in the centre. This person represents the street man in Scenario A. One at a time, mould this person to demonstrate a characteristic of him that could be represented visually. Imagine the person is a statue and you are sculpting it.

Using simple characters can be effective. We can recognise certain sorts of people by set characteristics, and this can be an easy way to communicate meaning to an audience, or to create comedy or fear. There are traditional expectations of certain sorts of characters.

<table>
<tr><td>**Action**</td><td>Turn to page 81 and read Scenario B.

What are the characteristics of the role of the security guard? Would they be different if the security guard was old or young? Would they be different if the guard was a man or a woman? How would the security guard be dressed? What would their voice sound like?

In pairs, try out the scene described from when the young person is leaving the checkout and walking out through the exit.

Try it with different outcomes. Focus on how the security guard speaks and behaves. After each run through, talk about what made a difference, and how you might change the scene by using different voices, showing a different character. How would you show the scene if the security guard was mean and nasty, or kind and understanding?</td></tr>
</table>

Characters such as the security guard of a supermarket may create in our minds a set of images, a set of characteristics that represent the idea of 'security guard'. This is often called a stereotype.

<table>
<tr><td>**Action**</td><td>Can you think of any other stereotypes? Use a still image and give the image a caption or title, such as 'The Grumpy Grandparent' or 'The Bad-tempered Teenager'.</td></tr>
</table>

Some plays use stereotypes deliberately, almost as a form of shorthand, a quick way to give information to the audience. The best examples are in television soaps such as *EastEnders* or *Coronation Street*, where characters become instantly recognisable because of the way they behave.

Some characters may remind us of people we know. When stereotypes are used in this way they become what are called stock characters, who represent a type or occupation, rather than an individual. So you might have the barman or barmaid, the flighty young girl or the drunken young man, the layabout who is always looking for a way to make easy money, the elderly couple, the nagging wife or husband, and so on.

Action

Look at the photograph below.

What sort of characteristics would you want to develop from the evidence you have from the photo? Be inspired by the photo and develop your own character. Be interviewed by someone else about your life.

There are other ways that character might be used.

In the medieval play *Everyman*, the characters all represent an idea or a quality. So, for example, the character named

Everyman represents all living people, while the character named Good Deeds represents all the good things Everyman has done in his life. Even things that happen are represented by a character in the play. For example, Death is portrayed as a character who comes to collect the body of the person who is going to die. This idea was used in many early plays. (You can find a brief summary of *Everyman* in Scenario E on page 83.)

Action | Can you think of any characters in plays or films who represent an idea or thing rather than a real person?

Review

When building up and shaping a character you need to consider:

- defining influences – information or clues that might define the role (see features listed on page 10)
- appropriate depth of character – stock character or rounded individual?

Learning how to select what will be best to make an effective character is an essential part of your course.

Context

The context for any drama is the situation or circumstances in which it is set or devised. This context may have historical, cultural or social influences. Probably the best way to understand this is to ask five questions of your script or stimulus for drama:

- What?   - Who?   - Why?   - Where?   - When?

What? Your answer will be a description of the action. What is actually happening? Is there a narrative, is it a representation?

Who? Your answer will explain who the main characters are. What is their background, what makes them what they are? Have they families or friends? How are they linked to other characters?

Why? To answer this you will need to decide what is the reason for or cause of what is happening. Is it happening because of an action, such as the burglary in Scenario C on page 82? Does the drama simply tell a story, or entertain? Or is there a message that the writer wants to transmit? Are the audience going to be educated or experience a spectacle? Is it a snapshot of real life of the type often presented in documentary theatre?

Where? Your answer will give the location of the action. The ancient Greeks restricted the settings in their plays to locations that could be represented in real life, where no imagination needed to be used. Shakespeare's plays often transport us to other countries, or even to imaginary islands where magic occurs. Many modern plays, for example those by Alan Ayckbourn, are set in ordinary people's living rooms.

When? Your answer will refer not only to simple time issues such as the time of day, but also to time in history. The time in history will bring with it different social conditions, different expectations, different customs, different ways of looking at things.

Use these five ways of establishing the context both when you develop your own drama and when you study existing scripts.

Action

Consider Scenarios A and B on pages 80–82. Then devise a short scene for one of them, but set it 100 years ago. What would change? How would the characters speak? How would they be dressed? What else might change?

Cultural differences caused by time or by cultural backgrounds can have a big impact. For example, the role of women has changed considerably over the last 100 years and in some societies the roles for men and women are very clearly defined.

Action

Devise a short scene using Scenario F on page 84. Prepare two versions: one set in the present, the other set in a time when women did not have the vote and were treated almost as the servants of men.

Remember that there are some cultures where the role of women is still very subservient to that of men.

In some plays, the context becomes more important than the characters. This might be the case where the horrors of war are the focus, or perhaps poverty and poor living conditions. Here the creator of the drama might use characters almost as part of the stage picture rather than using characters who are fully developed in their own right.

Action

Look carefully at the photograph below. If this was the stimulus for a drama, what do you think might be the context? What characters might you choose to be part of such a drama?

Develop a series of **still images** (sometimes called freeze-frame pictures) where the context is the most important feature. Repeat this, making the characters most important. How does the change of focus affect what you do?

Plot

This term is used to describe what happens, and when. It is the story that is to be told through the action and how the telling of it is organised. The plot can be linear (a straight line), telling the story chronologically (in time order), but this isn't always the case. Reviewers of plays sometimes write about a play's plot 'bending and twisting', suggesting that the storyline is not a linear, chronological account.

Plot will be influenced by the nature of the content of the drama. So, a plot based on historical events may well be more straightforward than one based on complicated personal relationships. The plot can also be centred on an object or other focus. Good examples here from well-known stories are the ring in *Lord of the Rings* and the sword, Excalibur, in the legends of King Arthur. Sometimes a quest may be the purpose of the plot or there may be several storylines in a plot running side by side until, later, they all come together.

Alan Ayckbourn has written plays that are linked to each other, e.g. *Separate Tables*, while Shakespeare wrote several plays that taken together cover a period in history, e.g. from *Richard III* to *Henry V*.

It is important not to mix up plot and structure. Plot is to do with content and the meaning and purpose of the action. Structure is how the meaning is communicated or the purpose achieved. In drama the two are sometimes interlinked. For example, in classical Greek drama, the device of *deus ex machina* was used when the playwright had a plot that could not be resolved easily, or happily. Here, the playwright arranged for a god character to swing in by crane, as if from the heavens. This god character was then able to use supernatural powers to dismiss the problem faced by the mere human characters on stage.

You can find out more about the seven basic plots on page 174 in **Unit 2.5**.

Social, political, historical and cultural contexts

Social, political, historical and cultural contexts can affect character, context and plot, so it is important to consider them both when developing your drama and when looking at existing texts. Ask yourself questions such as:

- Was the writer influenced by the culture in which they lived?
- Did the culture of the time in which they lived restrict what could be written about?
- Were there social conventions or political pressures that forced the writer to write in a particular way, or to avoid issues?
- Or is the opposite true? Did the writer deliberately set out to make a point, to challenge or even shock?

Social, political, historical and cultural contexts can be defined as the circumstances, influences, restrictions, messages that a context can bring both to the nature of a work and to the situation of a practitioner. This applies whether the practitioner is someone else or you.

▼ Italian political playwright Dario Fo is a big admirer of *commedia dell'arte*. You can see its influence in his plays such as *Accidental Death of an Anarchist* (below), which retells the story of how a police suspect managed to fall out of an upstairs window during questioning.

Examples include Blue Blouse theatre in Russia, where practitioners were trying to inform and energise the workers; Joan Littlewood and her theatre workshop, especially *Oh What a Lovely War*; Steven Berkoff's political comment in *Sink the Belgrano!* Scripts whose form has been affected by censorship include *The Falklands Play* by Ian Curteis. This television play about the Falklands War, written in the late 1980s, was banned by the BBC and not aired for seven years.

Another type of influence occurred when Dario Fo wrote

plays criticising the politicians and the police force in his country, Italy. The plays made the people he was criticising very uncomfortable, so they started turning up in numbers at performances and treating the plays as a send-up of what was happening. This spoilt the point Fo was trying to make, and he had to change the way he presented his plays.

Examiner hints

The examiners will expect to see that when devising, you understand and have thought about character, context and plot.

For **character**, they will want to see that you had a definite idea in mind when developing a character and that you have thought about what sort of character it is, and what factors will allow the character to communicate to the audience. They will also look at whether you have considered the intention of the playwright.

Aspects of design could also be very important here. What costume would be worn, and how might this add to the impact of the character? Is make-up appropriate or necessary? And if so, what sort of design might be needed?

With **context**, the examiners will expect you to have thought out what are the implications or consequences of where and when a play is set. They will expect you to show evidence of this in your devising as well. You need to understand what impact the time or location may have on how characters behave and speak.

The examiners will expect you to understand the purpose of **plot** and to recognise it in texts you have studied, as well as be able to demonstrate it in work you have devised.

You can use plot as a shorthand for describing story, or you might consciously reject story in favour of a different approach (see comments on *Waiting for Godot* on page 27).

Drama challenges

- Write or devise verbally with others the scenario for the next scene following Scenario C on page 82. What will we learn about the two characters from the scenario for the next scene? How will an audience learn more about the two characters just by looking and listening?

- Choose a character from one of the plays you are studying. Using the checklist on page 10, prepare a profile for the character as if you were going to play the role. Devise a short scene where your character meets one or more of the other characters in the play you are studying.

  What design issues might there be? How could you make your scene more effective through the use of lighting, sound, costume and make-up?

How to excel

Character and context go together well because they have an effect on each other. To gain higher grades, you will need to integrate your thinking about them so that the examiners can see that you know that for meaning to be communicated about a character, there has to be an understanding about the situation in which the character is placed.

Use the list on page 10 when thinking about developing character, or when assessing a character in a play.

Explain the function of the character. Is the character there to help the story along, simply a means of reflecting life, or is the character used as a way of telling the audience something?

Examiners will notice not just if you have thought out the characteristics of a role and the context that might affect the character, but also if you have a clear idea of the purpose and function of the character within the plot.

Stretch your skills

- Find out about *commedia dell'arte* and its stock characters. Look at the **Resources** list at the end of this book (page 254) if you need help in finding information.

INTRODUCING KEY COURSE CONCEPTS

SECTION 1

19

- If you would like to know more about *Everyman* look at Scenario E on page 83, and investigate medieval theatre. Constance Cox has written a modern adaptation.

- Stanislavski was a practitioner who did a lot of work on the development of a character. He wrote a book called *Creating a Character*. See if you can find out about his major points about creating a role.

- Find out about the Greek unities of time, place and action.

- Research the Blue Blouse movement and what came to be known as the Falklands plays of Steven Berkoff, e.g. *Sink the Belgrano!*, Edward Bond's *Restoration* and Nick Perry's *Arrivederci Millwall*. Discover how the political situations of the two time periods compare. How was each drama received by the authorities and by the people? What was the intention of each?

- What happened to Dario Fo when he tried to criticise the Italian ruling class through his plays? How did he change what he did?

- Have a go at developing one of Scenarios A, B, C or D (pages 80–83) into a complete drama.

- Design a set for Scenario A (page 80), considering how it could enhance the action.

Review

This unit has shown that when considering what goes into a play you need to identify and understand:

- the **context** – the situation or circumstances in which it is set or devised, which may have historical, cultural, social or political influences
- the **plot** – the content, meaning and purpose, the story and how it is developed.

1.2 Structure

Your aims

Structure: You will explore how a piece of drama can be put together and how episodes, scenes or acts can be connected.

You will learn about play form, the unities of time, place and action, different models that exist for dramatic structuring, as well as newer structural ideas, such as stream of consciousness, montage, vignettes and collage, the variation of chronological order, allegory and satire, irony and metaphor.

Structure

Many play scripts are divided up in some way, most commonly into **scenes** and **acts**. A change of scene usually means that a new idea is introduced, the location changes, or a new character is presented. The playwright does this to make sure that what they write will make sense when it is performed. You must work in the same way, so that any drama you produce does not appear haphazard or accidental.

Structure is the framework of the drama, the way sections are put together. If there is no formal framework, 'structure' refers to how the drama will proceed and progress.

Shaping is a term used to describe details of the structure and has a link with meaning. Shaping is the way the drama is constructed within the framework (structure) to create the meaning or effect intended by the creator of the drama. It may refer to small sections, or just a few lines or words, an entrance or exit, or a crucial event and when it occurs.

INTRODUCING KEY COURSE CONCEPTS

SECTION 1

Action

Take a look at Scenario G on page 85.

Copy the grid below and fill it in, or use it as a guide for discussion with your group.

Structure	Brief note of content
Scene 1	
Scene 2	
Scene 3	

What parts of the scenario might you want to consider in shaping the material?

Can you find any examples of the following in the scenario?

- Exposition: Giving the necessary information.
- Rising action: The things that happen build up in pace and perhaps excitement.
- Climax: Matters come to a head – there is a moment of catharsis, emotional release.
- Denouement: Everything is explained.
- Peripeteia: A twist in the plot.
- Obligatory moments: Moments in the action when the audience will expect something to happen and feel cheated if it does not.

Now let's look at some more ways of structuring and shaping drama mentioned in your course requirements. Then try out the **Drama challenges** on pages 25–26.

Stream of consciousness

In this style of devising there is no structure except to go with the flow. The 'flow' may be a series of ideas and almost random episodes. Stream of consciousness may be used in improvisation work to explore an idea or situation or when the participants want to see where the drama might lead.

For presentation purposes, there might need to be a more formal structure, although some theatre companies do follow a very flexible pattern of performance outcomes. Sometimes a play may have a variety of endings, with the one to be used depending on circumstances that happen earlier in the play, or even the intervention of the audience. For example, the audience might play the role of a jury and give a verdict that is not known before the performance, but will lead on to a set of circumstances that decide which ending is used.

Montage

This style uses a collection of stage pictures to show a series of events where perhaps the spectacle – what the audience sees – is as important as any characters, or as important as the plot, if there is one. Examples might show historical events, e.g. battles and other events on a grand scale.

Vignettes and collage

Vignette: A short, evocative episode, bringing to mind strong images, memories or feelings, which may focus on a particular character or event.

Collage: A series of illustrations or scenes with a common background, possibly a series of images where what is seen and experienced may be more important than what is heard in dialogue.

Varying chronological order

In what is often called the well-made play, characters are introduced, the action develops, rises to a climax and things are resolved. Here the action progresses in time order as would happen in ordinary everyday life. This structure can be varied however. The most popular variation uses flashback, where the meat of the plot is contained in events that occurred before the starting point of the action of the play. In such drama, the option is open for the beginning of the play to be the ending as well, with the thrust of the action being about the journey from earlier events. Alternatively, a twist can lead the audience to believe that the beginning will be the ending, but then, following the flashback, there is a further development after the action returns to the present.

UNIT 1.2: STRUCTURE

Sometimes introducing a narrator can help along flashback techniques and similar ways of flitting between the present and other times, past or future.

Allegory and satire

Scenario E on page 83 provides an example of an allegory. An allegory is a story or picture in which the meaning is represented through symbols. In the play *Everyman*, this is achieved through characters playing ideas like 'Good Deeds', and articles such as 'Wealth'. The play *Animal Farm* by Peter Hall, based on the book by George Orwell, represents both allegory and satire, using ridicule and irony to expose the foolishness of some politicians in the Soviet Union after the Russian Revolution. The pig Snowball represents Trotsky while the pig Napoleon represents Stalin.

You can find out more about these genres and how to use them in **Unit 2.5** on pages 177 and 185.

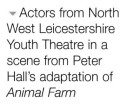
▼ Actors from North West Leicestershire Youth Theatre in a scene from Peter Hall's adaptation of *Animal Farm*

Irony and metaphor

Irony: Using language that says the opposite of what is happening in a form of sarcasm. Dramatic irony refers to the audience knowing something that the characters do not.

Metaphor: Using the imagination to describe something by saying it is something else. This is usually done to create an effect.

Examiner hints

In the **Drama challenges** below, you are asked a series of questions. If you answer these questions about the work you are doing and can provide evidence of what you have done, you will be meeting assessment criteria.

Many students just put down their ideas for a drama without any thought as to how they might be structured and work in practice. Always think about how work can be organised to create the effect you want, even with short pieces of improvisation.

Think as well about how changing the structure, or shaping or amending the plot might make the drama more successful or give it a different outcome and impact on an audience.

Top students will be able to:

- draw on a range of structures suiting the purpose of the piece
- demonstrate that they understand shaping by applying it to important moments in a drama
- provide sound evidence in their Working Record showing their processes, and cross-referencing to the Areas of Study.

Drama challenges

- What differences in structure might there be if you developed Scenario G on page 85 as:

  ◆ a short comedy sketch
  ◆ a play lasting about half an hour
  ◆ a play lasting for a full evening's entertainment
  ◆ a television play?

Prepare a short improvisation based on Scenario G. Supply two contrasting endings. Decide if, how and why your endings will change the structure or shaping of the drama.

- In *Unit 1 From Page to Stage* you will be considering another writer's text. Focus on:
  - the structure chosen by the playwright – why choose this one?
  - what shaping in the material has occurred that you, as a director or an actor, might want to understand
  - the plot – give a summary
  - if a different structure might have worked.

- In *Unit 2 Drama in the Making* you will be creating your own work. Ask yourself:
  - What structures might you choose and why?
  - What is the plot?
  - What in the plot will need shaping to ensure the meaning or effect is communicated successfully to an audience?

How to excel

A useful way to show the examiners that you have really thought about structure is to refer to scripts you have studied and to compare their various structures with the work you are devising. Even better would be to tell the examiners why you have chosen to use a particular structure or shape a particular scene by comparing it to something you have seen, studied or tried in the past.

Most important is that you demonstrate that you know what 'structure' means in theory and practice, and that you apply this understanding when looking at existing scripts and devising your own work.

There is no right or wrong way to structure a piece of drama. Audiences today will accept all sorts of structures and even a mix of them in a single piece of drama. So be prepared to experiment but always know your purpose for doing so.

Two famous drama practitioners had their own views on structure:

◆ **Konstantin Stanislavski** described the structure of a play as being like a turkey that a family might be having for dinner. The bird is the whole play, sitting there on the plate. Then the wings and legs are torn off, and the breast cut into big chunks. These are the acts. These pieces are then divided further into scenes, and even further until they are small morsels for the mouth. These morsels are small sections of the play, single lines or even words or gestures. This structure is described in Stanislavski's book *An Actor Prepares*.

◆ **Bertolt Brecht** held very different views to Stanislavski, and his plays, especially those described as Epic Theatre, did not have scenes that automatically followed on one from another. Instead they had a series of episodes, which together told a story, but each episode could stand up on its own. Brecht's views on the difference between Epic Theatre and the more traditional structure for a play can be found in many of his books. *Brecht on Theatre* is probably the easiest to find.

■ The unities of time, place and action used in Greek theatre provide an interesting insight into a view of structure introduced by Aristotle, but built upon by European practitioners throughout later centuries. This is explained in more detail in **Unit 2.5**, on page 190.

■ Samuel Beckett's play *Waiting for Godot* has a thought-provoking structure (see Scenario H on page 87). Beckett held the view that plot was not important because the focus should be not on what happens, but on how it happens. This means that as there is no real development in the story, the symbols and meanings become important. Bear this in mind when looking at **Unit 1.6 The Semiotics of Drama and Theatre** on page 72. Consider how the nature of a play might create a very specific structure.

INTRODUCING KEY COURSE CONCEPTS

SECTION 1

▲ This photograph, from 1898, shows a scene from Anton Chekhov's *The Seagull*. The play had already been premiered in St Petersburg, and failed, when Stanislavski took it up for the first season of the newly opened Moscow Art Theatre. Although he was taking a risk, he could see its potential for naturalistic presentation. Stanislavski's version, when it opened, created a sensation.

Stanislavski had prepared for the production in minute detail, keeping painstaking notes which he called his director's 'score'. These included a profile of each character's mannerisms and a storyboard recording the proxemics throughout. The actors spent over 80 hours in rehearsal, which was a lot for those days. Even then, Stanislavski felt that the play was under-rehearsed.

Stanislavski also played the character, Trigorin, who in the photo is smoking a cigarette.

Review

This unit has shown that:

- Structure and shaping are inextricably linked. Once the meaning, the content and the story of the drama have been established, decisions need to be made about how these will be communicated, what format the plot will follow. This framework for the drama, the way the different parts are put together, provides the structure.

- Shaping is applied to the basic structure. It is the way the drama is manipulated and constructed within the structure to communicate the meaning or purpose intended. Shaping can be applied to sections, a few lines or words, an entrance or exit, or to a key event and when it occurs.

1.3 Audience and Performance Space

What the course demands

The minimum requirement for Area of Study 3 is that more than one type of audience should be considered both in the study of script and in the preparation and devising of drama during your course. You must also consider more than one venue type or performance space for the performance of dramas. The impact, appropriateness and use of the performance space should be evaluated.

Your aims

Audience and performance space: You will explore how both the audience and the performance space relate to the intention of the playwright, and the issues that the drama raises. The work of Stanislavski, Brecht, Grotowski, Ayckbourn and Godber, for example, could be considered in relation to their view of audience.

You will learn about performance spaces such as the Greek amphitheatre, studio, arena, in-the-round, thrust, promenade, proscenium staging. You will also explore the use of different buildings for drama performances: purpose-built theatres across historical periods; museums, old country houses, factories and mills; street theatre and pub theatre; outdoor theatre.

The examiners will need evidence that you know what terms relating to audience mean. So let's have a look at some of these in more detail.

Audience

This is probably one of the easiest terms to understand but is often ignored by students of drama – it's very easy to take it for granted. The course definition makes it clear that the concept of 'audience' cannot really be separated from the intention of the playwright: the audience is *'those for whom the performance or outcome is intended'*.

When you are preparing work for assessment, keep to this approach in establishing your audience. Once creativity is under way, and ideas have begun to form, it is always worth asking yourself: 'Who is going to see this?' and 'What impact do I want this drama to have on those who see it?'

It is not necessary to have a complicated reason for the impact or effect you want. It is quite acceptable for your intention as playwright to be to entertain the audience, or to tell a good story.

What is required is for you to understand some of the different intentions that there could be with regard to audience, and to consider this in your work. Several examples of types of theatre that serve the audience in different ways are covered in this unit, although they are not the only ones – you can cover others. But you must consider more than one.

▲ A scene from *All Sorts* – a theatre-in-education drama

Simpler practical issues are also considered under *Audience and Performance Space*, such as an audience being able to:

- see what is going on
- see what is happening
- hear
- be safe.

Here is a selection of theatre types that might drive the playwright's intention and which you may like to use in your own drama.

Theatre-in-education

This form of drama has grown greatly over the years, and you may well have seen performances by visiting theatre companies. The content may have been related to drugs, or the prevention of smoking, or to do with road safety or the dangers of talking to strangers. Whatever the topic, the purpose of theatre-in-education is to educate the audience, to make a difference, to change outlooks.

Action As a group, what experiences can you remember from seeing a production that might be considered as theatre-in-education? Did it have an impact? Did it change you or others? If it did, why was this so? If not, why not, and what could have been done differently so that the production would have had an impact?

Documentary theatre

This style probably began with some of the social drama of the early 1900s, but it has become most popular for looking at historical events, significant people from the past, and issues of the day that cause comment or concern.

The problem for the playwright is to decide their intention. Is it enough to provide factual information, present it effectively, and leave the audience to make up their own minds about the rights and wrongs of what they have seen? Or should the playwright construct the drama in such a way that the audience have no choice but are confronted with stark opposites? The second option is what happens in the play *Oh What a Lovely War* by Joan Littlewood. Here the horrors of war are factually reported to the audience as a backdrop to the cavalier attitude of those in power, who casually order the deaths of hundreds of thousands whilst sipping drinks in the comfort of their offices.

The playwright will use authentic press cuttings, perhaps speeches of historical figures, and genuine factual information to develop dialogue and design elements.

Action Choose an idea from the local history of your town or village, or a character or incident in national history such as a strike or trade dispute. Prepare a scenario, decide on the plot and a structure. Then select one important part of your scenario and develop a short scene, shaping it to meet your intention. In other words, decide how you want your audience to respond to your scene.

INTRODUCING KEY COURSE CONCEPTS

SECTION 1

31

Agitprop

This style of theatre developed in Germany and Russia in the late 1920s and 1930s. It was linked with the Workers' Theatre Movement, and for its audience, it had a very specific intention. It wanted to move away from the traditional audiences watching plays – friends and relatives, the rich and comfortable – and to reach the masses of workers. Its intention was to give a more robust and realistic view of life and of social issues and to promote a particular cause.

Agitprop went out to its audiences, whether they were on the street corner, in the park, or in their workplace. It had a very direct approach to the audience so that they felt part of what was happening, and felt the actors understood what they were suffering. The actors took just a few days to prepare drama that had something to say about events that were actually happening.

You can find out more about this style and its uses on page 178.

Тов. Ленин ОЧИЩАЕТ землю от нечисти.

▲ Agitprop-style poster from 1920 showing Lenin sweeping the world clean of the rich

Political theatre

Agitprop is probably rightly considered as political theatre, but there are many more examples of political theatre where the audience being targeted is more general. The playwright's intention is usually to make the audience first consider certain events and why they occurred, then decide if what happened was right and reasonable. The playwright may well push the audience in a certain direction by the way the material is presented.

One example of political theatre is Steven Berkoff's *Sink the Belgrano!* This play is based on the sinking of an Argentine battleship during the Falklands War, but Berkoff deliberately waited several years before publishing it. He did this so that the writing of the play and the viewing of it would not be influenced by the closeness of the event, and to avoid the possible effects of the nationalism that inevitably arises when a country is at war. He wanted his audiences to examine the event in cool detachment.

Bertolt Brecht wrote many plays that are considered to be political theatre. In these works he examines issues of war, justice and social class.

Named theatre practitioners

Several practitioners are mentioned in the course details as playwrights who could be studied in relation to their view of audience, including Stanislavski, Brecht, Grotowski, Ayckbourn and Godber. Let's look at some of them in more detail.

Konstantin Stanislavski wanted his audiences to identify with his characters. He intended his audiences to see the play as a snapshot of real life. The expression 'the fourth wall' is often used to describe this concept. The audience are placed at the fourth wall of a room, peeping in and seeing what is going on. The actors take no notice of the audience, they do not acknowledge their presence in any way. The drama is devised so that the audience empathise with what is going on – that is, they are able to identify with the characters, feel what they are feeling, cry when they cry.

Bertolt Brecht rejected this viewpoint as being a means of hypnotising the audience, taking away their capacity to think and act, and not allowing them to make up their own minds. Brecht believed that the audience should view what was happening as a spectator, remaining detached, looking on rather than looking in. He described it as being a reporter giving an account. So, as a reporter, his audience should sympathise but not empathise, understand but not become involved.

Today, playwrights such as **Caryl Churchill**, **John Godber** and **Alan Ayckbourn** take a more mixed view. There may be moments when the audience is addressed directly, so no identification or empathy can develop. Then, in a later scene, there may be a very naturalistic episode.

Action

Read through Extract A on page 91. In groups of three or four, you are going to explore and present this extract **either** using the dialogue **or** improvising your own.

First decide what your intention as the playwright would be if you developed the extract as one of the following:

- naturalistic drama
- documentary drama
- theatre-in-education.

Focus on the impact on the audience. How will your intention be different depending on the audience you choose?

Now develop and present your piece. It would be interesting for each group to choose a different way to develop the extract and then perform their drama to the others.

Audience expectations

Whilst the intention of the playwright and their hoped-for impact upon the audience is important, audiences themselves also have expectations that may affect the playwright. Sometimes, these will cause the playwright to deliberately shock and surprise. Throughout history playwrights have done this at key points in the development of theatre. In the late 1800s and early 1900s, audiences had come to expect great stage spectacles involving complicated scenery and special effects. This reached a point where an audience would spend more time during a Shakespeare play watching changes of scenery than watching the performance itself!

At times, audiences have been affected so strongly that changes in society have occurred. The death of a prisoner at the end of the Galsworthy play *Justice* in the early 1900s caused Winston Churchill (then Home Secretary) to change the law on solitary confinement. The play *Love on the Dole* by Gow and Greenwood had such an impact on audiences that it created pressure for change in the regulations concerning the 'dole' (paid to people who were unemployed). In the 1960s, *Cathy Come Home*, a television documentary-style drama about a young homeless couple, led to the formation of the charity Shelter.

Action	It is fascinating that such changes came about after audiences had watched naturalistic theatre. Brecht said he did not believe an audience could have the capacity for change if watching a play produced using Naturalism. He described such audiences as being hypnotised. What do you think?

Performance spaces

This unit of the course also asks you to focus on *where* the drama will take place – the performance space. You are expected to know about formal places for presenting drama as well as informal ones. Sometimes the performance space will be linked with the intention for the drama.

You must make sure you understand and are familiar with three different sorts of spaces or venues. So let's have a look at some performance spaces in more detail. In the **Resources** list on page 259 you will find some web addresses which will give you good background information about these performance spaces.

In-the-round and arena

In-the-round: Here the performance space is in the centre of the audience and is surrounded by the audience on all sides. The space is usually circular or square, but may be any shape.

▲ In-the-round staging at New Victoria Theatre, Stoke on Trent – with a production of *The Wizard of Oz*

Arena: This is the same sort of staging. The name originates from the time of the Greeks and Romans, when the 'arena' was the space in the centre where action took place.

There are significant acting, direction and design challenges when the audience are looking at the action from all sides at the same time. Scenery and furniture must never be more than a metre high, and each member of the audience, wherever they are sitting, should almost always be able to see something happening. Entrances and exits need to be carefully set up.

In-the-round or arena is a very popular form of acting space. More and more new theatres are designed to have the flexibility to be used in this way. In the early 1900s, theatre practitioner Antonin Artaud suggested that more use should be made of this form then went a step further, suggesting that the action should surround the audience!

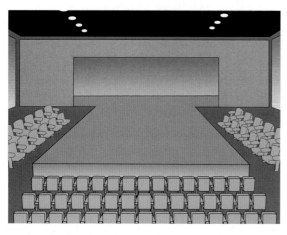

▲ Thrust staging

Thrust

In this staging, the stage sticks out into the audience, so that the action is surrounded on three sides. The challenges to designer, performer and director are not quite as great as with in-the-round. Thrust staging was very popular with theatres built in the second half of the twentieth century. This was because it was still fairly close to proscenium staging, but allowed greater flexibility.

Promenade

In this type of staging, the audience walk around from one set to another or follow the actors as they move from one location to another. Modern stagings of medieval mystery plays take in promenade.

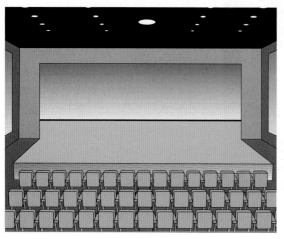

Proscenium

This type of staging is sometimes described as the 'picture-frame stage'. The term 'proscenium arch' refers to pillars and a crosspiece that make up a division between audience and acting space, framing the action on stage.

The name 'proscenium' has its origins in Greek theatre, although the meaning was

◀ Proscenium staging

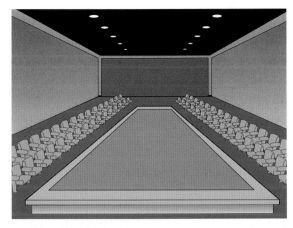

▲ Traverse staging

different then. The *proskenion* was a raised stage in front of the skene (the stage building) that formed a backdrop and allowed the audience to see the actors more clearly.

Traverse

This term for staging means that the acting area is between two opposing sets of seating. The Traverse Theatre in Edinburgh is the best-known theatre in Britain that uses this design.

How the building or space shapes the performance

Theatres

Theatres are buildings provided expressly for the performance of drama. Older theatres are likely to be in proscenium-arch format, while newer ones will have the option to add an apron and make the proscenium into a thrust stage. The latest theatres allow just about any sort of configuration.

▲ The Stephen Joseph Theatre in Scarborough has an in-the-round stage (lower photo) and a traditional proscenium-arch stage (upper photo).

Studio

This is a purpose-built theatre, but usually much smaller and more intimate, and not normally with a proscenium arch. The space will have rostra and platforms that can be used in a variety of ways. There is the opportunity to be very flexible as seating will often be 'loose' and so can be arranged in just about any configuration that the fire officer will allow!

Museums, old country houses, factories and mills

There has been a growth in recent years in the use of performance venues such as these. Sometimes it has been part of a marketing exercise, sometimes an attempt to bring to life the story of an event or person in history by performing the drama in authentic surroundings. Often such venues will use promenade devices and the audience will move around. Murder-mystery events in hotels and old houses have become very popular.

Street theatre and pub theatre

These forms of acting space are just what they sound like.

Strolling players have been performing street theatre for centuries. The performance can take place in any area big enough for the drama, and with access to an audience. Often it is for pure entertainment, perhaps with a focus on particular drama skills such as mime or clowning. There will be times when a story is told, or where issues are addressed, especially if it takes place at the location of some threatened event, such as the closure of a hospital, or demolition of a much loved building.

Theatre in pubs is similar in that it is an attempt to bring drama closer to where people are, rather than taking people away to a theatre. Companies around the country specialise in pub theatre, using upstairs rooms or the corner of a lounge or bar room.

In both street and pub theatre, lighting and scenery are minimal, but sound may play a bigger part. Props also become important, and in some productions there will be a lot of attention to costume and make-up.

▶ Street-theatre scene in a shopping centre by Natural Theatre Company

Action | Consider the photograph above. What is the scenario here? How does it suit the performance space? How have the players used props, costume and make-up to enhance their performance?

Outdoor theatre

There are a number of sites around the country that regularly feature outdoor theatre. It is relatively easy to find a production

▲ Some outdoor theatre spaces are quite spectacular. This is the Minack Theatre, an amphitheatre set into the cliffs of south Cornwall.

of a Shakespeare play in the grounds of a country house or castle. Some parks set up stages especially for such performances, and these spaces are very much like a traditional theatre but without walls and a roof.

How the space is defined: use of lighting, levels and materials

Whatever performance space is used and whatever its configuration, it will be defined by a physical barrier, such as the front row of seats or a wall. Alternatively, light may be used to define the area to be used by the actors. More and more stage spaces today are on more than one level, with the play using different levels for different scenes perhaps. Other devices include the use of back-projection and video images to create atmosphere or add to the plot. Sometimes the whole space is identified only by light.

▾ In the Birmingham Rep's production of *The Lion, the Witch and the Wardrobe*, the designer has used levels, light, colour, projection and shadow.

Upstage Right **USR**	Upstage Centre **USC**	Upstage Left **USL**
Centre Stage Right **CSR**	Centre Stage **CS**	Centre Stage Left **CSL**
Downstage Right **DSR**	Downstage Centre **DSC**	Downstage Left **DSL**
A U D I E N C E		

How do you describe where you are on the stage?

The standard method is to describe positions from the point of view of the performer, standing on the stage and looking at the audience. The plan on the left shows the terms used.

Action	In small groups, look carefully at the photograph below from a youth-theatre production of the *Mahabharata*. Decide how you would describe the position of each of the actors using the terms in the diagram above. From the photo, can you deduce who are the lead actors? Share your findings with the rest of your Drama group.

Designing sets for performance spaces

Once the director has decided what style will be used in the drama, and has decided upon the space where it will be presented, there will be some discussion with the designer to pass on the director's ideas. The designer will have some artistic input into this, giving ideas on the best way the director's ideas might be put into practice.

To get their ideas across, designers use two types of simple sketch.

▲ A designer's sketch for the settlement and fort scene from *Pocohontas*

The first is called the **designer's sketch**. For this, you need to imagine that you are looking at the space for the drama from the point of view of the audience. What do you see? This is what the designer's sketch will show – a picture of the acting space and what will be on it.

Turn to the **Resources** list on page 254 for more on designer's sketches and stagecraft.

The second type of sketch is called the **ground plan**. For this, you need to think of yourself being up in the air, looking down on the drama space. Imagine that the set and furniture are in place. What you see from the point in the air looking down is the view the designer draws.

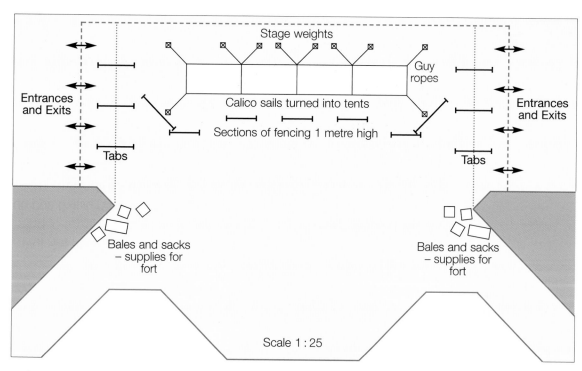

Stage weights

Guy ropes

Entrances and Exits

Calico sails turned into tents

Entrances and Exits

Sections of fencing 1 metre high

Tabs

Tabs

Bales and sacks – supplies for fort

Bales and sacks – supplies for fort

Scale 1 : 25

▲ Ground plan for the fort scene from *Pocohontas*. The scale marked on the plan is the scale the designer used on their (larger) original drawing.

Examiner hints

The examiners will want to see evidence that:

- you have had a clear intention in mind when devising work
- you have considered audience
- you know what will be needed to make the impact on an audience that you want in order to achieve your intention.

You need to show that you know about:

- more than one venue type or performance space
- how these performance spaces can be used
- what the potential is for each
- what the restrictions are, and how flexible each space is
- implications for designers and performers.

This advice applies to all three units of the course. Make sure you refer to audience, intention and performance space in your Working Record.

INTRODUCING KEY COURSE CONCEPTS

SECTION 1

- Develop a drama that could be performed in front of younger pupils. Choose **one** of the following:

  - a theatre-in-education piece about the dangers of playing in forbidden places, such as on the railway or in an electricity substation

  - a documentary piece based on a historical event of local importance.

- Be brave and develop a piece of agitprop drama to perform in front of your year group. The subject should be hard hitting and on a real issue. (It could be to do with school or the social life of boys and girls your age.) You will need to make your audience feel that you, as actors, really understand what it is like to be them.

- Examine the scripts you are studying and decide what sort of audience might see the play performed. Is it the same sort of audience now as when the play was first written? Will the play stand the test of time and still be performed in 50 years' time? What is the intention of the playwright? Is the audience expected to identify with the characters?

- What issues does a house manager have to consider for the safety of both performers and audience? Think about overcrowding, fire, equipment and anything else that you think might be a safety issue. Draw up a list of your findings and recommendations on Health and Safety issues.

- How would you meet the needs of sight- and hearing-impaired members of an audience?

- Imagine you are a director who has been asked to present the play summarised by Scenario A on page 80 at a theatre that has in-the-round staging. Describe your ideas for this. If possible, work with a group and improvise a scene based on the scenario, doing it in-the-round.

- Choose any script you have been working on and create some ideas for a set. Draw a designer's sketch and a ground plan. Don't worry if you can't draw very well – you're not trying to produce a work of art! Use labels to make sure everything you have sketched can be understood.

Get to grips with the views of some of the practitioners, and form your own opinions about audiences and the intention of playwrights. You can then refer to practitioners when talking or writing about audience and intention, both when looking at scripts and when devising your own work.

Never refer to a style of a performance as 'Stanislavskian' or 'Brechtian'. Instead use the terms 'naturalistic', 'non-naturalistic', 'episodic', 'Epic Theatre', or say that your ideas have been influenced by the thinking of the practitioner concerned.

Although Stanislavski and Brecht are the examples given above, your teacher may well have introduced you to other practitioners instead. If so, referring to them would be just as acceptable.

Look carefully at the potential for performance of work, and how to make it accessible to an audience. It is no good spending hours preparing a piece of drama if the audience fall asleep!

The course only requires you to know about *'more than one'* venue or performance space, but it is recommended that those you choose are contrasting ones. Consider how each poses different challenges for the deviser, designer, director and performer.

Stretch your skills

- The Blue Blouses were a collection of theatre groups in Russia in the 1920s that were part of the Workers' Theatre Movement. They got their name from their blue uniforms. Find out what you can about them and the way they staged their plays, and the response of their audiences.

- Find out about the origins of the word 'proscenium' by investigating Greek theatre. What did an ancient Greek theatre look like?

- Discover what you can about some British theatres that have a range of staging types. For example:
  - the different theatres in Stratford-upon-Avon celebrating Shakespeare
  - the National Theatre
  - the Globe (old and new)
  - newly designed theatres such the Curve in Leicester.

- What were the main features of the Restoration theatre stage?

- How were medieval mystery plays staged? Which of the types of staging listed in this unit most closely fit the way they were presented?

- Why do we use the expressions 'up' and 'down' when describing the position of a performer or piece of furniture on the stage acting space?

- Take a play or a devised piece you have been working on and suggest how the space might be defined by light, sound, furniture and props only. Do not use scenery, or a normal stage layout.

- Plan ways of presenting Extract B on page 81 using light and sound to develop atmosphere.

Review

This unit has shown that:

- Drama is devised with a purpose, and this purpose is reflected in who will experience it – the **audience**. Different dramas may have a range of different purposes.

- The purpose defining the audience may also define where the drama is to take place. Sometimes, the **performance space** may define the audience, as in street theatre, for example.

Considering audience and performance space should help to clarify what the drama is all about, who it is for, and how the intended effect can be enhanced or improved as an experience for the audience.

1.4 Improvisation

What the course demands

The minimum requirement for Area of Study 4 is that you must understand and use both spontaneous and planned improvisation skills to devise, perform and add insight to a drama. Evaluating the effectiveness of the use of improvisation in your work is also vital.

Your aims

Improvisation: You are going to experiment with performing unscripted drama, creating this either spontaneously or working within set parameters or guidelines.

You will develop confidence in improvising through a variety of activities. You will also use improvisation to gain insight into a role when working towards a scripted performance.

You will be able to research improvisation as a feature of medieval mystery plays, *lazzi* in *commedia dell'arte*, and some fringe theatre.

Improvisation

This word is used a great deal by those involved in creating drama. At its simplest level, improvisation is performance that is not scripted, that relies on the ability of the performers to make it up as they go along.

When this is happening without any preparation at all, and is an instant response to an idea, a character, a situation or a stimulus, then it is described as spontaneous improvisation.

Action

Look carefully at the photograph at the top of the next page. In small groups, respond to it with some action, without discussion or planning. Each of you should take on the role of one person in the photograph. See how long you can keep the scene going before either it breaks down, or it turns silly!

Improvisation often happens as part of the process of exploring an idea for drama. It may be done several times, with each run perhaps including elements of the previous one, but always with performers trying to improve the outcome. This is known as planned improvisation.

Action

In a group, discuss what ideas might be used to develop a scene from the photograph at the bottom of the facing page. As there are just two characters in this one, you may want to add more as part of your ideas.

Improvise one or more of these ideas. Repeat the best one, **editing**, **adapting** and **adding** to improve the quality. Polish your improvisation until you are happy that you have a piece of drama that communicates your idea from the picture successfully.

Improvisation may be used to get ideas in response to a stimulus, to explore a text, to develop a role, for rehearsal, or as a performance in its own right.

Action

In the planned improvisation you were trying out in the last **Action**, you took on a role. Stay in that role and let the other members of the group question you. Try to answer the questions truthfully as the character you have chosen to be. Sometimes you will have to think about what your character may do, or has done. You will have to invent a history for her or him, and know little details like age, likes and dislikes.

This technique is sometimes called hot seating, and is a useful technique to use when preparing a drama, and when exploring a text.

Examiner hints

The examiners will want evidence that you know what the term 'improvisation' means. They will want you to understand what 'spontaneous' and 'planned' refer to. They will want you to know *when* to use improvisation.

Examiners will also expect you to have taken part in lots of improvisation, as *Unit 1 From Page to Stage, Unit 2 Drama in the Making* and *Unit 3 From Concept to Creation* all require drama activities that rely on its use.

Drama challenges

- Repeat the hot-seating exercise but with a character from a play you have studied. Create **two** different ways of taking on the role in a performance of the play. You will find that the character begins to grow, and to develop some depth.

- Try out the improvisation below – it works best with a mixed group of at least seven. Invite one of your group to act as Director.

> Set out a few simple pieces of furniture and decide as a group where these will go. The context is the kitchen and front door and hallway of a house. Inside the house when the action starts is a woman. She has just seen the children off to school, and is making a drink. There is a knock at the door, the next-door neighbour walks in without waiting to be invited, and sits herself down for a drink.
>
> From this point on the Director tells the other members of the group when to enter the scene, and what is wanted from them. The Director could introduce some unusual happenings, e.g. the milkman/woman knocking and demanding payment for milk for a lengthy period, or the arrival of an old boyfriend, or the appearance of the husband's secretary to collect some clothes for a sudden business trip. The Director should secretly tell new characters who they are, what they are to do, how long to stay, and whether they are to get rid of any of the characters still 'on stage'. The Director can introduce any reasonable element they want, e.g. a large package arriving suddenly. Once a character is established, that character may enter or exit when necessary.

- Have another look at one of the improvisations you did on pages 47–49. As a group, make sure you are all familiar with what you did. Now develop the improvisation in terms of the key points about character, context and plot, structure, and audience and **performance space** from **Units 1.1, 1.2 and 1.3**. Consider what the examiners will want you to know. Can you apply these points to your improvisation? Note down any decisions you make.

- Take one of your improvisations and see how you might enhance it by using one or more design elements such as light or make-up or costume.

How to excel

Do not be casual in your use of the word 'improvisation'. When recording anything in your Working Record, be precise as to how and why you are using improvisation.

Show that you know how improvisation can be used to explore text and to help understanding of what is going on in a play.

Use improvisation to develop characters, both in deepening understanding of them and in creating a role for performance.

▶▶ **Stretch your skills**

▾ *Commedia dell'arte* stock characters wore costumes and masks that audiences would instantly recognise. One of the best-known masks is Pulcinella's with its beaky, drinker's snout. The character and mask of Pulcinella evolved in Britain into Mr Punch of Punch and Judy shows.

The course details provide some examples of drama where improvisation has been used. Find out what you can about improvisation in the following types of drama.

■ Medieval mystery plays were performed in the street and usually moved from stage to stage, a bit like promenade theatre. See what you can discover about the way improvisation might have been used.

■ The word *lazzo* (plural *lazzi*) is used to describe an improvisation performed around the text by the players in *commedia dell'arte*. It might include bits of stage business, verbal cleverness or word-play, tricks or showing-off of skills, or adding bits of made-up text, usually called 'ad libs'. Information about the content of *commedia dell'arte* isn't easy to find, but see what you can discover. You can find out more about the characters of this genre on page 124 in **Unit 2.2**.

■ Improvisation became very popular as a form at fringe theatre events such as the Edinburgh Festival Fringe. Some television shows also rely on live improvisation where presenters respond to questions from the audience. Research any companies that use improvisation extensively as a core part of their performances.

If you want to explore the theory of improvisation, read Viola Spolin's book *Improvisation for the Theater* (see **Resources** list, page 259) – you might find it interesting.

Review

This unit has shown that:

■ Improvisation is about creativity and allows you to explore how the creativity of devising can be immediate, how it can then be moulded, and structure and shaping applied to it.

■ From improvisation a plot may develop, so it could be said that improvisation has an effect on many aspects of the devising of drama.

1.5 Genre, Performance Style and Convention

What the course demands

The minimum requirement for Area of Study 5 is that two genres and two performance styles must be studied, explored and used. A range of theatrical and devising conventions must be demonstrated and evaluated in both planning and practical theatrical work.

Your aims

Genre: You are going to learn not only how each genre or category of drama is identified by common elements (usually characterised by subject matter or form of performance) but also how it may be linked to a historical period or to a particular group of practitioners.

Performance style: You will come to understand the implicit, unspoken agreement between the deviser, performer and audience on the set of conventions and codes to be used in various performance styles, among them:

- naturalistic
- non-naturalistic
- abstract
- representational
- physical theatre
- didactic
- masked theatre.

Conventions: You will look at **devising** and **theatrical conventions**, among them:

- ritual ceremony
- mimed activities
- still image
- narration
- interviews
- meetings
- re-enactments
- sound tracking
- thought tracking
- reportage
- giving witness
- collective drawing
- telephone conversations
- overheard conversations
- simulations
- mantle of the expert
- diaries
- letters
- defining space
- costuming
- games
- role-on-the-wall
- analogy
- journals
- messages
- folk forms
- noises off
- making maps
- caption making
- role reversal
- hot seating
- prepared roles
- interrogations
- marking the moment

- ghosts
- stock characters
- dramatic irony
- allegorical narrative
- prologue
- epilogue
- chorus.

Sometimes, the meanings of words in drama lead to discussion, debate, and even disagreement. 'Genre' and 'performance style' are terms that have stimulated such debate. This book gives you the definitions to use for the purpose of your Drama course. It these meanings that will be used by examiners when awarding marks.

Genre

The genre of a piece of drama describes what type of drama is being enacted. It usually relates to the content. Here are some examples of genres provided in the course details.

Comedy

The classic concept of comedy comes from Aristotle and the ancient Greeks. This concept sees each human as a social being, rather than as a private person. The purpose of the comedy drama is to change or correct something. A mirror is held up to society to reflect its follies and vices, hopefully leading to the mending of them. Through laughter the comic character is brought back into harmony with their society. The character will have abandoned the normal rules of society in some way in the early part of the drama. Unlike tragedy, which shows people who at the start of the drama are better than average, comedy shows people who are worse.

For centuries comedy was defined by what Aristotle set out and was opposite to tragedy in the following ways:

- Comedy centred on lowly types, while tragedy dealt with characters of high status.
- Comedy was concerned with the private affairs of everyday life, while tragedy was based on matters of great public importance.

- The events of comedy were fiction even though they imitated human nature, while the characters and events of tragedy were historic and to a degree based on truth.
- Comedy ended happily and was generally uplifting and optimistic, while tragedy ended sadly.

It has been said that comedy teaches by mocking things that are vile and tragedy teaches by means of pity and fear. In comedy, characters make efforts to live up to an ideal that is perfectly worthy, but is the wrong ideal for them. Shakespearean comedy has many examples: Beatrice and Benedick in *Much Ado About Nothing*, who must be made to realise that nature meant them for each other, not for the single life; the Duke Orsino in *Twelfth Night*, who is shown that it is not Lady Olivia whom he loves, but the disguised Viola; Lady Olivia herself, who changes her mind about mourning for seven years for a dead brother, when the right man comes along. These plays follow a common comic pattern, where characters move from foolishness and self-delusion to recognising who they are and what they want.

Today it is more usual for the term 'comedy' to be qualified with another word describing a specific sort of comedy. Here are some examples.

Comedy of manners: Its humour comes from observations on the way characters behave. A comedy of manners is usually set within a historical period when there may have been strict rules for social behaviour.

| **Action** | A comedy of manners could be set in any period in history. Try to devise a short drama that draws its comedy from the observation of a group of modern-day people. |

Black comedy: Its humour comes from the macabre and gruesome, often pushing the boundaries of what is acceptable.

| **Action** | Think of something gruesome and devise a short scene based on it that has a comic outcome or comic treatment. Be aware of the boundaries of good taste, and people's sensitivity, when dealing with gruesome or macabre content. This is a useful exercise in considering audience. |

Low comedy: This relies on the vulgar and the coarse. The comedy is unlikely to come about through clever wit or detailed characterisation and instead comes through obvious means, clowning, jokes.

Action	Devise a short scene that is within this genre. Be careful that it does not turn into slapstick, which is a different type of comedy. Make sure that you keep control, and that what you devise is funny for an audience rather than just funny for those taking part. As with black comedy, you need to keep in mind what is acceptable to an audience, especially in the context of a public examination, where work should be suitable for general audiences.

High comedy: This has a certain sophistication and is usually set in high-class social situations, where the comedy comes from the detail of characterisation, cleverness of language and use of wit.

Romantic comedy: Although usually applied to plays where the subject is love and all ends happily, this term can also be used to describe plays where sentiment is at the core, and even plays that have highly imaginative content.

Farce: This term is usually applied to plays that use extremely unlikely plots, stereotypes and exaggerated situations, often with the audience knowing things that the characters do not and guessing that some calamity is approaching. The pace is fast, involving horseplay.

Tragedy

This type of drama usually has a serious subject for its content, and will often have a sad, unhappy or disastrous ending. It may be based on an event or series of events that have unhappy consequences.

The Greeks used tragedy as their major form of drama, although their meaning for the word was not quite the same. In Greek tragedy there was often a battle with fate, and fate would win: a human could not escape what the gods had decided. There was a serious exploration of an event usually of historical or contemporary significance.

Greek tragic theatre asked questions about the nature of man, his place in the universe, the powers that govern his life, and was concerned with the problems of man's fate. Aeschylus, Sophocles and Euripides were three of the great writers in the fifth century BCE.

Aeschylus is concerned in his work with the moral issues that power and grandeur raise. He examines the dangers of overweening arrogance, the ancient rule of blood for blood, the inevitability of the misuse of power. His conclusions are his own, often breaking with traditional concepts.

Where Aeschylus supports and justifies the ways of the gods, **Sophocles** is content to accept them as they are, and treats them with awe and reverence. To Sophocles, any violation of the cosmic order creates suffering, but suffering can redeem and exalt. His power lies in his compassion, in his sympathy for his characters, however deluded or broken they may be. One of the best examples of this is his treatment of Oedipus in *Oedipus Rex*. Sophocles makes him a good-hearted but headstrong young man who kills his own father without knowing that he is his father, and marries his mother without realising that she is his mother. When he discovers what he has done, he blinds himself in horror and remorse.

Euripides is from a later generation of Greek thought, which questioned and showed signs of dissatisfaction. Euripides is the most direct of the three in his questioning of established beliefs. Where Aeschylus and Sophocles suggest the old ways may be wrong, Euripides criticises them directly.

▲ John Shrapnel plays Oedipus in the Royal Shakespeare Company's production of Ted Hughes' adaptation of *Oedipus Rex*.

Classical tragedy: Elements of this genre include:

- a catastrophic and unavoidable denouement to the plot
- the hero's suffering being disproportionate to their guilt
- the hero's anguish appearing to the audience as unjust and unfair
- the hero's pain seeming to be beyond human endurance.

Modern tragedy: Elements of this genre include:

- ordinary people in a tragic situation
- most central characters are destroyed or die

INTRODUCING KEY COURSE CONCEPTS

SECTION 1

- humour at the loss of humanity, laughter without substance
- simplified characters narrowed down to what is essential
- a fall from power or loss of status
- reality in essence, rather than Realism – the action is simple
- catharsis, with a significant impact on the audience
- no way out of dilemma
- a stylised manner.

Action

Think of a modern-day event or series of events that could provide the subject for a play that would be a tragedy. Prepare a brief scenario.

Tragicomedy: This is a hybrid genre which contains elements of both comedy and tragedy and is often bitter-sweet in its

outcome. For example, Peter Nichols' play *A Day in the Death of Joe Egg* presents the audience with the humour and warmth of a typical family. The audience spends time laughing at some very funny episodes, only to be brought up sharply as they realise that they are laughing at something related to a severely disabled boy and the impending tragedy looming in his young life.

Shakespeare's plays are often divided into tragedies and comedies.

Kitchen sink
Arnold Wesker and Harold Pinter are two of the playwrights whose work is described by this term. It refers

◀ Kitchen-sink drama: a scene from Harold Pinter's *The Birthday Party* to a type of drama that developed as a reaction to the context that provided most of the settings for plays in the 1940s and 1950s, that of middle-class, drawing-room, polite drama. Kitchen-sink drama can be set anywhere, including the kitchen, uses realistic language, involves the working class, and may use anything at all for its content.

Action	Look at Scenario I on page 87. Revise it so that it is set in an ordinary home. Improvise two dramas, the first using the original scenario, the second using your revised version.
	Consider how you will approach the **characters** and how the way they speak and behave will be influenced by the **context**. If you were to perform one of these dramas, how would you define the **performance space** – how would you stage it?

Melodrama

Melodrama – literally 'a play accompanied by music'– developed content and a style that made it a distinctive genre in Britain. At its height during the 1800s, melodrama had a number of recognisable features:

- content that was often based on a true story
- romance
- violence
- good battling against evil – often the working class being taken advantage of by the upper class
- sensational happenings
- justice coming out on top with wrongdoers getting their just desserts
- stock characters, e.g. the evil gentleman as the villain, the old parents, country yokels, the maiden wronged by the villain, the policeman
- emotional moments.

Religion, morals and the law were upheld in these plays, and the happy ending had to show that wrong did not win, and that the villain was dealt with. Usually, the villain would confess his guilt and express remorse.

Today, melodrama is often considered as a form of comedy where the actors overact and shout and declaim, and no one

▲ A scene from the melodrama *The Bells* performed by Northern Broadsides

really takes it seriously. This is very different to when it was first performed. There were serious matters being considered as content. People would react and respond to the violent portrayal of death and would identify with the characters who were being done down. Playwrights would often try to shock their audience. The content of Victorian melodrama was a good reflection of social class, performing a similar function for society to modern-day tabloid newspapers.

For a drama project based on the genre of melodrama turn to **Unit 2.3** on page 129.

Action	What types of people would provide stock characters today? Try to think of three examples across social classes and from different backgrounds. Devise a short scene where some of your stock characters meet together unexpectedly.

Miracle, mystery and morality plays

These were religious dramas of medieval times, developed from the liturgy (rituals) of the Roman Catholic Church. Content included miracles performed by the saints or scenes from the Bible. Miracle plays were presented at Easter and on other holy days, especially the feast of Corpus Christi. The plays were normally performed outdoors with each scene acted by members of one of the local trade guilds (mysteries). Each guild acted its scene on its own wagon, which could be moved from place to place for repeat performances. The plays were usually performed in cycles and important cycles were named after the towns where they were performed (e.g. Chester, Wakefield, York, Norwich and Coventry).

Morality plays instructed audiences in the Christian way of life and the Christian attitude towards death. They were allegories with characters personifying ideas such as, gluttony, lechery, sloth, pride, envy, hope, charity, riches, strength and good deeds. Examples of English morality plays include *Everyman* (see Scenario E on page 83) and *The Castle of Perseverance*.

Documentary theatre

This genre is looked at in **Unit 1.3 Audience and Performance Space** (see page 31). It is very much of the second half of the twentieth century, and Joan Littlewood's *Oh What a Lovely War* is one of the best examples. It is theatre that attempts to look at an event or issue through presenting evidence, filling in lack of knowledge with educated guesses.

Sometimes the focus of documentary theatre is something that is about to happen in a community. The drama may then attempt to demonstrate that it would be a mistake, by drawing on research and resources to show a picture based on evidence.

Theatre-in-education

This genre is popular, and has very definite educational aims. The style of presentation needs to fit very carefully the nature of the audience. You can find out more about this genre in **Unit 1.3**, on page 30.

Theatre of the absurd

The writer Martin Esslin invented this term. He used it to describe the plays of some post-1945 writers in Europe and the USA who felt that the values of society had disintegrated to the point where they no longer existed. Playwrights often included under this heading are Samuel Beckett, Eugene

▲ Pozzo leads Lucky by a noose in Beckett's *Waiting for Godot*, a play firmly of the theatre-of-the-absurd genre.

Ionesco, Harold Pinter and Jean Genet, although they never described their own work using this term.

Agitprop

Agitprop is tied up with political theatre, and is considered in **Unit 1.3**, on page 32. It is theatre where the main function is to make a political point, to address a perceived social wrong, or to create a change in society through influencing large numbers of people. The term 'agitprop' comes from the two words 'agitation' and 'propaganda'.

You can find out how to use this genre in **Unit 2.5** on page 178.

History plays

These plays tell a tale about or from a historical period. Some of Shakespeare's plays, e.g. *Richard III* or *Henry V*, are sometimes referred to as the Histories.

Restoration theatre

Charles II was restored to the throne in 1660, and it is this event that gives this genre its name. Plays from this time have very specific features, usually related to comedy of manners (see page 55).

Commedia dell'arte

Originating in Italy in the 1600s, this genre spread across Europe. Mainly an improvised form of drama, it has stock characters (e.g. the pierrot or clown, a master and his lady, and a naughty servant), uses masks, tumbling and other physical skills. Some modern playwrights, including Berkoff, claim to be influenced by its form. You can find out more about the characters in *commedia dell'arte* in **Unit 2.2** on page 124.

Poor theatre

This genre was developed by Jerzy Grotowski in the 1960s in Poland. Audience and actors share the same space, with no sets, props or technical features and only simple costumes. The actors follow a strict physical regime and may spend many months rehearsing a play. Grotowski was heavily influenced by Stanislavski.

Performance style

Your course uses the term 'style' to describe *how* a drama might be performed. Here are the main styles you will need to be familiar with and select from to use in your work.

Naturalistic

Naturalism and **Realism** are two words not always distinguished easily. Your course uses the term 'Naturalism' or 'naturalistic' to describe drama that is devised and presented on the basis that the action is to be 'believed in' as if it is something that is really happening.

So, movements, words, set and scenery, furniture and props, costume and make-up are designed to support this belief. It is as if the audience are peeping in through a keyhole, or as if the division between stage and audience is a wall that the actors can't see through but the audience can.

The audience 'suspend their disbelief' and come to identify with and believe in the characters and the setting presented to them.

| Action | Take a careful look at Scenario K on page 89. What approach might the director and designer take in preparing for a performance? |

Non-naturalistic

In this style, the drama is presented in a way that does not require the audience to believe in the characters or in what is happening. The audience are there more as observers or commentators, witnessing and experiencing rather than becoming part of what is going on. Playwrights and directors use a variety of techniques to do this. These may include:

- taking a minimalist approach to the setting with no attempt to reproduce the real-life setting
- having sets and props that are exaggerated
- using back-projection
- an actor addressing the audience directly
- an actor using exaggerated movements or gestures
- using dialogue that does not follow natural patterns of speech.

In non-naturalistic drama there is often a reason for not wanting the audience to empathise and for using non-naturalistic techniques. For example, in political theatre the reason will be the all-important message that the playwright wants to put across.

| Action | Turn to Scenario G on page 85. Imagine that this is going to be produced as a piece of drama to make fun of people who gamble, and to point out the misery it can cause. What ideas do you have for presentation that would prevent the drama from being naturalistic? Use the bullet points above to help you shape your ideas. |

Abstract

This style uses contexts that may be unusual, and will have non-naturalistic settings. Structure will not be standard, and there may be no pattern to it. There may not be a plot, and characterisation will be uneven, with the characters presenting an idea rather than any storyline.

The intention may be to present a series of ideas, or to provide an experience for the audience to go through. The drama may present a sequence of images about which the audience come to their own conclusion.

Theatre of the absurd (see page 61) is a genre known for using the abstract style – for example, in some of the plays by Samuel Beckett and Eugene Ionesco.

Representational

In this style characters represent an idea. Setting and props may also be used as symbols. This style can be useful for improvisation.

Extreme representational style may become allegory. The medieval morality play *Everyman* (see page 83) is a good example of allegory.

Masked theatre

Masks have been a part of drama for a long time. In early Greek theatre they were very important, as they were in

▶ 'Put on a mask and anything is possible,' says Eric Bornstein of Behind the Mask Theatre. 'Suddenly you can move, act, and think differently. The mask embodies the potential for transformation of all kinds.'

commedia dell'arte. In more recent times, Brecht and other contemporary playwrights made use of masks.

Some modern-day companies use masks extensively. Behind the Mask Theatre, a company working in the United States, bases its repertoire on telling stories with mask work forming an essential part of its performances.

Physical theatre

This style came about as a reaction against a heavy emphasis on text and words in drama during the twentieth century. It focuses on movement and visual images, treating the person of the actor as something that can be used. Some companies that specialise in physical theatre recruit actors who are extremely fit, as they are required to undertake very athletic moves. Some of these moves are similar to the moves clowns, tumblers or gymnasts might make. The introduction of physical theatre has narrowed the gap between contemporary dance and drama.

Several companies in the UK focus on physical theatre. DV8 is probably the best known and there is also 4DR, based in the south of England. Turn to the websites section in the **Resources** list on page 259 to research physical theatre.

▼ Frantic Assembly create work that puts equal emphasis on movement, design, music and text. This is an image from *pool (no water)*, their recent collaboration with playwright Mark Ravenhill.

▸ Gregor's transformation from the Woodhouse Players' production of *Metamorphosis*

| **Action** | In Steven Berkoff's play *Metamorphosis*, one of the characters, Gregor, turns into a beetle. He does this on stage without using a disguising costume. The actor represents the beetle through his moves, positions and stances. The photograph above is from an acclaimed amateur production of the play. |

Devise a short scene where each one of your group slowly turns into an animal or insect. Focus on the physical nature of what you do – the moves, speech, gestures and expressions.

Conventions

Conventions are used in two ways in your course:

▪ To describe points that are agreed by deviser, designer, director, performer and audience, that will be accepted by all. These points are often about the way something will happen. For example, in a piece of modern-day drama, there may be several characters in the acting space. A moment arrives when one character is required to deliver a short monologue. The other characters could leave, but will have to return very soon. Rather than disrupt the drama with unnecessary movement, the director may instruct the other characters to stand aside and turn their back on the audience, remaining perfectly still. The other characters know and understand what this means, and so will the audience. All concerned accept what is happening. This is a convention.

Another example is when characters help change the set. They may not be acting in role, but the audience accept the convention that they are preparing for the next scene and will ignore them.

■ To explain a set of conventions used when devising and exploring a piece of drama where there may be no audience. Here conventions may be used to help develop character or role, understand script, explore a subtext, or generate additional ideas.

Here is a selection of the conventions you will meet and should be familiar with:

■ analogy	■ journals	■ prepared roles
■ caption making	■ letters	■ re-enactments
■ collective drawing	■ making maps	■ reportage
■ costuming games	■ mantle of the expert	■ ritual ceremony
■ defining space	■ marking the moment	■ role-on-the-wall
■ diaries	■ meetings	■ role reversal
■ folk forms	■ messages	■ simulations
■ giving witness	■ mimed activities	■ sound tracking
■ hot seating	■ narration	■ still image
■ interrogations	■ noises off	■ telephone conversations
■ interviews	■ overheard conversations	■ thought tracking.

You can find out more about each of the conventions in blue in the **Glossary** on page 260.

Action	Using conventions such as these can be a very valuable way of improving your drama. Keep a record of the ones you use, explaining what you did and how you used each convention. You

may want to use a grid like the one below for this purpose. It could be included as evidence in your Working Record.

Convention	Explanation	How I used it

Examiner hints

Examiners want to see that you know how to apply a range of genres, styles and conventions. It is not enough just to know the terms for these. You need to know what each one means, how it is used and to understand its features.

With genres and styles, you must know at least **two** really well. Get into the habit when devising work of talking about what genre and/or style you are going to use, so that it becomes part of your natural process of devising.

When studying scripts, or watching live performances, identify the genre and style and try to recognise how it has determined the nature of performance.

In the today's theatre, practitioners may use elements of several genres to build up an individual approach to a piece of drama. So be aware of this too.

For the conventions, familiarise yourself with the lists on pages 53 and 68, and use a variety of them in your work. When preparing work for any of the three units, remember to use conventions in the exploration and development process, and to refer to them in your Working Record.

Drama challenges

■ Look through some tabloid newspapers and see if you can find a story that reminds you of the story in Scenario J on page 88. Then prepare your own scenario for a present-day melodrama and improvise a scene from it. Think about the stock characters you could use which would be relevant to an audience today. How would you shock the audience, and how would you get them emotionally involved?

■ Present a series of images on a theme you have chosen that will provide an experience for an audience, but does not have a plot or defined characters. If you like, combine some features of physical theatre with your final piece.

How to excel

Make a note in your Working Record whenever you gain experience of the same genre or style in drama that you:

■ study as script   ■ see performed   ■ devise yourself.

This will demonstrate clearly that you have had experience of the same genre or style but in a different context, and got to know this aspect of drama well.

Use a copy of the grid on page 69 to keep a log of the conventions you use and to comment on their effectiveness. Become expert in two or three conventions that work for you so that you can use them as your examples of successful ways of developing drama. This will also help you remember to use conventions in *Unit 3 From Concept to Creation* (the Examined Unit). Be aware that almost everyone knows about hot seating, so try not rely just on this one convention.

When recording evidence about genre in your Working Record, refer to features of the genre rather than just using its name.

Stretch your skills

■ Censorship has affected plays and theatres throughout the ages. Investigate censorship and the patents of theatres during the early 1800s.

■ It has been suggested that the Greek satyr plays are similar to what we now might call 'low comedy'. What can you find out about the content and method of performance of satyr plays?

■ Use the Internet to discover the allegedly true story behind *Maria Marten and Murder in the Red Barn*.

- Research the use of masks in Greek theatre.
- Find out about the form of drama called 'masque'.

Review

This unit has shown that:

- **Genre** describes the type of drama, and usually is linked with the plot, or the meaning.

- **Style** describes the type of approach, and usually is linked directly with the way the playwright approaches the drama.

- **Conventions** are a useful tool for the drama 'toolkit', something that performer and audience can relate to directly. Sometimes conventions act almost as a sort of shorthand of understanding between performer and audience. They are also a tool that can prove very useful in the preparation of drama, the development of character and plot.

1.6 The Semiotics of Drama and Theatre

What the course demands

The minimum requirement for Area of Study 6 is that an understanding should be shown of the actor as sign, proxemics, symbols in set, costume and properties to create specific meaning. The impact, appropriateness and use of semiotics should also be evaluated in your own work and in any scripts you study.

Your aims

Semiotics: You will come to understand how meaning is created and communicated through systems of encodable and decodable signs and symbols of drama – that is, the ways by which meaning is signalled to an audience. These will include:

- the actor as sign, e.g.
  - the way dialogue is structured to signal meaning
  - the use of verse and prose to create different effects (e.g. iambic pentameter, choral/chanting/rhythmic approaches)
  - how a character is signalled to the audience
- applying proxemics
- assessing practical set design opportunities
- understanding and using stage directions in a performance space to bring an intended image alive
- using lighting, sound and mixed media to create atmosphere and match the overall intention of the performance.

Be aware that these signs and symbols may be decoded in different ways by different cultures – in one culture white may signal purity, in another something quite different.

Semiotics

'Semiotics' sounds a bit of a scary word but once you get to grips with it, you will see that it draws together lots of ideas in drama that you've been learning about already. It is also a term used at A level, so gaining some understanding of it now might help you in the future too.

So let's see how the course explains semiotics.

The elements of semiotics provided by your course are quite specific and offer a good framework for study. Here's an introduction to each one.

Semiotics

How meaning is created and communicated through systems of encodable and decodable signs and symbols.

Put more simply, semiotics is about the signs and symbols of drama.

The actor as sign

A character in a drama will have various functions. For example, in Extract B on page 92, the character John has these functions:

- He is the father figure, and perhaps represents a particular kind of parent.
- He also represents a husband or partner, and depending on how he presents the role, there will be messages about that role. Is it stereotypical, does it represent the current views of society?
- What about him being out of work? Does he represent the result of the impact on people who are unemployed?

If he is all of these things, an audience will look at him not just as 'John', but as a character representing these different functions. Sometimes the name of the character will have a meaning, and this may be played upon or made use of within the text. Sometimes the actor's use of voice, accent and gestures can also communicate specific meaning and atmosphere.

Dialogue signalling meaning

The way dialogue is structured may signal content and different sorts of meaning. One example is the use of verse and prose – when each is used and why. Why is it that Shakespeare switches from verse to prose during a play? Why does Godber use verse?

Action

Traditionally, verse has been associated with tragedy and prose with comedy. Is this the case with Shakespeare and Godber? Give evidence for your views.

The usual form of dialogue is that characters take turns to speak. Within their speeches they will identify issues of importance and provide information about characters not on stage, about events in the past or events yet to come. The way the dialogue is structured can tell us something about the characters. Does one person take control or dominate the scene? Does this signify anything about their character or what might happen in the future?

Action

Turn to Extract A on page 91. Is there anything in the words used that suggest who might be the power figure, if there is one?

Sometimes the language used between characters does not move the action forward, or does not add to the audience's knowledge concerning the context or the character. In these cases perhaps the playwright is trying to make a point.

Action

Look carefully at Extract C on page 93. What is going on in the dialogue? What messages are there for an audience?

Rule-breaking devices are used by playwrights to make a point. For example, Caryl Churchill uses overlapping dialogue to:

- point up the use of the word 'I' and identify a collective female image
- speed up the pace of the drama
- develop tension.

She also writes dialogue in such a way that apparently sophisticated people come out with outrageous expressions that may seem the opposite of their character. She does this to give a pointer, to indicate a message, to give a sign.

Proxemics

This term is used to describe the meaning of the relationship in space between a character and another character, or a character and an object, or a character and a piece of set.

| Action |

Working with one other person, face them and say, 'What do you think?' Now have your partner sit on a chair while you pace up and down behind them and repeat the line. Then place them sitting on the floor, lean over them threateningly and repeat the line. Finally, say it with your face only inches away from their face. Notice how the way you position yourselves affects the way you say the line.

Develop **two** short improvisations using the line. Make one with both of you in a very relaxed position, and the other with one of you in a very threatening position.

You can change the whole meaning of a scene, and give a different message about the relationship between characters, just through the positioning of characters in this way.

Constructing stage pictures

This technique includes use of setting, costume, properties, lighting – in relation to the facial and physical work of the actor.

▾ A stage picture is used by Suffolk Youth Theatre to bring together several themes in this production of *Jane Eyre*.

If we read comics we experience a form of communication that relies on a still picture. Action might be suggested by the positioning of characters in the picture, but the picture itself is still. Cartoons in newspapers and magazines communicate in the same way: through a still image they tell us something. Sometimes there may be a caption or a word bubble, but the best cartoons are those with no words. The picture tells the story, has its message.

One of the most powerful ways still images can influence our lives is in an advertisement. Again, often without words, a still image will bring a smile to our faces, or we may be shocked by the message.

If applied to drama, the still image or stage picture provides another example of semiotics in action. Characters will be positioned (proxemics), gestures may be used, particular expressions on faces decided upon. If the deviser or director wants to put across a particular point, all of these will need to be thought through.

Action	In groups, imagine you are devising a piece of drama on the horrors of war. You want to end the drama with a still image that summarises the effect of the horrors of war on all sorts of people: soldiers, their families, ordinary people in towns, cities and villages. Devise this still image. Use the members of the group, think about props, and what sort of background you would want. Then decide what style it is going to be in. Will it be naturalistic or not? Try to identify each element of your stage picture and what message, what meaning it will have.

Stage directions

Stage directions and their relationship with a set can be used in different ways to enhance meaning and bring an intended image alive.

In a script, stage directions may guide the way an actor develops a character or performs a role. Examples include:

- a description identifying the character
- details of occupation, age and practical matters
- clues as to attitudes of one character to another
- movement to be used
- action to be taken
- reaction to another character's words or actions
- facial expression
- quality of voice, the tone in which something is said
- emotion to be shown
- the pace at which a line is to be delivered
- the volume to be used in delivering a line
- the rhythm to be used in delivering the line
- any emphasis to be used
- any mannerisms the character has
- asides
- pauses.

Stage directions may also cover these aspects of design:

- the setting – where it is
- levels and areas
- the whole stage picture
- time of day and season
- the weather
- costume – distinctive requirements
- mood (lighting and sound).

Action

Look at a text that has quite full stage directions. Find examples of as many of the items in the two lists above and opposite as you can.

Examiner hints

What is important here is not the terms themselves but how these elements of semiotics are used in drama to convey meanings. Examiners will be looking to see if you have grasped the concept of meanings being passed on to an audience through decisions you make as:

- *Deviser:* Considering how meaning will be passed on through the words to be used, stage directions, characters involved, or symbols

- *Designer:* Interpreting the meaning in ways that will communicate to an audience through aspects of design

- *Director:* Taking responsibility for making sure the sign system works, that there is thought about what is communicated and how methods of presentation can affect the audience's understanding

- *Performer:* Using the tools of an actor to communicate effectively to an audience in a way that reflects the director's and playwright's intentions.

Examiners will want evidence that you understand about how meaning can be put across in the way an actor acts and speaks, and in their positioning. Try to show the examiners that you understand the concept of the whole stage picture and the depth of meaning that can be transmitted from it.

INTRODUCING KEY COURSE CONCEPTS

SECTION 1

- Look at Extract D on page 93. In each of the seven versions a different word is highlighted. Work on a short improvisation of a scene involving two or three characters in which the pair of lines is spoken. Try it out with each of the seven versions in turn. Notice how emphasising different words changes the **meaning** of the scene. This is semiotics at work in script. The meaning changes depending upon how the words are said.

- Devise a scene from any stimulus. Make the words you say naturalistic. Then develop actions to emphasise what you are saying. Make moves and gestures. Exaggerate them to underline the meaning of the words you are saying. How does it feel to act like this? What would be the impact upon an audience?

How to excel

Become familiar with and use the words 'semiotics' and 'proxemics' when devising, developing and evaluating drama.

Look for semiotics at work in plays you are studying, not just when creating and directing your own devised work. When recording evidence in your Working Record, refer to signs and symbols that were effective in drama you have seen or read.

Make it clear in your Working Records for all three units that you have thought about signs and symbols in your work, and what might be transmitted to the audience. Link this with the intention of the deviser, whether playwright or drama student.

When you are writing your own scripts or extracts, make sure you use stage directions in the way described above, to help transmit meaning and your intention.

- There are a number of people who have written about sign systems in the theatre. See if you can find out about the Pavis Questionnaire (1985). It was designed for drama students with little or no knowledge of semiotics.

- Are there any examples of semiotics in the way theatres are built or organised? Think about the theatre buildings of the Greeks, the Victorians, and today.

- Consider this sentence: 'What on earth do you think you are doing?' How many ways can you find to present this line so that it has a different meaning? Can you find four, or more? Consider use of voice, proxemics, location and lighting. Number your ideas and use a grid like the one below to note down how you could use each idea.

Idea	Use of voice	Proxemics	Location	Lighting
1				
2				
3				

- Consider this photograph of a scene in a play. How has the director used semiotics in setting this scene? What are the possible meanings? How are the actors contributing to meaning?

Review

This unit has shown that:

- **Semiotics** is a useful way of thinking about meaning, about how ideas are communicated in drama, and about the many ways meaning can be expressed. It is an aspect that binds together all of the other Areas of Study and should be considered along with them when devising drama, looking at existing plays, or experiencing performances.

Scenario A: *The Job*

❝It had not been a good day. Cold, sleet sometimes, with a wind that cut right through him, caused John to huddle into the wall. He wrapped the old overcoat, several sizes too big, more closely around him. Remains of the rain earlier stuck to his beard and were turning into ice. The sores on his face itched with the cold and he wanted to scratch them, but he knew if he did, they would bleed badly and he would stand no chance of getting any money from the passing crowd. For he was not alone, except perhaps inside. He was sitting propped against the wall of a busy street, and sometimes people stepped over his feet, avoiding any eye contact, ignoring his pleas for their small change. Perhaps he should shave his beard off. Perhaps it was his woollen hat pulled down over his forehead that put people off. He wasn't asking for much. It was hours since the young girl had come across to him with a slice of pizza and a carton of hot, sweet tea.

As he sat, dripping with rain, and full of self-pity, he became aware of a shadow, something blocking the light from the shop windows opposite. Through the cracked lids of his eyes he saw a tall figure, imposing, straight backed, a full head of curly hair, and a strong-looking, well made-up face. As he looked up at the woman who was peering down at him with curiosity, he tried to tell if her face was kindly or cruel. Usually a good judge of character, in this case he couldn't tell. A frown of concentration covered John's brow as he stuttered, 'Any change, miss? Spare some small change?' He was ashamed at how weakly his croaky voice came out. The woman stared at him, stood up, decision made. She reached into her pocket and withdrew a wallet. John flinched – it wouldn't be the first time he had been hit. A hand went into the wallet, sorted, selected and then dropped a bundle of notes into the cardboard box John used to collect money. Silence – it was if the traffic had stopped, people frozen in their tracks, life on pause. The colour of the notes told John that there was a lot of money in his dilapidated box, at least several hundred pounds. He sat in silence, bemused, puzzled and apprehensive.

Then the woman spoke, a cultured, soft voice full of hidden power, someone who was used to giving commands, and having them obeyed. She said, 'I have a job for you.'

Scenario B: *The Security Guard*

Why had Mum sent me on this errand just when she had? I was watching TV, my favourite programme, and doing my homework at the same time – it was maths and I knew I could do the exercise – when Mum called. 'Run out of milk,' she said. 'Be a love,' she said. 'Run to the shop,' she said. 'Oh Mum!' I said.

So here I was, running up and down the supermarket aisles. Where did they put the milk? Thought it was by the entrance, but no, it wasn't. I spotted a display right on the back wall, hoofed it over there, grabbed the milk and ran to find a checkout queue that wasn't big. Decided to use the new 'scan' checkouts. Found one and was just scanning when someone crashed into me. No idea where she or he had come from, but they really winded me and I fell down. Wheezing, I got up and saw my scan had worked, fed my money into the slot, got my change and put the milk into my bag – one of those recycling ones, far too big for the task of a solitary bottle of milk, but Mum insisted, no plastic bags, need to be eco-friendly!

As I hurried out from the checkout I remember thinking my bag felt a bit heavy, especially with just one bottle of milk in there. I was just crossing through the exit doors when there was a shout. I noticed several things at once as I froze. First, someone outside who was taking a lot of interest in me; second, my maths teacher from school, who had just recognised me and was about to say hello; and third, the security guard in full uniform running down an aisle and shouting, 'Stop, thief!'

Scenario C: *The Burglar*

It was dark. The night was disturbed only by the dripping of the rain from broken gutters. The man crept quietly along the wall that divided the garden from the footpath. He stopped, listened, then moved on. He limped slightly, and as the light from a passing car shone on his face, the eyes looked frightened, the expression careworn. Quickly he climbed over the wall where there was a gap where some bricks had crumbled away. Squelching on the wet grass, he approached the rear of the house. All was in darkness. Yes, the window was open again. He had noticed the other day when passing that it had been left open. Probably the hot days recently had made the owners careless. He climbed in, careful not to knock the plant off the ledge. With his torch he crossed the kitchen into the hall, and turned into a room on his left. It was a study. Perhaps there would be some money on the desk. He sat on the chair, put the torch at his side, and started rummaging, looking for money, or anything he could use.

A noise startled him, and before he could identify it, the light was turned on.

'And what do you think you are doing?' asked a stern but not unkind voice. The face that looked up was full of desperation and hopelessness.

Scenario D: *The Head*

I was busting! Not just wanting to go, but absolutely busting! I didn't think 'the Doc' would let me out of class, but something in my face must have told him that I wasn't trying it on, that I really needed to go.

I hurried along the corridor. There was always something a bit exciting about walking along corridors when everyone else was in lessons. It sort of gave you a buzz.

Just as I came to the corner, I heard noises, then glass tinkling, then the sound of a bell. It wasn't lesson change yet, there was at least half an hour to go. What was going on? I soon found out as I turned the corner, saw glass on the floor, by the wall, just underneath the fire-alarm button, and heard running footsteps round the next corner.

I stood petrified, looking at the damage, hearing the bell destroying the calm. I was transfixed. Then came the voice.

'Robinson!' it thundered. 'Robinson, come here!'

It was the Head.

Scenario E: *Everyman*

Everyman is a play written in medieval times as a warning to everyday people about the way they behaved. People were very religious, almost all believed in God, and were frightened about what might happen to them if they did not do what God wanted. Like most people, however, their good intentions often disappeared, and this play was a reminder about how they should behave, and warned what might happen if they did not change their ways. It is a morality play, and is an allegory.

What follows is a brief summary of the play.

The play starts with God telling his messenger that he is fed up with humankind, because they have forgotten him and are behaving badly. He sends the messenger for Death in order to have an accounting of Everyman. This character is as the name suggests, and is meant to represent the whole of humanity.

Death is then sent off to find Everyman and to bring him for a 'reckoning'. When Everyman receives the visit from Death, he is dismayed, and asks for a delay, which is not granted.

He asks if he can take someone with him to the reckoning, the final judgement, and Death says that he can. Everyman decides to go to his friends, his family and his wealth. He asks each in turn about the good time they have had together. He asks each of them if they will do anything for him, and each of them say they will. Once Everyman reveals that they will have to die to go with him, they all desert him.

Finally, Everyman goes to Good Deeds to see if she will go with him. Unfortunately, Good Deeds can barely stand, because Everyman has done so little that was good. She is so weak that it seems impossible for her to help him. Everyman then says he is sorry and pays penance for what he has done, whipping himself. As he does this, Good Deeds gets stronger and accompanies Everyman to the final judgement. 99

Scenario F: *The Place of Women*

66 It is a lovely sunny morning, a Saturday. The man is reading the paper, sitting at the breakfast table. His wife is sitting opposite, trying to read the front page of her husband's paper. There is a pleasant, happy atmosphere.

The woman pours herself another coffee, asks her husband if he wants one. He grunts assent, and she pours. He asks her, from behind the paper, how the children got on at school during the week. She replies that they did very well and are enjoying their time at school. She obviously has something else she wants to say, and hurriedly goes on to talk about how much more confident they are, and how nice it is to have them at school and not to have to think about picking them up and dropping them off now they are so much older.

Plucking up courage, she then suggests that as the children do not need her now during the school day, she thought she might get a little part-time job. She says she has seen an advert in the paper for such a job that she thought she would enjoy. The paper is slowly lowered 99

Scenario G: *All's Well That Ends Well*

"The young man was delighted. To be trusted for the first time with the money to go and buy the lottery ticket for the syndicate at work! It might not seem much, but it was a lot of money, and it was usually the section leader who did that. And it was working time, too, not his own time. If he took it steady, it would take half an hour to get there and back, better than all that paperwork stacked up on his desk.

They all waved him off, as if recognising it was an adventure for him. Who knows, perhaps this would be the time that they won, and it would have been him who had paid for the tickets!

He checked to make sure he had the card with the set of numbers in his pocket: yes, it was there. Same numbers every week, paid on Tuesday for both the Wednesday and the Saturday draw. Fifty-eight pounds – one pound for each person in the section. The money was hot in his hand, the curled-up notes seeming to have a life almost of their own.

The newsagents was suddenly there before him, all too quickly. In he went, paid in the money and gave over the card. The girl serving him made some comment about training a new retriever for the money run. She must have been the one usually here on a Tuesday and was used to someone else paying in. He didn't care. The task was done. He took the ticket with the numbers on and began to move away. His eye caught the advert for an 'Instant'. His hand went into his pocket, out came a two-pound coin, and before he knew what he was doing, he was handing it over for one of the cards that promised a fortune. 'And I'll have a chocolate bar, please.' His eyes were fixed on the chocolate bar as he left the shop, almost colliding with someone who hesitated, as if she knew him, but he didn't look up, too engrossed in the wording on the back of the card. He decided to save it until he was home, opening the wrapper from the chocolate, clumsily dropping it and his card, and stuffing the chocolate wrapper into his pocket as he hurried back to work.

As he approached the street where his office was located, he realised he wasn't holding the lottery ticket. Must be in his pocket, he thought. A search revealed the chocolate wrapper, but no lottery ticket. His steps slowed as he got closer to the office. Where was it? Where had it gone? He looked around, but the street was clear except for a girl who seemed vaguely familiar walking back the same way he had come.

It did not matter how much he searched. He had just to accept it. He had lost it. His steps were now down to a positive crawl, and he was inside the building only seconds away from the office. Just have to face the music.

In he went, heads turned to see who it was, faces looking at him expectantly.

'Pay it in OK?' asked the team leader.

'Yes,' he replied.

'Why do you look as if you've just seen a ghost then?' asked the woman who worked at the same desk as him.

'Because, because,' have to tell them, no way out,'... I've lost the ticket!'

Silence. Everyone still, eyes fixed on him. The ultimate crime.

Just as the tension reached a pitch where he felt he would have to scream or run, a voice behind him from the door said,

'And still lost it would be if I hadn't seen you in the shop. Near knocked me over you did, so taken up with your Instant and your chocolate bar. Dropped it in the doorway you did, so I picked it up.'

'Sally ... Sally ... oh, thank you, Sally, and I'm sorry I

knocked you over and didn't see you and … oh, thank you!' The relief was so obviously enormous that several of the older workers had kind smiles on their faces. Sally picked up the Instant, which he had dropped on the floor in his agitation and started fiddling with it.

'Well, you just be grateful, and take more care in future.' Bill was about to lecture him when Sally, herself as white as a sheet, staggered to a desk and slumped in the chair.

'Why, what is it, lass?' began Bill.

'It's … Well, he may have lost the lottery ticket, but he's only gone and won on the Instant.'

'How much?' asked Bill incredulously.

'You'll never believe it.' She fixed the young man with a stare.

'You've won … .'

Note: This extract can be used with the characters playing male or female.

Scenario H: *Waiting for Godot*

This play by Samuel Beckett was written in 1948, and first performed in 1953.

Two men, Vladimir and Estragon, live in hope of the arrival of a mysterious being, called Godot. Although Godot sends messages that he is delayed, he never comes. The whole play consists of Vladimir and Estragon waiting, passing time just existing, meeting only two other characters, Pozzo and Lucky.

Scenario I: *Breakfast with Mary*

It is a lovely sunny day and the birds can be heard whistling in the garden. Mary is laying the table with a cloth, and setting out some cups and saucers. She pops outside and returns with a tray with a coffee pot on it, and some bowls. She goes over to the sideboard and pours cereals into the two bowls, returning to sit down. George enters, humming a tune, with the *Financial Times* under his arm.

He sits at the table with a cheery morning greeting to Mary.

'Coffee, dear?' she asks. George nods and she pours.

'What sort of day have you got, George?'

He puts aside his paper and chats to her about what it will be like at the office. He is a financier who deals in the stock market, has lots of important people as clients, and often has to take them out for lunch. He tells Mary about the lunch he will be going to today, on a luxury boat on the river.

'What about you, dear?' he asks.

Mary tells him that she will potter about in the garden later as the weather looks good, and perhaps visit a neighbour for afternoon tea before Nanny brings the children back from school.

George gets up. Mary then says she would like to pop over to the next village this morning, and asks whether she can use a car. George tells her to use the Mercedes as the Jaguar is in for a service. He sets off for work.

Scenario J: *Maria Marten and Murder in the Red Barn*

The story of Maria Marten has been told by a number of playwrights. Constance Cox has written a short version, and Brian Burton a full-length play based on the original plays.

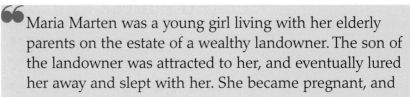

Maria Marten was a young girl living with her elderly parents on the estate of a wealthy landowner. The son of the landowner was attracted to her, and eventually lured her away and slept with her. She became pregnant, and he hid her in a cottage away from her parents. He promised he was going to marry her. She foolishly believed him until she discovered that he was engaged to another, wealthy woman.

By now, Maria had had her baby and came back to her home village to try and see William Corder, the villain. Corder kept promising to take her away. Then the baby became sick, and under the pretence of providing medicine, he poisoned it. Worried she was going to cause trouble, he tricked her into going to the Red Barn to meet him at night, where he discovered the baby was dead. When Maria continued to threaten to reveal what had happened unless he married her, they argued and he shot her. He buried the bodies of the baby and Maria using a spade borrowed from a country yokel, a friend of Maria.

Maria's parents were worried at her disappearance, and her mother had a dream that featured the Red Barn. There was a search and the bodies were found. An officer of the law put pieces of the puzzle together, and Corder was arrested. He confessed, and eventually expressed remorse for his actions.

There is a subplot involving a gypsy whose own sister had been treated in the same way by Corder, and who set up the meeting with Maria as bait to try and get vengeance. She assisted the police with evidence to catch Corder.

Scenario K: *Green Rain*

There were three of us. Jo, Martin and me. We were shopping. Just shopping, nothing more exciting than that. I was looking at some rather scrummy fudge, when my friend called out,

'Hey, hasn't it gone dark?'

'Suppose it has – but I don't care. If it throws it down we're in here nice and dry,' said Jo as she continued to sort through a pile of sale items. It wasn't very busy in the store and it was nice to be able to wander around without pressure from sales assistants, and the crush of busy shoppers in a hurry.

'It really does look odd out there,' said Martin as he wandered over to the display windows and stood peering out. 'The sky has gone a funny colour – and here comes the rain!'

I glanced over and saw Jo taking a bit more interest, edging slowly towards Martin.

'Hey,' shouted Martin, 'The rain's green!'

'Don't be daft,' I replied. 'Come and look at this fudge!'

'I think it is,' said Jo. 'The rain, that is. It really is green!'

'I'm going out to see,' said Martin.

Jo told him she didn't think that was a good idea, but he kept arguing, and I carried on ogling the fudge. Argument over, Martin went out and confirmed what we could all see – yes, the rain was indeed green. But why? Was it a chemical problem? If so, Martin shouldn't be out there. I turned to go and persuade him to come back in, only to see Jo run out to him. By now it was throwing it down and the pair of them were standing looking up, the water splashing all over them. 'They will be soaked to the skin,' I thought.

'I feel a bit funny,' I heard Martin shout.

'Me too,' I heard Jo reply as I reached the door.

I was just about to go out and join them and try to persuade them to come in when I saw others outside. They must have been caught earlier than Martin and Jo, must have been outside when it started raining. They looked strange. What was it that made them look strange? They weren't moving. Like statues they were, all of them, frozen in whatever state of movement they had been in when they froze.

Action needed, and quick. I reached out of the doorway and was just able to grab Jo, pulling her violently back into the store. She was shaking, but Martin wasn't. He was still, like the others. He didn't look dead, just frozen in time.

This was not the shopping experience I had come out for today! What on earth was I to do?

"

Extract A: *Child's Play*

(Emily is in her late twenties, and Philip, her partner, is about the same age. She works for a textiles company that makes exclusive clothes for mail order, for major boutique shops and for individual customers.)

(They have a young child of six, Sarah, and a new baby boy, Dominic. At the start of the scene, Sarah is playing with Dominic, pretending to be 'mum'.)

(Emily feels much pressured by her firm to succeed. Philip works from home, acting as a house-dad and writing short stories.)

Emily: I'm late.
Philip: Well, it's your own fault.
Emily: Not if it was my boss who kept me.
Philip: He must have known you were out with clients tonight.
Emily: He doesn't care – as long as the orders keep rolling in.
Philip: Well, you can only do what you can do!
Sarah: Mummy, look, Dominic's hungry.
Emily: Yes, dear. Did you get all the washing done, Philip?
Philip: No, sorry, I really got into the story I was writing.
Sarah: Look, Daddy, Dominic's going to have his tea.
Philip: Yes, dear. When do you have to leave to meet your clients?
Emily: In about ten minutes or I'll be late and that won't get orders!
Sarah: Here you are, Dominic

(Sarah is seen putting sausages left over from her tea into his mouth. Dominic starts to struggle to breathe.)

Sarah: Mummy, Daddy, Dominic is eating his tea.
Philip: Not now, darling, Mummy's busy.
Emily: Tell me later, Sarah.

(Sarah continues to stuff sausages into Dominic's mouth – he cannot breathe at all now and starts to choke. The noise alerts Philip.)

Philip: What's the matter with Dominic? Emily, what's the matter ...
Emily: Oh no, what on earth is sticking out of his mouth?
Sarah: Dominic's a good boy, he's eating all his tea, Mummy.
Emily: Sarah! What have you done? Philip, help quickly!

(Philip runs over to where Dominic is lying.)

Philip: Sarah, what have you done? He's not breathing ...
Emily: This is your fault, Philip!
Philip: I didn't stuff the sausages in his mouth!

Extract B: *Happy Home 1*

(John is in his thirties, father of Melissa, who is six. He is out of work. Lydia is also in her thirties and married to John.)

(This scene takes place in the kitchen of their small house. Melissa is playing at cooking a meal.)

John: Watch what you are doing!
Melissa: I am, I am.
John: You shouldn't be by the cooker.
Lydia: She's all right, John. She hasn't got many places where she can play.
Melissa: Can we go to the park?
Lydia: Not just now.
Melissa: But we haven't been to the park for ages!
Lydia: I'm sorry, but there just isn't time.
Melissa: Why not?
John: Because your mother's getting ready for work.
Melissa: Can't you take me, Daddy?
John: No. I've got to fill this form in.
Melissa: Why?
Lydia: Don't bother your daddy, Melissa.
Melissa: But why does he have to do the form now?
Lydia: So he can try and get a job, darling.
Melissa: Well, can't you take me then, Mummy?
John: Your mother's going to work. We need the money so stop asking.
Lydia: Do I look all right, John?
John: You'll do. You're only in reception, not on the catwalk.

Lydia:	I know, but you never know, I might catch the boss's eye and I might get promoted.
John:	He can keep his eyes off you!
Lydia:	The 'he' is a 'she', John.
Melissa:	Can't I go to the park then?
Lydia:	No!
John:	No!

(As they shout at her together, they both turn sharply towards her in anger. Melissa, frightened, jumps up. She has been playing with the cooker. On the top of the cooker is a pan of boiling vegetables. She catches the handle with her arm and knocks it off all over her. She screams.)

Extract C: *Happy Home 2*

(John is in his thirties, father of Melissa, who is six. He is out of work. Lydia is also in her thirties and married to John.)

(This scene takes place in the kitchen of their small house. Melissa is playing at cooking a meal.)

John:	Watch what you are doing!
Melissa:	I am, I am.
John:	You shouldn't be by the cooker.
Lydia:	I wonder if the fridge door will squeak when I open it.
Melissa:	Can we go to the park?
Lydia:	The car is very noisy.
Melissa:	But we haven't been to the park for ages!
Lydia:	I think I might suck a lemon.
Melissa:	Why not?
John:	What are our cups made out of, china or plastic?
Melissa:	Can't you take me, Daddy?
John:	I've got to fill this form in.
Melissa:	Why?
Lydia:	Don't jump in the water.

Extract D: *The Theft*

| Pete: | Why are you looking at me like that? |
| Janet: | I think you stole the phone. |

2 Pete: Why are you looking at me like that?
    Janet: I think you stole the phone.

3 Pete: Why are you looking at me like that?
    Janet: I **think** you stole the phone.

4 Pete: Why are you looking at me like that?
    Janet: I think **you** stole the phone.

5 Pete: Why are you looking at me like that?
    Janet: I think you **stole** the phone.

6 Pete: Why are you looking at me like that?
    Janet: I think you stole **the** phone.

7 Pete: Why are you looking at me like that?
    Janet: I think you stole the **phone**.

Extract E: *Two's Company*

Person A: I would like a word with you.
Person B: What about?
Person A: I want to know what is going on.
Person B: What are you on about?
Person A: It's no good coming the innocent with me.
Person B: I really don't know what you are talking about!
Person A: How could you?
Person B: Look, I've had just about enough of this.
Person A: Oh you have, have you?
Person B: Yes, and I think you should watch out.
Person A: Well, I think you are the one who should be watching out!
Person B: You're the one who started this!
Person A: No I'm not! You started it.
Person B: No I didn't – but I'm not taking any more of this rubbish.
Person A: What an actor!
Person B: Right! That is it!

> The scenarios and script extracts above can be used either as indicated in specific activities in this section or as stimulus for your drama work.

SECTION 2
Creating Drama and Developing Skills

▨ Introducing the Drama Projects

This section offers seven free-standing drama projects that give you:

- background information and ideas for creating drama
- some 'rules' and standard ways of structuring drama
- a variety of texts and performance styles to choose from.

These resources will allow you to build on your understanding of the Areas of Study and to learn how to combine them in your own drama work. The knowledge you have gained already about each Area of Study should be applied when relevant in the practical dramas you create.

As you work as Deviser, Designer, Director and **Performer**, you will deepen your knowledge and understanding of the craft of drama, learning mainly by doing. Applying the knowledge you have and are given is the best way to develop understanding, and once you understand, you will gain the freedom to apply what you have learnt in new contexts. As you begin to master the medium of drama, you will be able to take control of your work, which is what you will need to do in the two Controlled Assessments and final Examined Unit.

So the projects in this section will encourage you to work as an emerging dramatic artist in your own right. Plenty of advice, information and tips are given along the way, but in each project there are points where you will take over and control the drama.

As you become more confident, you can select from and alter the structures, genres, performance styles and general ways

of working you are introduced to. You may decide to bend the 'rules' or even radically break them. Great artists are always pushing the boundaries, creating new ways of communicating their ideas. As well as entertaining an audience, an important function of all artists is to throw a little bit of 'grit' into the system, to help society ask the important questions about how we as human beings are organising our societies and how they might develop. Use these projects as a chance to grow within and as part of your drama group.

2.1 Creating an Ensemble Performance

Your aims

You are going to work as a whole class to create a piece of ensemble theatre based on an adapted version of Shakespeare's *Julius Caesar*.

Rationale: Drama is a social art – you work together as a whole class or in small groups. Therefore your Drama class has to become a supportive unit if you are all to achieve good results on this course. You must help each other to take drama risks knowing you will be respected and without fear of being mocked or undermined. Creating a piece of ensemble theatre together is a great way of developing this important team spirit.

Skills and understanding you will develop

- *Genre:* You will be working with a classic text – even though it has been adapted it mostly sticks to the genre.

- *Performance style:* Ensemble theatre

- *In rehearsal:* You will be making decisions about audience and **performance space**, and semiotics. You may also use improvisation as you experiment with the script. The script itself provides many opportunities for you to consider character, context and plot, and structure.

- *Contexts:* You will be working principally as **Director** and **Performer**. You may also have an opportunity to work as **Designer** if you really like the script and decide to take it to a full performance.

At the end of the project you will find additional ideas for working as **Deviser**.

Record which of the four Contexts – Performer, Director, Deviser or Designer – you focused on. List the skills you are developing, your level of competence and what you need to improve.

For your information

Ensemble theatre is a specific way of shaping and performing drama. Famous theatre practitioners who have worked in this way include:

- Bertolt Brecht, who founded the Berliner Ensemble in the 1950s. His play *The Caucasian Chalk Circle* works very well as an ensemble production.

- Joan Littlewood, who with Ewan McColl set up the Theatre Workshop in the East End of London, producing a classic ensemble play *Oh What a Lovely War* in the 1960s.

- Northern Stage Company, a current theatre group who have used this dynamic approach to adapt *Animal Farm* and other works.

You could look at these plays with your teacher and consider them for use with **Unit 1 From Page to Stage** or to help develop your understanding of the six Areas of Study.

Defining features of ensemble theatre

- Deviser, designer, director and performer work together as a team, often over a long period of time. (You will be working with your Drama group for two years.)

- Functions merge, e.g. performers contribute to the script and design, designers contribute to direction.

- The script evolves during the devising and writing process. Writers often work with a company to create the script.

- There are no star parts and often actors play many parts.

- Content is often dealt with in an episodic or broad sweep rather than in the format of the well-made play with a clear plot line.

- Content often centres on 'big' events or sweeping novels, as in *Oh What a Lovely War* (which deals with the carnage of the First World War) or the Royal Shakespeare Company's adaptation of *Nicholas Nickleby*.

- Ensemble theatre can be an ideal way to work with large casts and create exciting big-group scenes.

- It makes possible imaginative approaches to setting and communication that rely more on the resources of the performer than on technical effects. Songs, music, sounds, symbolism or physical theatre may be used to keep a continuous flow of action.

- Design has to be flexible and is not necessarily descriptive – not totally realistic or naturalistic. Symbolic or representational design is often used. One large branch may symbolise a forest, a flag and rostra may represent the battlements of a castle. The main concern is to keep the performance flowing.

Why use Shakespeare?

Of course it is possible to do a GCSE Drama course without using a Shakespeare play, but why would you want to? He is one of the world's greatest playwrights, his works are performed throughout the world and have been an inspiration for generations of artists: musicians, film makers, painters as well as those who make theatre.

So what is special about Shakespeare's plays?

- The plays demand to be acted out. They really work on stage, reading them doesn't do them justice.

- The themes are universal. They don't date, they are the issues that affect all human beings in any period of history: jealousy, greed, love, war, the struggle for power, compassion, the state of the nation.

- The language, at its best, is wonderful to speak aloud, it cries out to be performed. Don't be put off by the old English. Decode it together, then let the rhythms and rich ideas contained in the text take over.

- The plays are complex, you don't just get simple characterisations. The plays are **dialectical**, that is, they are written from two or more points of view. In this way varied and contrasting views are represented and allowed to battle it out. The audience is forced to think about the themes and whether they sympathise with or despise the characters or a bit of both. Shakespeare's characters are human beings with both virtues and faults.

'Shakespeare is a very modern playwright, he is our contemporary.'

When you have finished this project discuss as a group whether you agree with this statement.

Preparation

The play chosen for you to work with is *Julius Caesar*, which is based on actual historical events. It is a political play, a story of assassination, an examination of power, pride, ambition and the volatile, changeable nature of public opinion. It is ideal for your group to work on as an ensemble, as there are strong group and crowd scenes.

There is no intention in this project for you to tackle the complete play: the adaptation you will be using is a 15 minute version. It focuses on the lead up to the assassination and the assassination itself. This distilled, heavily edited version works with the essence of that section of the play. (You can find this adaptation on pages 104–109.)

There are also parts not written by Shakespeare at all, often a necessary step when you edit a text, for example to add links to compensate for what has been cut. Cassius's lines have been cut down and redistributed among the Conspirators. This means some of the intrigue of Cassius convincing Brutus to move against Caesar that is in the original has been lost. The opening Soldier and Citizen lines are not Shakespeare's and have been devised to rapidly set the context of the Rome of those times. They are very blunt, direct scene setters. You could add to them or write your own versions if you want something less simplified.

The thinking behind the cuts and adaptations is to turn a powerful 3 hour play into a dynamic 15 minute ensemble play – one that can work with a GCSE Drama class in a studio, which is likely to be your chosen performance space.

Exploration

1 Read the script with your Drama group.
2 Work on the opening scene (page 104) of the script. Split into three groups: Soldiers, Citizens and Senators/Nobility.

▲ One student group's interpretation of the entrance and postures of the Soldiers, Senators and Citizens

■ Decide and rehearse how you will enter: your posture and collective group shape – proxemics. Practise this so that you create a strong visual impact, one that will tell the audience the type or class of people you are even before you speak.

■ Consider whether you should add sound or percussion to your entrance. The Soldiers could be backed by a drumbeat and brass, the Citizens by improvised shouts and words, the Senators/Nobility by silence. Try out some ideas.

■ Now tackle the words of each group's opening speech. How will you split it up? What will you all say together and what will be said by individual or smaller groups of voices?

■ Put all you have rehearsed together to perform the opening of the play. Does it capture the sense of a powerful state and that Rome is a volatile society where peace is fragile?

3 As one group, work on the first Conspirators' speech. (This speech is made up of excerpts from lines spoken by Cassius to Brutus in the original.) The Conspirators are jealous of the power and current popularity of Caesar.

■ Each take two or three parts of the speech you'd like to say. Walking around the room, practise saying your lines aloud with expressions of contempt and jealousy – try spitting them out. Then try saying each line rather coolly as if it doesn't really trouble you, then try saying it as if you are worried someone might hear you.

■ Next, as you walk around the room, your teacher or one of the class will call out either 'Spit it out' or 'Cool' or 'Secret'. When they do this, perform in the appropriate manner to the first person you pass. Keep rotating the three calls for as long as it is useful.

■ When that voice exercise is over, decide how you think the lines you have selected should be performed. Collect as a group and run through the speech. It is quite all right if more than one of you are saying the same line. If there are any bits of the speech that no one is saying then someone needs to take those on. Now, as a whole group, be a collective set of Conspirators. Create a suitable shaping on stage (sort out the **proxemics**) and perform the speech.

▼ Getting contempt and jealousy into the Conspirators' speech

4 You could do the same for the Citizens' speeches. Here the voice exercise could be speaking the lines loud and loutishly or as hero worshippers or as if you're having great fun or slightly drunk. Alternatively, you could use the Mark Antony 'Friends, Romans' speech on page 107, saying it pompously or sincerely or sarcastically.

5 Try working in pairs on the Caesar/Calpurnia scene, developing the concerned, fearful wife and the masterful, confident Caesar. It could be fun to try this completely over the top, send it up. Then do it as it should be done in the script. You may discover that your over-the-top version was not very far from how it needs to be played. Did some of you find it hard to go over the top? What might help you be more adventurous when performing drama? Taking more 'risks' can add impact to your performance.

6 As you will perform this script as an ensemble, the cast will remain on stage at all times. When not directly involved in a scene you could sit/stand around the edge as interested spectators, as happens in many **Brecht** productions. Or you could provide some **supporting images** for the action on stage. For example, as the Conspirators talk, the audience could see in the background Caesar being offered a crown by the Citizens and the Soldiers holding back the crowds. Look through the script and identify where else you could use supporting images.

7 Are there any design images you could use to support the themes of the play? Will it be set historically or are you going to make it an analogy for modern-day politics. A simple idea would be to use two large graffiti boards with suitable political slogans on them. These could be general slogans about politicians in any age, plus graffiti relevant to the text. In one production, the assassination scene was backed by white screens which were splattered with artificial blood by the assassins as they killed Caesar.

In Shakespeare's theatre the play was most likely performed on an empty stage. The words and actors would have had to conjure up the pictures in the audience's minds, accompanied at certain points by sound effects created by stagehands.

66

Julius Caesar
(Enter Crowd.)

Citizens: The Roman mob.
You either humour us,
Or control us.
If you can!

(Enter Soldiers.)

Soldiers: Caesar's power depends on his army.
Rome, the mightiest army the world has ever seen,
Disciplined, trained, invincible.

(Caesar, Senators and Nobility enter.)

Citizens: It's Caesar, Caesar and the Senators. Caesar, Caesar, Caesar, ...

Senators and
Nobility: The rich,
The beautiful,
The mighty and influential.
All powerful.
Cassius, Casca, Brutus, Mark Antony, Calpurnia, Tebarius.

Caesar: I am Caesar.

Senators: We are the Senate.

Citizens: Caesar! Caesar! / Caesar wear the crown. / Be our King. / The people's King.

Voices: What the soothsayer said is coming true.
Pride before a fall.
Beware the Ides of March. Beware the Ides of March.

Caesar: The Ides of March have come.

Voices: Aye, but not gone.

Citizens: Caesar! We offer you the crown! / Refuse us not, Caesar. / Caesar, we offer it thrice. / Listen to them. / You blocks, you stones, you worse than senseless things. / Look at them strewing flowers in Caesar's way.

(Caesar declines. Is he tempted to take the crown offered? Caesar exits.)

[Following text taken from Act 1, Scene 2.]

Conspirators: This Caesar would soar above the view of man and keep us all in servile fearfulness. / I was born free as Caesar, so were you,

> **Note**
> Slash (/) marks indicate how lines might be divided among several actors.

we have fed as well and can endure the winter's cold as well as he. / And this man is become a god, while we wretched creatures must bend our bodies if Caesar carelessly nod his head. / Why, man, he doth bestride the narrow world like a Colossus, and we petty men walk under his huge legs and peep about to find ourselves dishonourable graves. / Why should his name be sounded more than ours?

(Noises in background, from a distance.)

Citizens: Caesar! Noble Caesar! Caesar! Caesar!

Caesar: Let me have men about me that are fat, sleek-hearted men, and such as sleep o' nights: Young Cassius has a lean and hungry look, he thinks too much, such men are dangerous.

Antony: Fear him not, Caesar, he's not dangerous, he is a noble Roman.

Caesar: Would he were fatter! But I fear him not. He reads much, he is a great observer, and he looks quite through the deeds of men: he loves no plays as thou dost, Antony; he hears no music; seldom smiles. Such men as he are never at heart's ease, whiles they behold a greater than themselves, and therefore are they very dangerous.

[Link line below devised to cover large cut in text.]

Voices: Beware, beware the Ides of March. Beware, beware.

[Script moves on to Act 2, Scene 2.]

Calpurnia: Do not stir out of our house today. Horrid dreams have I seen. Fierce fiery warriors fighting upon the clouds in ranks and squadrons, which drizzled blood upon the Capitol. Ghosts did shriek and squeal about the streets. Oh I fear for you, Caesar.

Caesar: What the gods decide is decided. Caesar shall go forth, for these predictions are for the world in general not just Caesar.

Calpurnia: When beggars die, there are no comets seen, the heavens themselves blaze forth the death of princes.

Caesar: Cowards die many times before their death, the valiant never taste of death but once. Death will come when it will come.

Calpurnia: Do not go forth today.

(Caesar, joined by Senators, goes forth to the Senate.)

[Lines below devised to cover large cut in text.]

Citizens: To the Capitol to see great Caesar. / Such days are not common, not to be missed. / You doting fools, remember you not Pompey who not long since you 'adored' also. / And now in your best holiday attire you salute Caesar who comes in triumph over Pompey's blood. / To the Capitol to see Caesar.

[Script moves on to Act 3, Scene 1.]

(The Conspirators gather around Caesar.)

Brutus: I kiss thy hand, Caesar.

Cassius: As low as to thy foot doth Cassius fall, to beg enfranchisement for Publius Cimber.

Caesar: It cannot be done, Cimber shall remain banished.

Cinnar: Oh Caesar.

Caesar: Hence! Arise, man.

Decius: Great Caesar.

Caesar: Doth not Brutus bootless kneel?

Casca: Speak hands for me.

(Caesar is stabbed.)

Voices: Blood pouring, blood pouring. / Caesar dying, Caesar dying. / Stab, kill, stab, kill. / Die Caesar, die Caesar, die Caesar, die Caesar.

Caesar: Et tu, Brute? Then fall, Caesar!

Cinna: Liberty, freedom! Tyranny is dead. Run hence, proclaim, cry it about the streets.

Cassius: Liberty, freedom and enfranchisement.

[Devised section of text follows to involve Soldiers and Citizens in the scene.]

(Mayhem by the Mob, improvised lines and action, reflecting mixed views on the assassination as news spreads across the city.)

Soldiers: What now? / Who commands? / It's done. Caesar's dead. / What faction rules? / Who do we follow? / What shall we do? / Revenge or jubilation? / Ah to hell with it!

(The Soldiers join the mayhem.)

Voices: Oh piteous spectacle / O noble Caesar / O woeful day / Traitors, villains / O most bloody sight / Revenge, revenge / We will be revenged. / Revenge! About! Seek! Burn! / Fire! Kill! Slay! Let not a traitor live!

[Back to Shakespeare's script.]

Brutus: People and Senators, be not affrighted. Fly not, stand still, ambition's debt is paid.

Casca: Speak to the crowd, Brutus, go to the pulpit.

Tebarius: Men, wives, children stare, cry and run as it were doomsday.

Brutus: Stoop, Romans, stoop and let us bathe our hands in Caesar's blood up to the elbows. Let's all cry 'Peace', freedom and liberty.

We must appease the multitude. They are beside themselves with fear. I must explain why I, that did love Caesar, struck him down.

Mark Antony, take Caesar's body. You shall not in your funeral speech blame us, but speak all good you can devise of Caesar, and say you do 't by our permission.

[Act 3, Scene 2]

Citizens: We will be satisfied. / Let us be satisfied. / Hear Brutus speak. / Silence.

Brutus: If any here demand, why Brutus rose against Caesar this is my answer; not that I lov'd Caesar less, but that I lov'd Rome more. Had you rather Caesar were living and die all slaves than that Caesar were dead, to live all free men? Who is here so rude, that would not be a Roman? If any, speak, for him have I offended. Who is here so vile, that will not love his Country? If any, speak, for him have I offended.

Citizens: None, Brutus, none. / Live, Brutus, live, live. / Take Brutus home in triumph. / Give him a statue with his ancestors. / Let him be Caesar. / Caesar's better parts shall be crown'd in Brutus.

Silence, let us hear Mark Antony. / We'll hear him. / Noble Antony, speak.

Caesar was a tyrant. / We are blest Rome is rid of him. / Peace! Let us hear what Antony has to say.

(The following speech could be made a collective role, with the lines divided among several actors.)

Mark Antony: Friends, Romans, Countrymen, lend me your ears;
I come to bury Caesar not to praise him:
The noble Brutus hath told you Caesar was ambitious:

If it were so, it was a grievous fault,
And grievously hath Caesar answered it.

He was my friend, faithful and just to me;
But Brutus says he was ambitious,
And Brutus is an honourable man.

I thrice presented Caesar with a kingly crown,
Which he did thrice refuse. Was this ambition?
Yet Brutus says he was ambitious;
And sure he is an honourable man.

Citizens: There is a lot of truth in what he says. / Yet when you consider it Caesar has been greatly wronged. / There may come worse in his place. / Antony is right he didn't take the crown so he was not ambitious. / Listen, Antony speaks again.

Antony: Here I have Caesar's will.

Citizens: Read it, Mark Antony. / The will, the will! / We will hear Caesar's will.

Antony: I must not read it. You must not know how much Caesar loved you all. It will inflame you, it will make you mad.

Citizens: Read the will. Read the will.

Antony: I should not have told you of the will. I fear I wrong the honourable men whose daggers have stabb'd Caesar.

Citizens: Honourable men! They are traitors. / Read the will. / They were villains. / Murderers! / Read the will.

Antony: Look where Cassius' dagger struck.
See what a rent the envious Casca made.
Here the well-beloved Brutus stabb'd
Oh how dearly Caesar loved Brutus
This was the most unkindest cut of all.

Citizens: O piteous spectacle / O noble Caesar / O woeful day / O traitors, villains / O most bloody sight. / Kill. / Let not a traitor live. / Burn the house of Brutus. / Let's seek out the conspirators.

Antony: Wait, you have forgot the will. To every Roman citizen he gives seventy-five drachmas. He has left you his walks, his private arbours and newly planted orchards, left them to you and your heirs for ever.
Here was a Caesar! When comes such another?

Citizens: Never, never. Come, away, away! / We'll burn his body in the holy place, / and with the brands fire the traitors' houses. / Take up the body.

(Exit Citizens with the body.)

Antony: Now let it work: mischief, thou art afoot,
Take thou what course thou wilt.

[In the original play there is one more scene in Act 3 and two further Acts follow.]

,,

 **Stretch your skills**

After completing the Exploration tasks you could read the original complete text of *Julius Caesar*. Watching the excellent 1950s film version, starring Marlon Brando and James Mason, would also give you a flavour of the whole text before the Rehearsal stage.

Rehearsal

Divide the parts and lines of the *Julius Caesar* script amongst the whole group. Take the best ideas from your Exploration work and create the performance.

As the rehearsals progress add any sound, lights, properties, costume or setting you think relevant. Introduce these aspects one at a time, covering as many as time allows. For example, focus on ideas for sound then have a run through incorporating the selected ideas. With that mastered try adding some lighting. This keeps the process more manageable than trying to tackle all aspects at once. If you run out of time then at least each element tried has contributed fully and added something extra to each rehearsal.

The script can of course be performed without any design or technical elements, letting the actors alone bring the words to life. However, if you have time and resources, design and technical support can aid communication and help you raise your level of performance. It also gives a chance for you to develop your skills in these areas. This is good preparation for the Designer Brief in *Unit 3 From Concept to Creation*.

How to excel

Managing your time effectively is one of the key factors in creating a quality performance. Adding elements one at a time is an effective way of ensuring there is always a workable play ready to perform. Extra elements can be added time permitting. This is vital in **Unit 3 From Concept to Creation**, when you are working to a tight examination schedule.

Performance

Decide whether the performance will be for yourselves and the teacher or to an audience, e.g. another drama class, a different year group, another school. This decision will influence the degree to which you refine and rehearse the performance.

In *Unit 1 From Page to Stage*, you could use this project as the basis for your Controlled Assessment and consider a different section of *Julius Caesar*.

In the full text of *Julius Caesar* there are key scenes between the main characters and there are two group scenes that play well: Act 3, Scene 2, with Antony, Brutus and four Commoners, and Act 3, Scene 3, with Cinna and four Commoners.

The first of these scenes is rather long, so you might only do part of it or share it with one or two other groups. Likewise the roles of Antony and Brutus have a lot of lines to learn so these could be split between two or three actors or edited down, as has been done in the adapted script you have used for this project.

Editing and adapting is a key drama skill. Scripts are not sacrosanct and can be played around with. Shakespeare himself regularly drew from other plays and stories to create his works. So practise these skills. Working on the scenes from *Julius Caesar* suggested above could be good practice. Cut them to the key essentials, but not so brutally that they lose their impact and sense.

Try adapting *Macbeth* to a 15 minute version that is fast and furious, but has all the essential elements of the original 3 hour play.

▲ High-speed *Hamlet*. This energetic performance managed to deliver the gist in a blistering 12½ minutes.

Test out your editing skills on *Coriolanus*, another play by Shakespeare which explores some of the same themes as *Julius Caesar*, especially the relationship between leaders/heroes and citizens. It is also set in Ancient Rome: Coriolanus has been a great warrior and hero of the people of Rome, but when he steps into the field of politics he finds the people turn against him. The scenes with Coriolanus and the Citizens are strong engaging episodes that you may like to compare with those from *Julius Caesar*, and/or use them for performance. Two examples to start you off are Act 2, Scene 3 and the second half of Act 3, Scene 1.

Additional devising option

The 15 minute *Julius Caesar* script on pages 104–109 is an example of how deviser skills can be applied to an existing script, something you could opt for in **Unit 3 From Concept to Creation** (the Examined Unit) if you choose the Performer (devised) Brief.

Shakespeare's plays are good enough to take any amount of 'messing about'. The Drama group who first worked with the adapted script for *Julius Caesar* added songs to it. The song below was inserted following the assassination of Caesar. It gave the cast a chance to be Devisers, adding a commentary on the action, acting almost as a chorus. It also incorporated the skill of singing and allowed them to play around with genre, adding a 'Lloyd Webber' musical-theatre touch to this classic text.

An approach like this is particularly relevant to **Unit 2 Drama in the Making**, where you need to present three different items for assessment and show that you have experimented with ideas. Devising a song to add to a drama or comment on the action could be one of the three items required for the Controlled Assessment.

Stretch your skills

Try performing this song in the script or write your own song for the moment after Caesar's assassination.

> # 66 Song for *Julius Caesar*
>
> Voices: The deed is done
> This bloody day
> Don't look back
> What's done is done
> It was never meant to end this way.
>
> The deed is done, now walk away
> The tears are spilled, this bloody day

Don't look back, just close your eyes
What's done is done, you've said goodbye
It was never meant to end this way.

His breath is gone he is no more.

Deathly words are spinning round your head.

He was our leader
He was our saviour
Not so long ago
You would have thought the same.

Review

This unit was designed to:

- build some team spirit in the group by working as an ensemble
- perform a script which uses Shakespeare's language
- work with a classic theme in the tragedy genre
- explore staging and performance styles.

Discuss with your teacher your views on:

- what you have learnt about yourself and others on each of these four aspects
- any performance skills you have improved
- any directing skills you have developed
- any design and devising skills you have used.

2.2 Improvising Drama

Your aims

You are going to develop your confidence and expertise in the skill of improvisation.

Rationale: Improvisation will be used as both a devising and a performance process. It will be defined clearly so you understand exactly what the key elements are. This should help you plan dramas more effectively and ensure your work has **substance**, **detail** and **quality**. The activities will allow you to practise and develop your improvisation skills.

Skills and understanding you will develop

- *When improvising:* You will learn that it is best to think first, speak second, to be relaxed about doing nothing, to stay in the improvisation as you think of something appropriate to say or do. You will build the discipline of staying in a fiction that is evolving for a sustained period, not stepping out of it at the first pause/problem, but solving the problems from within the improvisation.

- *Contexts:* You will work principally as **Performer** as you act out the improvisations. You may also work as **Deviser** when improvisation leads on to planning dramas and creating characters and plots.

    There may be some input as **Director** when you make decisions or give advice on the performing and staging of the improvisation. Finally, there may be a chance to work as **Designer** if you create the setting for any of the scenarios presented.

    Record which of the four Contexts – Performer, Director, Deviser or Designer – you focused on. List the skills you are developing, your level of competence and what you need to improve.

For your information

Improvising is, in effect, verbal table tennis where, instead of a ball, ideas are batted backward and forward. An improvisation can be spontaneous or planned around a loose or tight structure.

Spontaneous improvisations can be fun and will help you to:

- develop your confidence as a performer
- become comfortable working with the unknown and taking risks
- think on your feet.

Planned improvisations are a way of working you will often use during your course. When devising your own dramas, you will:

- sort out a framework for the plot/situation
- improvise the actual dialogue as you go along
- review what is working as you work, keeping bits, editing bits and adding new bits.

You can find out more about different improvising styles on pages 47–49 in **Unit 1.4**.

Defining features

Whichever style of improvisation you use, there are three key features to become familiar with:

- offering
- yielding
- not blocking.

Each must be implemented correctly and with discipline if you are to improvise successfully. So let's look at each one in turn.

Offering

For the improvising 'game' to start, someone has to bat the ball into court, so they offer their partner an opening. For example:

Look, you can trust me. Tell me what's upsetting you.

Straight away there is an implied plot: someone is troubled and someone else is offering to help. It's a positive offering, so it's quite easy to bat the ball back and make the next offering. If it is a planned improvisation, you may have already decided who the characters are and what the problem is. If it is spontaneous, you have to think on your feet. In this case you may want to stall, because you can't think of a problem straight away, but you will still have to offer something to keep the game going. So return the ball with:

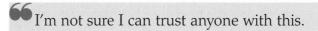

> I'm not sure I can trust anyone with this.

And so the improvisation proceeds, continuing for as long as **legitimate** offerings are made. For offerings to be legitimate each participant has to work with the logic of what is offered to them. The trick is to take your time, **think first, speak second** and don't be afraid of silences. A silence can be an offering, it can be used by your partner. It is a mistake to think that the best improvisers are those who give the quickest responses. The best improvisers make the most thoughtful, relevant responses. You have to be **drama intelligent**, which means the role play has **integrity**, and you use well the knowledge you already have and speculate creatively or avoid areas where your knowledge is weak.

Yielding

During an improvisation you sometimes have to adapt to your partner and change the line you thought you were going to take. You are in effect building a story together so don't ignore your partner and plough on with what you already had fixed in your head. Allow your partner's responses to open up new possibilities for the evolving drama. It is best to operate in **now time**. Don't get ahead of yourself. It's a team game, so listen first then respond.

Think again if your partner says:

> Look, actually I already know what's upsetting you. The police have been to John's house and taken a statement. He said he didn't mention your name and he's already told you he's going to keep you out of it. But what do you feel about that? Are you going to let him carry the can on his own?

Aspects of the first problem are now fixed, so you have to play the game with this new information.

Not blocking

This is all about dramatic discipline. There are a hundred ways you can **block** the improvisation – that is, create a situation where it is forced to stop or it loses its integrity. All good acting needs integrity, an honesty that makes the fiction being created work for an audience. You block by going outside the fiction being worked on. For example, you might block by:

- being 'witty', making jokes that are outside the fiction
- not paying attention to your partner
- using negative body language
- giving up
- not taking the exercise seriously.

Sometimes people block because of lack of confidence. Improvisation exercises are a good way of fighting this and building confidence. If you practise this core drama skill it will become something you use almost every day without thinking about it. Of course everyone can 'corpse' (the actor's word for getting the giggles) in improvisations, especially comic ones. However as GCSE Drama students you are expected to be able to improvise with full dramatic discipline, working within the fiction being created. This word **fiction** is vital, as Performer you must try to take the audience into the imagined world you are creating.

▶ Creating a spontaneous improvised dialogue

1 Try this offering task. In pairs, one of you makes an offering and the other has to pick up on it. See if you can keep the improvisation going for 1 minute. Switch the starting person and use a new offering, this time keeping the improvisation going for 2 minutes.

Make your initial offering something quite general and move gradually during the improvisation to the more specific. With the initial offerings you and your partner are like boxers sparring, looking for a good context. Here are examples of some general offerings:

- Are you going to sign it?
- Well, that's the way it goes if you don't stick up for yourself.
- Do you think your parents will let you go?
- Did you see who took it?
- Why does she always have to do that?

2 Have a go at finishing off the scenario below. Remember, yield to any new information offered by your partner and try your best not to block their offerings.

'Look, you can trust me. Tell me what's upsetting you.'

'I'm not sure I can trust anyone with this.'

'Look, actually I already know what's upsetting you. The police have been to John's house and taken a statement. He said he didn't mention your name and he's already told you he's going to keep you out of it. But what do you feel about that? Are you going to let him carry the can on his own?'

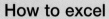

How to excel

Practise spontaneous 2 minute improvisations as a warm-up activity throughout your course to develop and refine your improvisation skills.

A framework for planned improvisation

Now that you have had some practice using the three elements of improvisation, let's take a look at a framework for **planned improvisation**. Considering each of the following questions will help you build in quality:

■ Where? ■ When? ■ Who? ■ What's up? ■ Why?

Where?

The location can create or add to the tension within a scene as well as **defining the performance space**. All good drama needs the 'magic T' – tension. If your location suggests the start of a plot and sets up a tension then it will prove a good choice for the setting of a drama. The setting will have what's called dramatic resonance, which is a good starting point for an improvisation.

Remember: Low-key, ordinary situations can create just as effective drama as exciting, 'all singing and dancing' situations. The same is true for locations.

Exploration	**1** In groups, look at the locations listed below and rate each one for dramatic resonance on a scale of 1 to 5, with 5 the highest rating:

    ■ a graveyard   ■ the top of a mountain
    ■ an aircraft cockpit   ■ a supermarket checkout
    ■ a car   ■ a trench on a battlefield
    ■ a sitting room   ■ the gate of the local infant school
    ■ an interview room   ■ a sports changing room
    ■ a headteacher's office   ■ a television studio.

2 Share your results with the rest of the class, summarising which locations got the highest rating and which the lowest. Give your reasons.

3 Back in your group, choose one location and set it simply with whatever you have in your drama space to suggest the location. Now devise the entrance into the space, without any dialogue. The aim is for your entrance to capture for the audience where you are meant to be.

4 Now compose the first speech that is spoken after the entrance. These lines should establish for the audience **where**

you are. Of course, a good set design can do this, but in improvised work you don't always have much set.

What you have done is slowed things down for the audience, given them time to adjust to what is happening and given them time to enter the fiction with you. They are now ready for you to move forward with the plot. Such **detailed work** is one of the keys to creating quality dramas.

When?

The when of an improvisation has two parts: the time frame it is set in and the time of day.

- **Time frame** falls into four broad categories: past, present, future or limbo.
- **Time of day** could be midnight, breakfast, dawn, for example.

But without some detail, there is little **dramatic significance** in these categories. You can add dramatic significance to the time frame and time of day by:

- how you combine them
- giving a specific date that has historic implications
- linking the time frame to a specific issue that makes it significant
- being mysterious.

For example, the following scenarios all imply some direction for the drama:

- Past, 1862, a few weeks before the Bryant & May match-girls' strike. It is early evening as the girls leave work.

- Present (a very specific example), teenagers talking about a curfew imposed in Redruth on young people under 16 being in the street after 9.00p.m. It is 9.30p.m.

- Present (a vaguer example), it's 10 minutes to kick-off.

- Future, 2040, sea level has risen globally by 30 metres in 30 years and is expected to rise another 30 metres in the next 30 years.

- Limbo, there is no time, people wait and wait, no past, no future.

Exploration

Divide into groups, each taking one of the five scenarios above, and create a short improvisation that grows out of the information provided.

When you have finished, discuss whether the time-frame information you worked with offered enough significant information to help you make a quality improvisation.

How to excel

Have this question in mind when you plan your dramas: 'What is *worth* doing a drama about?'

For instance, how much potential is there in the 'It's 10 minutes to kick-off' scenario? For an improvisation exercise it may have enough, but not for a planned drama of the sort you might prepare for assessment. It is the type of material that leads to what drama examiners call **skits** – short, often shallow improvisations based on an everyday situation. This is not to say you cannot create very good observational dramas that accurately show life as it is lived. The television programme *The Royle Family* is such a case. Skits, however, do not fulfil this potential and tend to be somewhat pointless and lack theatricality.

The match-girl scenario probably seemed hard if you didn't know the historical background. However, you could use your drama intelligence to speculate about a Victorian strike meeting and produce a reasonable improvisation. Simply googling 'match-girls' will lead to material that opens up lots of possibilities and real historical characters. This would enable you to devise a much more detailed and interesting drama.

The limbo scenario could be a stepping stone to something more abstract and mysterious. It would need further improvisations, discussions and experimentation to come up with an interesting storyline and characters.

Improvisation is a very effective process for developing stories. Many famous playwrights have worked like this with actors to develop their plays, e.g. Caryl Churchill. Even so, it is important to be critical as you devise, drawing on research and observation.

▼ 'Now, can you take a little bit of criticism?' Beverly's famous advice to Angela in *Abigail's Party* (1977) on how to wear lipstick came from an awkward moment in Selfridges observed by actress Alison Steadman (below). *Abigail's Party* director, Mike Leigh, is well known for developing his work using ensemble improvisation.

Who?

A good question to ask yourself when selecting characters is: '*Who* would this situation matter to?'

For example, consider a drama set in the Second World War where children from the city are to be evacuated to the country to escape the bombs. Who would this matter to?

It would matter to the parents of the children or the children themselves. So a scene based on parents deciding whether to send their children away to strangers has the potential to work well. If you played one of the parents you would have an interest in and concern with the situation. In other words it would be possible to **put yourself in their shoes**, which is the basis of good role play.

Any scenario where the situation does not really matter to your character has little scope for drama. There are some exceptions to this rule, such as when the character fulfils some other dramatic function – for example, setting the scene, bringing a message or creating an entertaining observation of everyday life.

Exploration

1 Choose one of the roles listed below. Create a specific context and make this character a particular person.

For example, a soldier might be scared about what is coming tomorrow when they go into battle – they have a family at home. Or an officer with a strong family military tradition might not want to let down the family honour by showing fear in front of the other soldiers.

- Soldier
- Mother/Father
- School pupil
- Famous celebrity
- Politician
- Worker, e.g. supermarket checkout operator
- Police officer
- Teenager
- Grandparent.

2 In pairs or in a small group, take it in turns to hot seat the role you have started to create.

3 Using the background you have built up, take it in turns to deliver a spontaneous improvised monologue. Set where it is, the time and make an entrance just as you did for the 'Where?' activity on page 119.

What's up?

This is the **context** which fixes the **scenario** for the improvisation and creates the potential for **tension**.

This context is influenced by all the other choices made – 'Where?', 'When?' and 'Who?' In reality, you are likely to decide them almost together as a package, not one at a time or always in a specific order. You have been developing much of 'What's up?' as you have gone through the other planning elements. But now from your experimentation you need to select a context that will create an engaging improvised drama, one that is worth giving some time and attention to.

Remember: You need a situation that matters to the characters involved.

Alternatively, you could choose a more observational type of drama (as used for a lot of comic work), where you would recreate everyday incidents showing how people behave in these situations. Again, beware of skits.

Exploration

Select from the work you have done in the activities on pages 119–123 and plan a quality improvisation for performance to the rest of the class. Work in pairs or small groups. Use one lesson to prepare and rehearse then perform your improvisation in the next lesson. Enjoy your performance then take feedback.

Why?
There is just one more point to consider. This is the intention of your improvisation or drama. What is the purpose of your work? To make people laugh? To make them aware of a particular issue? To shock them? To tell a good story? To work in a particular style or genre?

Adding genre and performance style to the mix
So far in this unit on improvisation, **genre** has not been mentioned. If you consciously select the genre and performance style, this will have a big impact on the devising and performance of your drama. You will find it can give your work an overall direction, helping you both to organise the drama and to communicate to the audience. This is because they will be familiar with the conventions of telling that type of story, so to an extent they will know what to expect.

For example, *commedia dell'arte*, with its established comic traditions, plots and stock characters, is instantly recognisable. The best known characters that appear most frequently are:

- Harlequin (sometimes called Arlechino), the mischievous acrobatic servant, very clown like

- Colombina, the female servant, who is clever, crafty and untamed
- Pantalone, wealthy, greedy, licentious, an old miser
- Il Capitano, swashbuckling, bold, but not always heroic and very foppish
- the Innamorate, the two lovers, often called Isabella and Flavio.

Each character will have their own typical mask and costume.

As part of your course you are expected to understand how genre influences the shaping of drama. So let's look at improvising within a specific genre and an appropriate performance style.

Exploration

1 Consider the list of lines below. They are all typical of a particular genre. Discuss in groups what genre you think they belong to.

Next decide what performance style would best fit these lines:

- It comes down to can you live with your conscience if you do this? That's what you have to ask yourself. I'm not sure if I could.
- If you let him get away with it again it will just go on happening. You can't keep burying your head in the sand.
- It's time to forget the past. You need to extend an olive branch. You need to let bygones be bygones.
- I can't say that to her, she'd take it the wrong way and then we'd be back where we started.
- I think you should complain about it. It's no good moaning to me all the time if you don't let her know how you feel.
- We can do this if we stick together, but if we let them split us, talk to us one at a time, you know what's likely to happen.
- How can I tell him? You know what he's been through recently. It's the wrong time at the moment. Can't it wait or can't someone else less emotionally involved tell him?

Turn to page 128 to find the name of the genre and notes on performance style.

2 You could take one of the lines and use it as a starting point for devising an improvised drama. However, don't jump into doing

that yet. In groups of two to four, each take one of the lines and dig deeper into what is implied. Use these questions to 'interrogate' your line and 'mine' it for meaning:

- Who do you think is speaking to whom?
- What history is implied between them?
- What sort of people talk like this?
- What clues are there about the relationship and status of the speaker and the person they are talking to?
- Where and when is this taking place?
- What is the issue they are talking about?

When you have completed the interrogation you should have created a solid basis for an improvisation.

3 Take the line you interrogated and in pairs develop it into an improvisation. Stick with the kitchen-sink/slice-of-life genre and Naturalism for the performance style. So, when you perform your drama, it should seem an honest representation of life as lived by these characters. Making it true to life is not an easy option. As an actor you will still have to work hard to communicate this to an audience.

▼ Kitchen-sink improvisation based on: 'If you let him get away with it again it will just go on happening.'

4 After your performance, assess whether you managed to devise well within the kitchen-sink genre and to perform throughout using a naturalistic performance style. Take feedback from your audience.

How to excel

When working in a naturalistic performance style, many young actors are too casual, even sloppy in the way they speak, sit or move. Often they sit slouched on a plastic school chair speaking as if there is no audience needing to be communicated to.

'Casual' never works in performance. To create a casual character in a performance is hard physical work. To create a natural effect in any performance you have to exaggerate, using your voice and body just as precisely as with other performance styles.

Stretch your skills

Experiment further with another genre and performance style to widen your range of improvisation skills.

1 Write each genre in the list below on a slip of paper. Each small group should select one of the slips 'blind' making sure no other group sees it. Then devise a list of lines that are typical of the genre you have picked.

- Melodrama
- Farce
- Greek tragedy
- Whodunnit
- Modern romance
- Historical romance
- Mythical quest.

2 Practise delivering the lines you have devised with the appropriate performance style and theatricality. In this activity you can go a little over the top. When you have perfected your performance, present it to another group and see if they can guess the genre. Repeat your performance to a different group to test out how convincing you are.

Review

This unit was designed to:

- develop your knowledge of improvisation and your confidence in using it as a performance and devising skill
- provide examples of how to structure improvisations
- help you consider content and what is worth creating a drama about
- help you create quality work.

Discuss with your teacher your views on:

- how the unit has helped you in each of these four aspects
- what you will take from this unit into future dramas you devise by improvisation.

Notes for Exploration, step 1 on page 125

These lines are typical of the kitchen-sink genre.

For this genre, Naturalism is the obvious choice for performance style (see page 63 in **Unit 1.5**) – in other words, making the drama as true to life as possible. Of course, in an art form like drama rules are made to be broken and you can get some interesting outcomes by going against the grain and using an 'inappropriate' performance style. This is often deliberately done for comic effect. In this case, however, stick to using Naturalism.

2.3 Making Melodrama

Your aims

You are going to work with a specific genre, melodrama, and develop skills and confidence as a performer to apply this genre.

Rationale: Melodrama, as both a genre and a performance style, is a strong contrast to working in the naturalistic style (as you did in **Unit 2.2** – see page 126). This project will make new demands on your performance skills. It is designed to develop your acting confidence and your willingness to take some dramatic risks.

Skills and understanding you will develop

- *Genre:* Melodrama

- *In rehearsal:* You will expand your range of acting skills by experimenting with exaggerated gesture and expression. You will work in groups to contribute to drama action.

  Overall you will be fulfilling the part of the course that requires you to know two genres and two performance styles in detail.

- *Contexts:* You will all be working in the Contexts of **Performer**, **Deviser** and **Director** and there will be the option of working as **Designer**. As you will be working in a team, you may begin in the role of Deviser, then switch to Designer, followed by Director, back to Deviser, then to Director again, and finally Performer. Therefore you will be extending and practising your performance skills, as well as devising/directing sections of the drama. This will mean working with the mindset of all these Contexts rather than being allocated total responsibility for any one of them.

  Record which of the four Contexts – Performer, Director, Deviser or Designer – you focused on. List the skills you are developing, your level of competence and what you need to improve.

Defining features

▣ Melodrama – the **genre** – originated in the late 1800s, as a sentimental drama accompanied by music. There is often an

unlikely plot that concerns the suffering of good characters at the hands of the villains but ends happily with good triumphant. Melodrama features stock characters such as the noble hero, the long-suffering heroine, and the nasty villain. Stock characters are very much the same from play to play and some actors would specialise in playing them. This was very similar to type casting now.

▲ Just as the appeal of melodrama was beginning to wane in theatres, the technical limitations and mass audiences of early film created the perfect conditions for its survival in cinemas. Here Fay Wray is the stock heroine and Bruce Cabot the protecting hero in a tense moment from *King Kong*.

▣ Melodrama can be a bit annoying for students who like things cut and dried. It is especially annoying for those who want an absolute definition, for it is both a genre and a **performance style**. But that is one of the beauties of drama: there aren't always simple 'correct' answers or a standard 'right' way of doing things. This applies especially to modern theatre, where genres and performance styles are often mixed together. Audiences have come to accept a very varied menu and it can seem that the rule is: 'There are no rules.' However, here a few features of the extreme melodramatic performance style:

▣ larger than life gestures and facial expressions

▣ dialogue and delivery that is strongly emphasised by the actor

▣ all action emphasised with the actor making sure the audience gets the point – it's like acting within apostrophes

▣ direct address of some lines to the audience as well as exaggerated stares/glances

▣ a plot line and actors' performance that are predictable and all the more enjoyable for that.

You can find out more about key elements of melodrama on page 59 in **Unit 1.5**.

1 In groups, take one of the following television programmes and list the names of the stock characters. If someone can be described as a 'stock character' you should be able to identify the same type of role in another programme.

Also list the particular features of that role that stand out.

- *EastEnders*
- *Coronation Street*
- *Emmerdale*
- *Midsomer Murders*
- any of the Agatha Christie dramas, e.g. *Miss Marple*, *Poirot*.

2 Watch some extracts from Charlie Chaplin films like *The Gold Rush* and *The Tramp*. Identify in each the Villain, the Heroine and the Hero.

Observe the performance style and note the big, strongly defined gestures. Are some what we would call today 'over the top'? For example:

- the Villain's glowering looks at the audience or other characters

- the Heroine's downcast look when faced with the Villain or her coyly fluttering her eyelids when with the Hero
- the determination and innocence of the fresh-faced Hero.

How many other melodramatic stylistic performance 'tricks' can you spot the actors using? If you have time, track down some of the Keystone Cops films, for the chase scenes. You have some chasing to do later in this unit.

Exploration and rehearsal

1   Get into groups of three, one to play the Villain, one the Heroine, one the Hero. (In any groups of four you can have two Villains.)

2   Next all the Villains, all the Heroes and all the Heroines get together. Each of these three groups forms a circle. The task is for each group to come up with three physical motifs for their character, e.g. moustache twiddling for the Villain, eyelash batting for the Heroine. Experiment together then fix on the three strongest motifs. Give yourselves only 4 minutes to do this.

3   When you have selected the three motifs, send each one round the circle in turn. One actor starts and as it is passed on the motif should become more and more defined and exaggerated, so that when it completes the circle it is huge. This will develop your 'over the top' melodramatic style of acting.

4   Return to your original small groups. Share the motifs for each character within your group. If a motif has become too exaggerated, too ridiculous, tone it down to what your group decides is the correct level of definition.

    Reminder: The melodramatic style of acting covers a wide spectrum from the almost ridiculous to the heightened Naturalism of acting in soaps like *Coronation Street*.

5   Listen to the song *Along Came Jones* by the Coasters. It has three episodes: the rescue from the dynamite, the rescue from the buzz saw and the rescue from the railway track. Each group should choose **one** episode to work on but make sure that equal numbers of groups are working on episodes 1, 2 and 3.

6   Rehearse the action for your episode to fit the timing of song. Include the three motifs you have been developing, especially at points where your character has nothing else to do.

7 You will notice that between episodes 2 and 3 there is a long musical interlude. During this all those who have completed episodes 1 and 2 can act as the railway train that is coming down the track as the song approaches episode 3.

8 Rehearse the action for the whole song twice.

Performance

Run the final version of *Along Came Jones*, making a mental note for later of what you think worked best.

Review

Reflect on the performance of *Along Came Jones*. What did you see or hear that you liked? In the next 2 minutes, go over to the actors involved and tell them what it was in their performance that worked well.

Moving on to music hall

Along Came Jones is a fun way for your Drama group to work together and get to grips with the old silent-comedy style of melodramatic acting. It should also have been a boost to your acting skills, encouraging you to let your hair down a bit. So let's build on that and look at a longer melodramatic form – a music-hall comic **sketch**. *The Thwarting of Sir Jasper: A Victorian Melodrama* (see pages 136–138) is not an original Victorian sketch, but derives from one. It has been rewritten so that a whole Drama group can perform it as an ensemble piece.

This sketch is demanding, as comedy is a serious business and to make an audience laugh the actor has to perform with great discipline and seriousness. It works best if you play it straight and don't try consciously to send it up or perform it tongue in cheek. That would weaken the comedy. Trust the material and the melodramatic performance style, and the comedy will look after itself.

As well as the Villain, the Hero and Heroine, the script has additional melodramatic character types, e.g. the Mother and Father of the Heroine. It also has a common melodramatic-sketch plot line: the desperately poor family looking for a way out of poverty by marrying their beautiful daughter to a rich gentleman. Such plots have their roots in the economic conditions of the 1800s or early 1900s: in this case, in Victorian Britain.

To the original audiences of Charlie Chaplin films like *The Tramp*, the situations and plot lines of melodrama would not have seemed so artificial as they do to us, because they would have connected to the audiences' own experience of life. The **pathos** (action intended to raise feelings of pity or sadness) which is such a feature of Chaplin films would have touched the emotions of the audiences of the day. For modern audiences it can seem sentimental and twee. The script you are going to work with doesn't go in for pathos. It's more of an over-the-top comic music-hall sketch.

Preparation	*1* Start by reading the script of *The Thwarting of Sir Jasper* on pages 136–138 right through as a class.
	The original sketch has been adapted so that you can use it as a whole-class ensemble piece. Remember what was said in **Unit 2.1** (page 97) about the advantages of working as an ensemble for building a good team spirit in your Drama class.

2 Decide whether you are going to perform the sketch as a whole-class ensemble or in groups with one Mother, one Father, one Sir Jasper. Distribute the parts.

Exploration and rehearsal

1 Rehearse, considering staging, properties, costume, lighting and the performance. Will you develop these fully or just add simple items for key roles, e.g. a sailor's hat for the Hero?

2 Investigate any aspects of the music-hall style that you want to add to your interpretation of the melodrama. These might include:

- direct appeals to the audience
- stage business, e.g. using props
- sound effects, e.g. hooters, whistles, in certain action
- songs or ditties.

You can create your own sound effects vocally or with instruments.

Performance

It may be possible to perform to another group in the school. Having a live audience will enable you to test out the effectiveness of your comic delivery and timing.

The Thwarting of Sir Jasper
A Victorian Melodrama

> **Note**
> Slash marks (/) indicate how the role can be divided between more than one actor. This works with the convention of using collective roles. You can edit these slash marks if you wish and give parts to individuals if that suits your group better.

(Tableau of a poor Victorian family.)

Mother: Our daughter Mary has grown into a fine girl. / She is such a great comfort and help to my husband and me. / So good and kind to her younger brothers and sisters.

Father: So many mouths to feed / So little money / If only we could find a rich husband for our eldest daughter, Mary.

(Creditors surround the family.)

Creditors: Your rent is in arrears. / Pay now or it's debtors' prison for you! / Your coal bill needs settling immediately. / Your slate at the grocer's needs clearing at once. / Mr Jones says no more credit until you pay.

(A romantic interlude where the seeds of love are sown – a mime of the Sailor picking up a handkerchief dropped by Mary. They gaze into each other's eyes. Musical accompaniment.)

Narrator: Oh! Isn't that sweet. / He loves her. / She loves him. / So go and ask her dad if you can marry her. / Go on, be bold, faint heart never won fair lady. / Nothing ventured, nothing gained.

(Mime of Sailor asking for Mary's hand. Father asks about money, Sailor shows empty pockets, but puts hand on big heart. Father shakes his head, no. Mary and Sailor part. Suitable piano refrain to accompany the exit of the Sailor.)

Father: My daughter will never marry a pauper.

(Mary and Sailor gaze longingly and disappointedly as the Sailor departs.)

Narrator:	Devastated yet determined, away to sea he went to make his fortune in far-off lands. / Mary nursed her broken heart. Meanwhile the local squire, Sir Jasper, had cast his roving eye upon Mary and thought …
Sir Jasper:	Hmm, a handsome young filly. I will make her my wife. / Time I settled down to domestic bliss. / I will go to her father and offer him gold. He's poor as a church mouse so he's sure to agree.

(Mime of Sir Jasper and Father making the marriage deal. Suitable musical accompaniment.)

Narrator:	And so the *happy* couple are introduced.

(Mime of the introduction, much moustache twiddling by Sir Jasper.)

Sir Jasper:	Hello, my dear. Sir Jasper is my name and marriage is my game. / I have chosen you to be my bride. Aren't you lucky?
Mary:	*(horrified thinks)* Oh no, it can't be true! My love is far away. Oh, what can I do?
Father:	Come, come, Mary, show some gratitude.
Mother:	Just think, you'll be a lady.
Father:	Sir Jasper has promised me a job on his estate.
Mother:	He has helped us out with all the bills. Oh thank you, thank you, dear sir.
Sir Jasper:	Think nothing of it. / Come, my dear, let us make you more presentable as befits your new status in society. / Your first appearance as my fiancée shall be at the hunt ball.

(Suitable musical link.)

Hunt Ball Crowd:	My word, Sir Jasper's got himself a fine new filly. / Still life in the old dog, eh, ha ha ha. / Champers all round. / A new asset for the estate, I see, Sir Jasper. / Damn good haunches, sturdy little wench. / Where've you found her? / You always had a sharp eye for a good thing, you old goat.
Narrator:	And so the day grew near / When Sir Jasper and Mary were to be wed.

(Wedding-march music hummed or played. Sir Jasper and Mary are dressed for the wedding by the Narrators, using simple props, e.g. bonnet for Mary, cloak for Sir Jasper.)

Narrator: It should be the happiest day of her life, but look at Mary's face. / Her heart is not in it. / Oh, it's cruel, it's cruel. / Yes, it's a cruel world. / But help is at hand. / You don't think our handsome hero would allow such a carry on? / He has arrived home from foreign parts / with a tan / and money in his pocket. / But where is Mary? / She is to be wed this very morning! / He arrives at the church just in the nick of time.

Sailor: Hey! What's going on? Mary!

Mary: My one true love.

Sir Jasper: Unhand my wife, you bounder! You arrive too late.

Sailor: Not too late yet, mate! *(Knocks out Sir Jasper with a single blow.)* Come on, Mary, let's scarper.

(Chase sequence, with suitable music. Finally the Narrators throw confetti over the couple. Ends in melodramatic pose, which mirrors the outcome – Sir Jasper livid, Lovers enraptured, Parents apologetic.)

Narrator: And so, as in all good tales, true love triumphs and evil is put in its place.

(A theatrical bow, cast in line linking hands, all raised together, all bow together. Extravagant thank you, thank you in suitable 'luvvie style'. A few kisses blown, brows mopped.)

Stretch your skills

- If this work has captured your imagination, test yourself by trying to create a melodrama that uses pathos as much as comedy. Or forget the comedy element and act out a melodramatic plot line seriously, concentrating on the social injustice. This could be done by altering the script of *The Thwarting of Sir Jasper*, changing its tone completely. You could perform the drama as an experiment to see if the old melodramatic genre and its associated plot lines, where villains and heroes are clear cut, can still engage the sympathies of a modern audience.

- Look at the melodrama *Sweeney Todd* by Christopher Bond. This is at the other end of melodrama's wide spectrum. It is quite sinister and dark and deals with some strong social issues. Its plot is that of the classic Victorian melodrama *Sweeney Todd – The Demon Barber of Fleet Street*. Sweeney exacts revenge with his razor on those who have wronged him and they end up in pies made by his partner in crime, Mrs Lovett. It was Bond's play that inspired Stephen Sondheim to write his dark musical *Sweeney Todd*. Both the play and the musical are excellent and will give you a chance to explore a very different type of melodrama.

- Another classic Victorian melodrama is *Maria Martin and the Murder in the Red Barn* (see Scenario J on page 88). Like us, the Victorians loved crime dramas.

Review

This unit was designed to help you to:

- widen the scope of your performance skills
- gain knowledge of melodrama as a genre and performance style
- explore how genre influences structure, plot, use of character and performance style
- consider when you might use the genre of melodrama in the dramas you create.

Discuss with your teacher or in your group what you have gained from this unit in terms of:

- what you have learnt about melodrama and the possibilities it offers
- two things you will you take from this unit into future dramas you work on
- what performance skills you have improved.

2.4 Brecht's *The Threepenny Opera*

Your aims

You are going to use the plot of the opening of *The Threepenny Opera* by Bertolt Brecht (music by Kurt Weill) to create an improvised drama. You will also explore the genre of political theatre and some of Brecht's ideas on performance style, e.g. gestus and representation.

Rationale: Brecht's ideas on theatre are very distinctive and his influence on European theatre has been great. Your own practical work may already be influenced by ideas that he championed, without you realising it. This is an opportunity to become familiar with some of his ideas through the play that was his first commercial success.

Skills and understanding you will develop

■ *Genre:* Political theatre

■ *In rehearsal:* You will continue to extend your understanding of different genres and performance styles.

■ *Contexts:* You will be considering how all four Contexts – **Performer, Deviser, Director** and **Designer** – are affected when they are influenced by a specific political or philosophical stance. Politics are central to Brecht's work, so social, historical and cultural influences are placed centre stage.

Record which of the four Contexts – Performer, Director, Deviser or Designer – you focused on. List the skills you are developing, your level of competence and what you need to improve.

As you will be working on the actual script of *The Threepenny Opera* or taking ideas from the text as a stimulus for creating your own drama, this material could be used as the basis for your Controlled Assessment for either *Unit 1 From Page to Stage* or *Unit 2 Drama in the Making*.

For your information

Brecht was a German who lived through the tumultuous first half of the twentieth century – through the First World War, the Russian Revolution, the Great Depression and the collapse of the German economy, the Spanish Civil War, the Second World War to the start of the Cold War. Like many who lived in those turbulent times, Brecht was very politically conscious. Again like many others at that time, he saw Communism as the answer to the inequalities in the world around him.

Brecht fled Germany when the Nazis came to power. He worked in America until the end of the Second World War, then returned to East Germany, the Communist half of the newly divided Germany. East Germany, like the rest of the so-called Eastern Bloc, was under the influence and, largely, the control of the Soviet Union. The East German government gave Brecht a theatre in Berlin which became the famous Berliner Ensemble. Here he continued to develop his ideas on theatre and stage in highly acclaimed productions of his plays until his death in 1956.

Brecht's whole life's work was about putting politics and philosophy on the stage in an entertaining way. He wanted his audience to think about the issues he presented.

He was innovative in his approach to staging. For example, it was in his productions that the famous half screen was introduced, which could be drawn across the stage to interrupt the action while a song was sung. Songs were often used to provide a commentary on the themes being explored. His plots were episodic – each scene could, to a degree, stand on its own, so the order of the scenes could be rearranged without making too much difference to the play as a whole.

Typically, Brecht would use captions before each scene telling the audience what they were going to see. This meant the audience were immediately focused on the issues rather than the plot. As he believed in using the latest technology, the captions were often projected.

His plays were performed in full white light, with no attempt at creating atmosphere and illusion. The actors often changed or moved the scenery in front of the audience's gaze, with no blackout. Brecht believed the audience knew that it was a play and that the scenery had to be moved, so why hide it from them or 'pretend' it didn't happen? This approach is often referred to as breaking down the fourth wall – the line that separates audience from actors. Brecht wanted to break down the 'stuffy' formality of going to the theatre, and his work was heavily influenced by cabaret, circus, music hall and Eastern theatre.

▲ In this old photo from the original production of *The Threepenny Opera* you can see many of the distinctive features of Brecht's approach to theatre, including stage captions and minimal scenery.

All these ways of working link to Brecht's political standpoint as a Marxist.

Brecht would have argued that every director's, designer's, deviser's and actor's work is political. This standpoint was supported by another practitioner, Augusto Boal. If you are interested in political theatre, take a look at Boal's influential book *Theatre of the Oppressed* (see page 259).

⟩ Epic Theatre

The term Epic Theatre was first used by another practitioner, Erwin Piscator, who influenced Brecht's work. Here are some key ideas in Brecht's Epic Theatre which you are going to explore in this unit:

- ▨ *Familiar story:* Essentially, Epic Theatre follows a familiar story, often a fable or a story based on historical events. By not using an original story Brecht hoped to focus the audience's attention on the issues.

- ▨ *Episodic structure:* Each scene stands on its own, often ending with songs or captions giving the audience time to reflect critically on the action they have just seen. This episodic structure allows many different viewpoints to be explored, each person seeing the events in a different light. This is a **dialectical** approach (see page 99).

- ▨ *Making strange:* This means making the audience see something familiar in a new light. (It is often called alienation, but this is a bad translation from the German – making strange is more accurate.)

- ▨ *Representing types:* Performers represent types of character or humankind rather than being a distinctive individual character. The actors in Epic Theatre are demonstrators of action or narrators helping the audience to understand an issue. They always remember that they are actors and do not lose themselves in the role. To do this they use the technique of **gestus**. Gestures or positions are taken up at key points to draw attention to the feelings of the character at that moment. The action stops briefly so that the audience is forced to notice the effect of the action on the character, as in Brecht's *Mother Courage* where the character Mother Courage is frozen in a silent scream.

- ▨ *Technical elements:* All the technical elements of the production – lighting, music, scenery changes, costume changes, projection of captions – take place in full view of the audience. This is a reminder that they are watching a play that has been 'manufactured'.

These techniques can be explored through working with Brecht's most famous plays: *The Caucasian Chalk Circle*, *The Good Person of Szechwan*, *Mother Courage*, *The Life of Galileo* and *The Resistable Rise of Arturo Ui*.

All the features of Epic Theatre work towards Brecht's aim to put philosophy and politics onto the stage and make the unfolding drama a discussion, where opinions are put forward. The audience are treated as 'thoroughly intelligent'. The play presents them with questions and possible solutions, encouraging them to think, take a stance and perhaps take some future action in the real world.

The starting point for creating your own improvised drama from Brecht's *The Threepenny Opera* will be the mocked-up set design with properties on pages 146–147.

Preparation

Split into groups of three or four. You are going to work as 'theatre detectives'.

1 Take a close look at the set design on pages 146–147. This is a rough mock-up of a set for the first scene of *The Threepenny Opera*. Work out as much as you can about the play from the clues in the mock-up and note your ideas on a copy of this grid:

Cracking the code	
In what period of time is the play taking place?	
What is the theme/content of the play?	
What part of the play is going to be acted out in this scene?	
What characters are going to be involved in this scene?	
What performance style would suit this play?	
What genre or type of story is being signalled?	

2 Feed back your ideas to the rest of the class and listen to theirs. From what you hear, what do you think is the most likely scenario for this play?

3 For further clues about how the play starts, have another look at the list of begging character types and the licence to beg that the beggars could be issued with.

Exploration

Use the instructions below to help you improvise a drama using the mock-up of set and properties for *The Threepenny Opera* on pages 146–147 as the stimulus.

1   Working in groups, choose which character starts the play and write their first speech with any accompanying stage directions.

2   Link with another group and as Directors instruct that group how you want your speech performed. Let them enact it. Give them feedback and do it once more. Swap over, letting your partner group take on the role of Directors with their script.

3   Take turns to stage the speeches within the setting, making an entrance, using any relevant props and generally using the designed space. You are working with the semiotics of this setting to create the best effects.

4   Share some or all of these openings of the play with the rest of the class.

5   Which uses of set or props in the openings you watched did you like? Decide which you liked best and why this worked well.

▶ 'What I liked best was ...'

Rehearsal

1   Now continue working in your original groups and **devise** the full opening scene of the play. Use your partner group for feedback as before.

2   When your scene is complete, perform it to the rest of your class.

LICENCE TO BEG

NAME in FULL ....

CONDITIONS

I agree that the firm will designate a location that will become my allotted pitch. This will be in one of the firm's fourteen begging districts and is not negotiable.

I will be allotted a beggar's outfit and pay the standard hire charge.

I will pay fifty per cent of my takings to the firm.

I understand that my **LICENCE** may be revoked at any time without notice.

I understand that the organisation will take no responsibility for my actions at any time, nor recognise that they are in any way bound to my person.

Signed ....

Witnessed ....

FOR OFFICIAL USE ONLY

Date processed ....

LICENCE NUMBER ALLOCATED ....

Signed:

J J Peachum

Outfit for Beggar A

Item: Green sleeping bag, ripped
Item: Check blanket, stained
Item: Blue woolly hat
Item: Windcheater, silver, grease stains on contact points
Item: Odd trainers, one black, one white, different sizes
Item: If female, pink ribbon; if male, copy of old *Beano*

LAUNDRY

11.15 a.m. Tuesday

Report of a beggar in Section 12.

Madonna and Child may be moonlighting.

Urgent! Call them in.

11.45 a.m. Tuesday

A Mr. Tiger Brown seeks urgent meeting with Mr. Peachum.

The matter won't wait.

10.30 a.m. Tuesday

Constable on beat in Section 4 wants an urgent meeting to discuss "current arrangements".

The SIX Basic Begging Types

A The Scruffy Waif with Plaintive Whine
gets results by inspiring sympathy.

B The Tiresome Trembler
molests passers-by, gets
results by inspiring nausea.

C The Madonna and Child
gets results by inspiring guilt.

D The Bold as Brass, Cheeky Chappie or Lassie
gets results by embarrassing
people they confront.

E The Victim of Accident/ Disabled Person
gets results by making
passers-by feel sorry for them.

F The Beggar with Dog
appeals to animal lovers,
inspires sympathy for dog.

How to excel

Notice that you have devised the scene in small bites, each part having a tight focus. Planning in this way helps you gradually develop your drama, adding in extra elements one at a time. The small elements gradually build a complete scenario.

By doing this, you slowed down the development of the action – you devised one small speech, which made you as Devisers focus on the importance of the words you selected. You then had to make an entrance into the setting. Then, as Performers and Directors, you had to deliver the speech within the setting, so you had to consider entering the space, action, use of setting and timing the delivery of the speech.

These are all vital elements in creating a script and making a text come to life on stage. These practical 'craft' considerations are as relevant as character and motivation and are essential preparation for creating engaging roles. Adding new elements one (or two) at time like this is called **layering**. It is a very effective way of devising or rehearsing a play.

Stretch your skills

You could extend your scene from *The Threepenny Opera* into a complete devised drama. Try applying Brecht's principles by making it politically thought provoking and using gestus in your performance style.

Comparing with the actual script

Now let's look at the actual script that this setting was devised for – Brecht's *The Threepenny Opera*. Here is Jeremiah Peachum's opening speech from Act 1, part of which is sung as a hymn.

I: *[Caption/Announcement]* To combat the increasing callousness of mankind, J. Peachum, a man of business, has opened a shop where the poorest of the poor can acquire an exterior that will touch the hardest of hearts.

(Jonathan Jeremiah Peachum's outfitting shop for beggars.)

PEACHUM'S MORNING HYMN

You ramshackle Christian, awake!
Get on with your sinful employment
Show what a good crook you could make.
The Lord will cut short you enjoyment.

Betray your own brother, you rogue
And sell your old woman, you rat.
You think the Lord God's just a joke?
He'll give you His Judgement on that.

PEACHUM: *(to the audience)* Something new is needed. My business is too hard, for my business is arousing human sympathy. There are a few things that stir men's souls, just a few, but the trouble is that after repeated use they lose their effect. Because man has the abominable gift of being able to deaden his feelings as well, so to speak. Suppose, for instance, a man sees another man standing on the corner with a stump for an arm; the first time he may be shocked enough to give him tenpence, but the second time it will only be fivepence, and if he sees him a third time he'll hand him over to the police without batting an eyelash. It's the same with the spiritual approach. *(A large sign saying 'It is more blessed to give than to receive' is lowered from the grid.)* What good are the most beautiful, the most poignant sayings, painted on the most enticing little signs, when they get expended so quickly? The Bible has four or five sayings that stir the heart; once a man has expended them, there's nothing for it but starvation. Take this one, for instance – 'Give and it shall be given unto you' – how threadbare it is after hanging here a mere three weeks. Yes, you have to keep on offering something new. So it's back to the good old Bible again, but how long can it go on providing?

Preparation | Read Jeremiah Peachum's opening speech from Brecht's script.

1 What is the scam Peachum is running? He's turning begging into a commercial enterprise. This is an example of **making strange** of the familiar (or **alienation**) so that we see it in a new light. Who would have thought it, begging as an organised business?

▸ Erich von Ponto was one of the first actors to play Jonathan Jeremiah Peachum, shown here with Roma Bahn, who played Polly Peachum.

2 Experiment with this opening speech as Performers. As it is a long speech, present it as a collective role, with groups of you sharing out the lines. Or you could do it as a whole class, again dividing up the lines. It doesn't matter if more than one person delivers some of the lines.

3 Try singing the speech in the style of a hymn. Be brave, don't worry too much about the tune, look on singing as merely heightened or intensified speaking.

Exploration

1 Split into six working groups and each take one of the six basic begging types listed in the mock-up on pages 146–147. Write the spiel (speech) that your beggar would use on the streets. Remember that these are professional beggars so what they say needs to be high quality and convincing, even cunning.

2 Now rehearse your spiel. A professional beggar would know just how to deliver it for maximum effect. But remember that in the context of the play this is a scam and the audience are 'in on it' with the actor. So use techniques like looks and gestures to show the audience that they are in the know and help them spot any false moments. Don't use an aside to make this obvious as that would be working in a different genre. You need to work with Brecht's **performance style**, where the actor clearly **demonstrates** to the audience. The actor's job is to make sure spectators notice what is being demonstrated and its relevance.

3 Now, working in groups, you are going to look at the example of an outfit for Beggar A in the mock-up on pages 146–147 and, as Designers, suggest outfits for Beggars B–F.

In the opening scene of Brecht's script, Peachum lectures Filch on 'the five basic types of misery'. They have been adapted to create the beggar types in the mock-up and to connect with modern-day street beggars, so that you can draw on your own observations. How do your costume suggestions reinforce the idea of each beggar type?

4 Set the scene: the streets of London (say). The actors from each group playing the beggars should select their pitches. The rest of the class slowly make an entrance one at a time. They are the public walking through the streets and are addressed by the beggars as they pass.

Discuss how effective the beggars' requests were. In terms of Brecht's performance style, would the audience have been aware that this is a con, but a very convincing one?

5 Set up Peachum's office and improvise the beggars' return to the office. One of you or your teacher should take the role of Peachum. The beggars arrive one at a time to face Peacham's assessment of their begging work. Peachum has eyes everywhere and he has reports on their 'performance' and appearance. He is a tough task master – if he grants you a licence to beg, then you must maintain the standards of the company. Peachum has a cynical, detached view of the world.

You could also include his wife, Mrs Peachum, as she is in charge of creating the begging outfits. She might have a view on how the beggars were wearing them or looking after them.

Stretch your skills

Put together the costumes and properties for the beggars and the Peachums. Then rehearse your devised speech adding the costumes and props (part of **semiotics**). Also develop some interaction between Peachum and the beggars, collectively this time, and include some interplay between Peachum and his wife. She can also comment on how the beggars should use their costumes to maximum effect.

Make sure your work addresses these questions:

■ What should the power relationship between Peachum and the beggars be?

■ How should the relationship between the Peachums differ when they are alone from when the beggars are present?

■ How do Peachum and the beggars handle the money that was collected?

Evaluate how well your work matched the tone and situation indicated by the mocked-up set you started with.

How to excel

Asking yourself questions like the ones bulleted above will help you to devise authentic, textured dramas rather than shallow skits.

These questions indicate the sort of detailed thinking that typifies Brecht's style. No one in a Brecht production handles money casually – the audience has to see that the commodity of money is a crucial governing factor in people's lives.

For example, in Brecht's play *Mother Courage*, Courage has to barter for her son's life. She offers what she thinks will secure his release; she doesn't offer all that is in her purse. The actor playing the part very pointedly takes coins from her purse and then returns some to the purse. Brecht's point is that she has to carry on and survive whether her son lives or dies.

Review

This background work has provided you with a bridge into the actual script of *The Threepenny Opera*.

In the sequence of tasks you have worked within all four Contexts and mindsets: Performer, Director, Designer and Deviser.

You should also be able to identify where you used each of the Areas of Study – all six have featured somewhere in the tasks.

By the time Brecht wrote *The Threepenny Opera*, defeat in the First World War and the harsh terms of the Treaty of Versailles had turned Germany into the beggar of Europe. It is as a once proud war veteran reduced to begging for survival that German artist Georg Grosz, a contemporary of Brecht, depicted the plight of his country in this cartoon.

Working directly with the script

The Threepenny Opera was a huge commercial success when first produced in 1928 and had a significant effect on the careers of both Brecht and Kurt Weill, the composer of the musical score for the work. This was an ironic turn of events given Brecht's political ideas about money.

Now examine the script in more detail. Your teacher will select sections for you to use and provide you with copies.

Preparation

1 Read Scene 1 from the play and discuss:

- In what ways does it link to the improvised drama you created?

- How do the descriptions of the basic types of human misery in the script compare to the six basic begging types listed in the mock-up on pages 146–147?

2 Your teacher will give each group a small section of script for two or three characters from Scene 1 or other scenes. You are going to rehearse your section using one of Brecht's rehearsal techniques.

- Before the first actor in your script section says their character's opening line, they should describe in detail what actions and stage moves they are going to make. Once they have done this they deliver the line, putting in the actions and stage moves they have described.

- The next actor in the section does the same, describing their actions and stage moves before going on to combine this with their speech.

- Continue this process speech by speech until you have completed the section of script you are rehearsing.

- Once you have been through the section in this way, run the scene without stopping and without the description. The description is now in your head, but put in all the actions/moves you rehearsed as you speak the lines.

- Join with another group and show your rehearsed sections to each other. Switch to another group and repeat.

- Now discuss as a whole class whether there was anything about the sections you have just performed that made them different from scenes you rehearsed earlier in your course without using this technique.

How to excel

This system is a very efficient way of rehearsing if you are going to develop a scene to performance standard. It will be particularly useful for the early stages of rehearsal for the text extract in *Unit 1 From Page to Stage* or if you choose the Performer (text extract) Brief for *Unit 3 From Concept to Creation*. It adds lots of detail, makes you 'physicalise' your performance and blocks in all the moves.

Exploration and rehearsal

Your teacher will give each group a different short extract from the script (no longer than 2–4 pages) selected to represent a key moment from the play.

1 Rehearse your extract, applying what you have learnt so far about Brecht's approach to theatre. Devise a caption that can be spoken or projected to introduce your scene.

2 Run all the scenes in order.

3 Ask your teacher to select a song from the script that appears close to one of these scenes. Look at the lyrics. What commentary is made on the themes of the play in this song?

4 Go back to your own script extract. Compose a song or poem for the end of your scene that breaks from the text and acts as a commentary on the themes of your section. Note that a commentary should not simply state or describe what has just happened. It needs to comment like a spectator or audience,

giving a critical response to the situation and behaviour of the characters or spotting some angle the characters missed.

5 Rerun the scenes and include your sung commentaries.

Performance

If you want to go further with *The Threepenny Opera*, ask your teacher to extend the length and number of extracts from the script so that you have a montage that captures the essence, the key ingredients of the play. Rehearse these extracts and perform them as an ensemble.

Note: If you are short of time you do not have to reproduce all the script extracts as written. You can use the standard drama approaches of read then improvise the situation, or physically represent it or tell it as a story. This will allow you to cover the plot line more rapidly and get your head out of the script more quickly.

Review
This unit was intended to:

- introduce you to some of the ideas of an influential theatre practitioner, Brecht

- consider a playwright's purpose when they create their play

- work with a different performance style – gestus/ demonstration – and so extend your performance skills.

Discuss with your teacher or in your group what you have gained from this unit in terms of:

- what you have learnt about Brecht and his approach to theatre

- what performance skills you have improved

- how the work you have done might influence your approach to directing, devising or designing

- two things you will take from this unit into future dramas you work on.

2.5 Structuring Drama

Your aims

You are going to explore a range of structures for devising drama which you can select from and adapt when you create your own dramas.

Rationale: It is vital as you come to develop your own ideas that you know the possibilities for structuring drama that are available. Most playwrights draw on standard, well tried and tested structures – their scripts are never totally original and draw to a large extent on what has gone before. Similarly, you shouldn't burden yourself with thinking that everything you devise has to be totally original. Of course, within any standard structure or plot line, there are infinite ways to make it distinctively your own. But, especially when you are devising as a group, it is helpful to have a basic unifying structure to give the drama an overall shape.

Skills and understanding you will develop

- *Genre:* You will continue to extend your understanding by working with different genres and performance styles.

- *In rehearsal:* You will work with a range of practical drama techniques and experiment with some of the standard ways of structuring drama.

- *Contexts:* You will be acting as **Performer** and **Designer** as you implement each structure. You will also draw on the other two Contexts – **Deviser** and **Director** – whilst focusing on *Area of Study 2: Structure*.

The projects will provide ideas and develop devising skills that will prepare you to tackle *Unit 2 Drama in the Making* and the Perfomer (devised) Brief and Deviser Brief for *Unit 3 From Concept to Creation*.

Record which of the four Contexts – Performer, Director, Deviser or Designer – you focused on. List the skills you are developing, your level of competence and what you need to improve.

Let's start by looking at a range of structures that you might choose to use at any point in your course.

The 'dead warrior'

In this structure, you will be **starting with the end of the story**, using as your starting point the example of a 'dead warrior'. Take a look at the warrior's costume on the right.

A drama based on this would recreate the warrior's story through a series of flashbacks. This is exactly the approach in Orson Welles' classic film *Citizen Kane*, where the plot works backwards from the starting point – Kane's dying word, 'Rosebud' – and asks: 'What did it mean?' In *Citizen Kane*, Kane's life is revealed to the audience through the eyes of different 'witnesses', each seeing him in a different light. This adds an extra element to the structure.

Preparation

1   With a partner or in small groups, you are going to decide what is being signalled about the story of the warrior by the items in the photograph above – the semiotics of the scene. Speculate about the following:

- Who was the warrior and what was he doing here? (His character and motivation)
- What has happened here and why? (Plot)
- Where is this taking place? (Setting or location)
- When is it taking place? (Time frame)
- What genre of play is this?

Look at the improvisation activities in **Unit 2.2**, pages 119–124, which build quality into the drama by adding detail. These may help you build up your information on the warrior here.

2 Share your speculations with another group or do this as a whole class. Take a 'forensic' (crime investigator's) approach to analysing the suggestions, to check if your ideas match the evidence in the photo.

Exploration

As a whole class, use this activity to explore a location for the dead warrior:

1 Working on a large sheet of paper (A1 or A0, if possible) and with coloured pens/markers, collectively draw/plan the location surrounding the dead warrior.

2 Producing this sketch will help you think about location, but it will not be a set design. Turn it into a set design that could be created in your studio space. You are limited to using **three** items for the setting. Select these from your sketch using these questions to guide your choice:

- What needs to be communicated to the audience to support this drama?
- What is it practical to create?
- What will signal most effectively and efficiently to an audience?

3 Create your setting in your performance space.

How to excel

Don't think too realistically. Symbolic representations are often easier to create. This is not a film set you are creating. A simple flag can communicate a lot – you don't have to build a castle! Or as the influential set designer Edward Gordon Craig asked, 'How much tree do you need to have on stage to signal forest?'

▶ In his 1970 production of *A Midsummer Night's Dream* for the Royal Shakespeare Company, Peter Brook famously set the entire play in a white box to create an 'empty space' for the performers. In this scene, a single coil of dangled wire has been used to signal forest.

CREATING DRAMA AND DEVELOPING SKILLS

Another device for coping with action or settings on a grand scale is the chorus. In Shakespeare's *Henry V*, Act 4 Prologue, the chorus apologises to the audience for the battle scene about to take place:

> O for pity! – we shall much disgrace
> With four or five most vile and ragged foils,
> Right ill-disposed in brawl ridiculous,
> The name of Agincourt. Yet sit and see,
> Minding true things by what their mockeries be.

Here, and throughout the play, the chorus tells the audience they must use their imagination. In this case four or five people with foils (swords) will represent great armies. With this structuring device, instead of having an elaborate set, the chorus or narrator sets the scene in words.

Devising

Now you need to start devising the script.

1 As a class, agree on a **genre** that suits the material. For example, will the drama be:

- historical and realistic
- similar to Arthurian legend
- fantasy
- a spoof in the style of a historical saga (such as the film *Monty Python and the Holy Grail*)?

Once you have decided the genre, make sure you stick with it.

2 Working in small groups, create an opening narration for the drama. You may find it useful to write on big sheets of sugar paper. This narration will eventually be spoken by a **chorus**.

Each group should choose one aspect from the following list and write three sentences or phrases on it:

- the location
- the weather
- the sounds
- the clothes of the corpse
- the face of the corpse
- the broken sword
- the general atmosphere.

At this stage do not name characters or places, because the class has not agreed these yet. What you are writing will set the general atmosphere or tone of the play.

3   Place all the sheets created by the small groups in a random order, one after the other, on the floor. Now invite your teacher to do a modelled reading of them, bringing your words to life. As you listen, try to spot the techniques your teacher is using to communicate through both voice and body.

What were the techniques used? Pace, pitch, expression, use of particular words, stillness, eye contact, gestures with hands? Remember that the voice is like a musical instrument through which you can communicate with and engage the audience. Your ordinary conversational voice will not be enough when you have to communicate ideas and feelings and be heard by an audience.

4   Rehearse the lines you have written, deciding how you will use your voice to bring them alive. You will be speaking them as a chorus so split the lines as you think best. Narration has to be performed as well and rehearsed as thoroughly as character dialogue.

5   As a class ensemble, set the scene. Enter and deliver the opening speech of the play as a chorus.

<hr>

Exploration

Next you are going to build on your opening narration and create a scene showing the ritual burial of the dead warrior. Ritual is a powerful dynamic structure to include in any drama. *Royal Hunt of the Sun* by Peter Shaffer, about the destruction of the Inca empire by conquistador Francisco Pizarro, contains some fantastic examples of ritual theatre.

1   Divide the scripting amongst groups, each with a different task. You could use some of the following as well as your own ideas:

   ▪ an oration (formal speech) from a priest
   ▪ family members coming to the body to say a few last words or place a token
   ▪ a fellow soldier(s) speaking of their dead comrade
   ▪ someone speaking against this war
   ▪ a patriotic speech on the noble cause the warrior has died for
   ▪ ghosts of the battle returning to give their thoughts.

As well as the scripted words, add a soundscape to the ritual using any of the following: percussion, music, chants, orations. This will be a highly stylised piece of theatre that is in no way naturalistic.

When you use your voices, heighten them (don't use your normal conversational tone), declaim the lines a bit like a priest in a church or like a public speaker.

2 So far you have devised:

- *Scene 1:* The opening narration spoken by the chorus
- *Scene 2:* The ritual burial of the warrior

Either as a class or in small groups, add to your work by making a list of scenes that writers might use if they were creating a play from this material. What possible scenes have the potential for the magic 'T' – tension – which is the key to good stories and dramas?

Here are some classic scenarios used over and over by writers in tales of battle and war:

- the night before battle
- the soldier says farewell to their family
- facing the enemy across the battlefield
- the ghost of the warrior returns to speak to their family about danger coming.

Select from this list the ideas that you think have most potential or add others of your own.

Rehearsal and performance

1 Working in small groups, take one of the scenarios and create a short improvised drama. Start and end your scene with a tableau/still image. Also identify the key moment of tension within the scene and pause the action at that moment, in effect creating another still image. This still image should be more of a portrait, like those created by artists. It will be full of meaning not just a frozen moment.

2 Perform all the new scenes you have devised. Add them to the two you already have and decide on a final order. The class can now perform the complete drama.

Your dead-warrior drama will not have a well developed plot line – it will be more of a montage (see page 23) of moments in the life of the warrior. You could probably rearrange the order of the scenes and still have broadly the same play, as every scene can stand on its own. The structure is episodic, like Brecht's Epic Theatre (see page 143). In other words, you could tackle the selection and development of scenes in a very different way to starting with the dead body and working back through his/her life.

Stretch your skills

This devised drama can be expanded with ideas from existing texts, such as Shakespeare's *Henry V*, Act 4, Scene 1. Here Henry, disguised as a common soldier, goes amongst the troops the night before battle. This is a terrific scene for exploring the implications of war for the common soldier.

You might link the dead warrior to an actual historical figure. What if the body represents Boudicca, the Celtic warrior queen who took on the Romans? Hers is a fantastic story and provides rich material for devising a drama. There is also a good play about her you could use: *Song of a Dark Queen* by Nigel Bryant, which is very ritualistic and challenging in how it is structured.

Sections of the Bayeux Tapestry, charting the story of the Battle of Hastings in 1066, would also make a good stimulus for devising drama around the theme of the dead warrior.

▼ This scene from the Bayeux Tapestry shows the bloody closing stage of the Battle of Hastings. Harold's army, who are all on foot, are surrounded by the Normans attacking on horseback.

A day in the life

This is a classic and beautifully simple structure for drama. Your starting point would be a stimulus for a character. This might be:

- an invented name – for example, Angela Pascall
- a description, such as:

> 66 He was painfully thin, his eyes sunken, rimmed with dark circles. His broad warm smile exposed a collection of jagged broken teeth. On the back of his hand his veins stood out like cords. Tufts of hair sprouted about his head in assorted clumps. Yet while his appearance was slightly alarming he radiated a warmth of spirit and fellowship that inspired trust. 99

- a powerful photograph or picture like the one below.

Preparation

1 As a class, speculate about your character using the What, Who, Why, Where, When planning technique from pages 13–14 so that you can build their background. Alternatively, you could hot seat one of your class in role as the character to start off the character development.

2 Use the ideas that you generate to create a day in the life of your character, dividing it into five or six episodes or scenes. Devise titles/captions for the scenes, for example:

Scene 1: Another morning, another day. What now?
Scene 2: A decision is made.
Scene 3: I'm all right, don't worry. It's something I've got to do in my own way.
Scene 4: I can get through this.
Scene 5: I am somebody, I'm important – OK!
Scene 6: Night creeps in, the close of the day, but not the end of the story.

The captions you devise will be influenced by the starting stimulus you used – the type of name, picture or description.

3 Split into working groups and take one scene each. Take 15 minutes to devise the scene. Start your scene with a **still image** and round it off with another.

4 All sit down while your teacher starts the drama as narrator with a prologue something like:

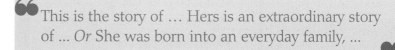

> ❝ This is the story of … Hers is an extraordinary story of … *Or* She was born into an everyday family, … ❞

Next, your teacher moves to the group who have devised Scene 1. This is their cue to make their starting still image and run their scene through to the still image that ends it. They then sit. The teacher does a narrative link inspired by the improvisation then moves to the group who have devised Scene 2. This continues until every group has performed.

Your teacher then improvises the epilogue. When this is over, individuals can stand, join the narrator, or stay seated. At this point, you could improvise echoes of words already heard, or repeats of actions or incidents as short motifs.

5   You have created your play *A Day in the Life of* … . As a class, review this structure and how it might be useful for future work.

This simple structure can be elaborated and enriched in many ways. For example, it might be expanded to a whole life rather than a day in the life, as in the film *Citizen Kane*. In this case, each episode in Kane's life is seen through a different character's eyes. The next example will show you another way of elaborating this structure.

The journey or pathway metaphor

The idea of creating a drama based on a character's journey through life goes back centuries to plays like *Everyman* (see page 83) but can also be seen in productions today.

Preparation

Working as a whole class, you are going to use a pathway or journey as a metaphor for someone's life to create your own play. This work might form the basis of your work for the Controlled Assessment in *Unit 2 Drama in the Making*. For your Controlled Assessment, you might perform in separate small groups but in the following activities you should work together to create an ensemble piece.

1   To create a character, use as a stimulus either role-on-the-wall or an artefact (object) or an item of costume, such as a pair of shoes or jacket. Someone from the group can volunteer to collect together the starting stimulus or you can ask your teacher to create it. Look at the list of features that define character on page 10 to help you create a role and context that has plenty of potential.

2 As you create the journey through life of the character, map it out on a large sheet of paper (A1 or A0). Draw the starting line – this can be any point in the character's life. Using forum theatre, create a **still image** which fixes a common drama moment for everyone. The still image will fix the 'where' and 'when' of your character and the drama, and maybe give a hint of the 'what'. You can add any other characters you think relevant.

3 The journey now begins. Decide whether you will travel forwards in time, backwards or a bit of both. For example, you might choose mostly the past with just a little bit of the future.

Next you need to establish five key points on the journey:

- a crossroads
- an accident
- a bridge
- a tunnel
- a brick wall.

The full journey, your play, will have five scenes, one based around each of these key points. Mark each key point/scene on your route map. Discuss what order should they be in. If the brick wall ends the play, will that make the play less hopeful than ending with the bridge? Ending with the brick wall might fix the genre as gritty Realism.

Once you have put the five scenes in order and mapped them in, you will be ready to create the full drama.

Exploration and rehearsal

As you are working as an ensemble, the play needs a unified style for both structure and design. First, try the following approach, but review and alter it if you don't think it suits your play.

As a team of Designers, create a starting and finishing line for the journey. Use a screen on castors that can be moved about the space for pinning up signs, pictures, anything! Draw road signs for the five key points so that they can be incorporated into the play.

The performance space should be designed as for a promenade play – so that the audience moves with the action rather than staying in one fixed spot. In effect, they go on the journey as well. That might give you some novel possibilities, such as selling them a bus ticket for part of the journey.

▲ Using road-sign props at key points in your drama will reinforce the journey metaphor.

Any properties or set you use should be kept to a minimum and must be moved on and off the performance space as needed. This must not interrupt the flow of the play, so items must be capable of being brought on and off efficiently. When not performing, the actors should surround the performance space.

1 Split into five working groups and each take one of the scenes. Your scenario should match the metaphor you are working with. So, if you are working with the crossroads, the scene you create needs to be a crossroads in the main character's life. The way you devise must match the performance space and the ensemble way of working. Also consider the best performance style – for example, should the scenes be naturalistic, abstract or a mixture? Fix a time limit and set to work.

2 When the group scenes have been completed, you will probably have five different people playing the main character. As a whole class, decide how to signal this to an audience. Will you pass on a prop or piece of costume to signal 'passing the baton' to another actor, for example? Decide also whether you need a narrator to lead the audience through the journey and link the scenes. In your first run through, your teacher could improvise this role.

Performance

Perform your play, keeping your chosen performance style in mind and making the most of the promenade approach to your performance space.

Stretch your skills

Divide into two groups. One group should script a prologue for your play, while the other group scripts an epilogue. Perform the whole piece again. Decide what difference the new elements made.

Review

Did it go well? Was this an interesting way of devising and staging a play? If you decide to perform your play to an outside audience you will need to consider editing, adapting, adding and rehearsing. What sort of audience would it suit?

How to excel

Use of the journey metaphor gives drama work a direction and can help you select and create a design and performance style. Now that it is not just *A Day in the Life of …*, but the journey along the road, you can use all sorts of dramatic gimmicks to make your points to the audience if you follow the metaphor through. Along with the road signs, you might add beeping horns, crashes, punctures, being towed away, or the main character can meet an AA person or a speed cop, each adapted to work with the metaphor.

Separated lives

This structure is used to great effect in the classic Willy Russell play *Blood Brothers*. There the plot follows twin brothers separated at birth, showing how their paths through life differ and how they eventually intersect. The powerful, emotive use of twins in this structure is a beautiful plot idea, creating a context with dramatic resonance.

The ideas for drama which follow are another variation of this structure.

Your drama work will grow from the photograph below taken in the Gorbals in Glasgow in 1948. You are going to create the boys' story as a whole-class ensemble or in smaller groups.

Take a close look at the photo of the boys. Research the social, cultural and historical context for this picture – post-war poverty in Glasgow. Discover something about the nature of the Gorbals, what life was like there at the time the photo was taken, and about the photographer. This information will influence your drama.

▼ 'Gorbals Boys', taken by Bert Hardy in 1948

Exploration and performance

1 Name the two boys and create a background for them at this point in their lives. This can be done using any of the techniques you have been introduced to already, e.g. improvisation, hot seating, the 'W' questions (What, Where, When, Who, Why?). Select what you think will work best.

2 Now create the drama, making sure you include these four elements in the plot:

■ In the first part of the story the boys are inseparable pals throughout school. This is the exposition, setting the background.

- The boys go different ways after school, so you will need to devise two parallel life stories. These must develop the audience's interest and build to the next stage. This is the rising action.

- Each story must have a key moment, that magic 'T' – tension (see page 119). These are the climaxes of each story.

- After a lifetime the boys make contact again. Each brings a very special memento of their early times together to the reunion. This should be used to add a strong emotional kick to the drama. This is the plot's resolution or denouement.

3 Perform and evaluate your completed drama about the two boys.

Adapting a well-known story

The advantage of taking a story that already exists is that you don't have to spend time working out the plot and all the characters – someone else has already done that. You have devised lots of plots and characters in the examples above. This time these elements are provided for you.

Preparation

You are going to take the pantomime *Cinderella* and perform it in a naturalistic style – as if it were real life. Concentrate on the storyline and accurate observation. The traditional elements of pantomime such as hissing the villain or shouting 'He's behind you' will now be inappropriate. A naturalistic style will turn the tale of *Cinderella* into a story about a dysfunctional family within the kitchen-sink genre. It will become a contemporary story of a boy or girl who has a step-parent.

1 Select a sequence of events from the story – for example:

An invite arrives for a big posh party → The family can't afford for everyone to go → Cinderella tries to tell her father how she feels about her stepmother → The stepsisters make life unpleasant for Cinderella → Cinderella talks to a friend about the problems of her new stepmother and stepsisters → She dreams of a more romantic life.

2 Discuss these events then split into acting groups. Each acting group is going to perform a scene based on one event. The number of people in the group should match the number of characters in the scene chosen. So, if only two characters are needed, then work as a pair. Your scenes don't all need to be different – several groups could work on the same event in the plot. For example, a planning group of four could split into twos for the acting.

Perform your scene in a naturalistic style using the kitchen-sink genre. If you are successful it should turn out like something from a soap opera such as *EastEnders*. Spend a maximum of 20 minutes on this.

Exploration and rehearsal

1 Using the kitchen-sink or **slice-of-life** genre again, create an improvisation between two or three characters of different ages (who), which is set in a hostel near a channel port (where), in the middle of a weekday afternoon in the present day (when), where there is a problem or tension of some sort (what). When you plan the scene refer to the features that define a role on page 10.

Working in a naturalistic style means that you will have to make the drama as authentic as possible. Spend a maximum of 10 minutes planning the scene then 15 minutes improvising it. Remember: the challenge is to make it as accurately observed and true to life as possible.

2 Write up your scene as a script. This will be handed to another group to perform. Remember that you are writing it for performance in a naturalistic style.

Note: Writing dialogue is good practice for working as a Deviser. You can opt for the Deviser Brief in *Unit 3 From Concept to Creation*.

Performance and evaluation

1 Join with another group and give each other your script to perform. As Performers you must turn the words on the page into a dynamic piece of drama. If the script you are given is brilliant, you'll have a head start. If it's not, you'll have to use your performing and directing skills to make a little piece of magic. Take 10–15 minutes to rehearse the scenes, then perform them to each other. This way the original Devisers get to see their 'play' performed.

2 In your groups, review what it was that you were trying to communicate in the scene you devised and performed. For example, is it about a teenager not being able to communicate with an adult? Is it about love? Is it about fear? Is it about isolation? Write down a sentence, phrase or word which sums up what each scene is about. This is not the plot, but the essence or 'core' of the scene.

Stretch your skills

Have a go at communicating this essence of the scene not in a naturalistic way as in your original script, but in an **abstract** style. So it's the same story but a different play. Read the information below then spend 10 minutes planning and 20 minutes trying it out.

You could spend longer, if it is profitable, using improvisation to explore the potential of the scenario. This is something you have to do for your Controlled Assessment in *Unit 2 Drama in the Making*. Make sure you review your understanding of abstract style once you have completed your drama.

Naturalistic and abstract style

The difference between naturalistic and abstract style is a bit like the difference in painting style between Constable's *The Hay Wain* and Picasso's *Guernica* (see pages 63 and 64 for a full definition). Don't worry too much about this at the moment – when you have finished the work suggested, you should be much clearer about what is meant by an abstract style.

Some issues that could be tackled in the abstract version of your scene are:

- outside pressures the characters face, e.g. with officials, with the law
- personal issues, e.g. health, family loyalty, friendship, love.

These issues can be built into the script by:

- using drama conventions such as pressure circle, conscience alley, good angel/bad angel, freeze frame (For an explanation of these techniques, turn to the **Glossary** at the end of this book, page 260.)
- creating a sound collage to match the mood or thoughts or fears of a character
- using symbolic props, specific colours of material or light to communicate atmosphere and ideas, e.g. the character feels physically threatened so a red strip of material is wrapped around them by one of the cast as they sink to their knees.

How to excel

Whenever you devise or work with a script during your course, try performing it in at least two styles. It's a fun exercise, but it also builds up performance confidence and will help you develop an insight into how effective different styles are for communicating ideas dramatically. Content can be viewed with a completely different perspective.

Professional actors often do such exercises. When Brecht was working as a theatre director on Shakespeare's tragedy *King Lear*, he got his actors to perform in a pantomime style in the early rehearsals. Working in different genres will develop your knowledge and improve your drama skills.

For your information

In addition to the storylines explored above, you may like to work with one of the seven basic narrative plots identified by Christopher Booker (see **Resources** list, page 255), as follows:

- *Overcoming the monster* – e.g. *Jaws*, *Dr No* and any number of Greek myths

- *Rags to riches or disguised potential* – e.g. *Cinderella*, *Superman*, *Pygmalion*

- *The quest* – e.g. *Jason and the Argonauts*, *Lord of the Rings*, *Raiders of the Lost Ark*

- *Voyage and return* – journeys to somewhere beyond the known world, e.g. *Robinson Crusoe*, *Lord of the Flies*, or to some magical mythical world, e.g. *The Wizard of Oz*, *The Lion, the Witch and the Wardrobe*, *Peter Pan*

- *Rebirth* – e.g. *Sleeping Beauty*, *Snow White*

- *Comedy* – a story with a mass of misunderstandings and chaos but ending in reconciliation and celebration, e.g. Shakespeare's *Twelfth Night* or the vintage film comedy *Some Like it Hot*

■ *Tragedy* – usually a story where a hero or heroine comes to power or achieves glory then goes too far in some way, it all goes wrong and their life is violently cut short, e.g. Shakespeare's *Macbeth* or R.L. Stevenson's *Dr Jekyll and Mr Hyde*.

You can find out more about comedy and tragedy in **Unit 1.5** on pages 54–58.

Review

The first part of this unit was designed to:

■ develop your knowledge of different structures and your confidence in using them to devise your dramas

■ enable you to combine your devising with other groups, so that all groups were contributing to the same play

■ collaborate and share ideas as a whole class group

■ put extra emphasis on developing your devising skills.

Discuss with your teacher your views on:

■ the advantages of the whole class combining and contributing to one play

■ what you have learnt about structuring a drama

■ two things you will take from this unit into future dramas you devise.

More Genres to Try

Here is some information on more genres you might like to work with and options to try for creating drama within these.

Pastiche

Pastiche is a 'patchwork quilt' of typical material taken from a particular genre. Many television and film comedians take a popular genre and then proceed to lampoon or affectionately send it up. You can send up the horror genre (as in the film *Young Frankenstein*), the Western genre (as in the film *Blazing Saddles*) or the disaster movie (as in the film *Airplane*) or create send-ups of Shakespearean tragedy, war films, musicals, soap operas, for example. Pastiche is a very popular and successful way of working, particularly within the comedy genre.

Pastiche relies on you being able to identify the standard elements that are used again and again in a genre or, to put it another way, the clichés of the genre. Creating a pastiche from a genre is a very good way of developing your understanding of this part of the course. You can't lampoon or gently poke fun at something successfully unless you understand it. *Four Plays for Coarse Actors* and *More Plays for Coarse Actors* contain short scripts which send up genres and the theatre generally (see **Resources** list, page 255).

Preparation

Over a few weeks, identify examples of pastiche in television and films you see and note which genre they are making fun of. Record this ready for discussion with your teacher and the rest of the group.

Exploration

In groups or working as a whole class, choose a genre and list as many clichés relating to the genre as you can think of (or better still, make still images of them). Spend a maximum of 15 minutes on this. Repeat this activity for as many genres as you can think of as long as it remains interesting or fun.

How to excel

Use this exploration throughout your course as a warm-up activity to help you fix in your head what each genre is all about.

Stretch your skills

Choose a genre and devise your own pastiche. Create a planned improvisation for presentation to the rest of the group. Producing this will take two to four lessons, depending on how far you wish to develop the work. It would help if you could watch some short video clips of pastiche work. Vintage TV programmes with comics like Morecambe and Wise or Stanley Baxter are full of excellent examples of pastiche.

Satire

This genre is very effective at making fun in a critical way of individuals, groups of people or organisations. Satire can be cruel and hurt people's feelings, as the people on the receiving end of the humour may not always see it as 'only having a laugh'.

Satire is never just comedy, but is comedy with a political purpose. Satire can be a way of striking back at powerful people or groups who it is otherwise hard to influence. For instance, using satire to criticise politicians has a long history. Comedians and satirists like Bremner, Bird and Fortune work in this way, having a dig at the mighty, rich and famous. *Ubu Roi* (by Alfred Jarry, 1896) is a bizarre play that satirises power and jumped-up officialdom (a contemporary update exists called *King Baabu*).

For satire to work, it must make the audience sympathise with or think about the observations being made. To do this, there must be some truth in the implied criticism. The observations will be distorted and over the top, but they must also be recognisably true. It is the truth of the situation that makes the audience laugh and think. Effective satire doesn't just make you laugh, but makes you annoyed or even angry about some issue or injustice. In order to be truthful, satire has to be based on a topic you know something about.

| **Exploration** | You are going to devise a satirical sketch of your own. Decide on an issue in your life experience that is worth satirising. It needs to be something that actually matters. Remember: for satire to work it has to be based on something important to you and something you have knowledge of. Here are some possible areas to get you thinking. You might satirise: |

- your own age group by looking at how teenagers follow fashion, seek to keep in with the cool group or try not to be seen to work too hard at school

- the world of adults and how they relate to young people, or how adults build a false world for young children: the tooth fairy, Father Christmas

- teenage anxiety and moodiness, in the vein of Harry Enfield's Kevin and Perry or Catherine Tate's schoolgirl, Lauren – 'Am I bovvered?'

1 In working groups, make a list of subjects suitable for satirising. Choose one and devise your sketch. Planning and rehearsing your sketch should take one or two lessons.

2 Perform your sketches to each other.

3 Decide whether you would like to develop the work for another audience. If the answer is yes, you could put the sketches together to create a revue. To perform it to an outside audience you will need to edit, adapt, add and rehearse.

A revue usually has songs and dancing in it. Creating satirical songs and dance routines on your chosen theme could be a challenge and fun. Devising and performing them will be good practice for *Unit 2 Drama in the Making*, where you have to present three different items for your Controlled Assessment. A song or a dance/physical theatre could be such an item.

Stretch your skills

Beyond the Fringe was a very famous revue first performed at the Edinburgh Festival Fringe at the start of the 1960s. It poked fun at the British establishment of the 1950s, a time of great change in British society, and it had a huge influence on the development of comedy and satire in Britain. Some critics even argue that its irreverent approach had a greater influence in changing British theatre than John Osborne's *Look Back in Anger*, which is usually named as the play that moved British drama from being centred on cosy middle/upper-class drawing rooms to realistically portraying working-class people on the stage.

See if you can track down the scripts and sound recordings of *Beyond the Fringe* with the original cast performing. Reading or listening to some of the sketches will give you an insight into the recent history of comedy in Britain. Decide whether you think the material is still relevant and funny.

Agitprop

This term is a combination of 'agitation' and 'propaganda'. One of its origins is plays presented by revolutionaries during and just after the Russian Revolution of 1917 to promote their cause and educate the audience (see page 32).

Agitprop is very much theatre as an 'advertising poster' for your own particular cause. The idea is not to present an issue in an even-handed or critical way but to promote your cause and get the audience on your side. It is not such a common genre in Britain as it was during the first half of the twentieth century, when there was more social and economic turmoil. A famous example of this genre is the American play *Waiting for Lefty* by Clifford Odets (1934), which has as its theme the New York taxi drivers' strike of that year. In Britain during the miners' strike of 1984/5 a number of theatre companies toured the coalfields performing plays promoting the miners' cause.

Agitprop developed its own distinctive performance style using sketches, cabaret and mime. Setting was minimal, actors dressed in dungarees and the audience was encouraged to participate. Companies composed their own music and songs to fit their themes. The Unity Theatre Company, which was a British group, had a big hit with one of their tunes: *Sing a Song of Social Significance*.

Preparation

In working groups of up to six, you are going to create a piece of agitprop theatre.

1 Pick an issue you all feel strongly about. Make sure you all support the stance you are going to take on the issue. Possible issues include:

- global warming
- battery farming
- sweatshop or child labour
- homelessness
- nuclear weapons

- road protests
- genetically modified crops
- fox hunting
- school uniform
- worldwide banking crisis.

2 Make six **still images** which promote your cause. They should be like posters putting across your viewpoint, and each should have a caption, which will be spoken to accompany the image. Spend a maximum of 20 minutes on these images. (Later you could develop this by putting the captions on a CD and adding musical links or songs, raps and poems to play between the images.)

3 When the time is up, all groups should perform at the same time, running the images in sequence as if they were quick changes on a slide projector. Someone calls the numbers 1 to 6 and you make the images and speak the caption lines. This is a test of group organisation and co-operation. A successful group will be able to do this with no discussion and no fuss. You can now watch each group individually and concentrate on each message.

Exploration

The still images are the bare bones or plan for your agitprop drama. Next develop the drama, linking the images together with movement, dialogue, narration, songs, raps, poems, etc.

Rehearse, edit, adapt and add to create a quality drama. This could take two to four lessons. When your drama is complete, decide whether you wish to perform it to an outside audience, e.g. in school assembly.

Stretch your skills

- Research the sketch *Art is a Weapon* (1931, adapted by Workers' Laboratory Theatre) on the Internet. Rehearse and perform this sketch in the style of the political theatre groups. You can achieve this using the techniques introduced above and the clues that the script gives you.

- The folk songs of the American Woodie Guthrie and Britain's Ewan MacColl and Peggy Seeger are very political. Ewan MacColl wrote many songs for the theatre, particularly during his collaboration with the theatre director Joan Littlewood. Popular music also has its political songwriters, such as Bob Dylan, John Lennon (during his solo career) and Billy Bragg. Which recent and current pop groups or solo artists do you know of who have produced songs with political lyrics?

How to excel

Use songs, raps and poems in your drama. They are excellent devices for making a commentary on the action: they can draw the attention of the audience to the points you are making or give a viewpoint on a character or incident in the drama. A poem can be used to make a point or move the plot on more quickly than conventional scripting. Agitprop and music hall commonly used such devices but they are now used in all forms of theatre.

Breaking into song or playing music is conventionally used for moments of heightened emotion. These are the moments when words are not enough – for example, love and death scenes. They are also tricky moments to act, so putting on music or breaking into song can be a solution!

Living newspaper

This is a form of agitprop that has virtually disappeared in Britain. Hot political news items were turned into theatre and taken onto the streets as the events were still unwinding. The idea was to confront people with these issues and make them think. Often the play would stop in full flow and a debate take place with the audience. This didn't matter in the eyes of the actors, as their aim was to get people thinking about the issue rather than just entertain them.

When this type of theatre was popular, during the first half of the twentieth century, a higher percentage of people couldn't read. The drama used the agitprop style, political satire, songs, music and action.

Preparation and exploration

Have a go at reviving this form of political theatre. Bring in newspapers, school newsletters, a radio, etc., on a particular day and choose a national, local or school news item to turn into a sketch. The sketch must have a point of view, which you are trying to push.

Your news item must be hot off the press, so you'll have to select the theme there and then on the day. Have one or two practice runs, so that you get used to devising and performing a sketch in one lesson.

Now do it for real, taking the sketch you devise in the lesson out onto the 'streets' of the school the same day as you devise it. You can perform it in the playground, the hall, to the tuck-shop queue. As you are not in Russia during the revolution, make sure you clear the project with the Headteacher to ensure you are not being a nuisance or creating a health-and-safety risk. Repeat with a different news story on another day so that the school gets used to its daily 'living newspaper'.

Documentary theatre

This form of social drama presents historical events, significant people from the past, and issues of the day that may cause comment or concern. Its main strengths and attractions are the combination of real documentary evidence and fictional layers of the drama.

You will find more on documentary theatre on page 31.

You are going to look into the issue of 'street children' as the basis for a piece of documentary theatre. Street children are children who have, through life's adverse circumstances, been forced to fend for themselves without the support of caring adults. Such children have existed through history right up to the present day.

You will need to do some research to provide factual documentary material, which might then be woven into your drama as:

- narration
- voice-over
- songs
- actual testimony/statements from children or adults
- music
- news items
- depictions of events from history or the recent past.

Some starting points on street children are given on the next two pages. Use the Internet, your school history department or your local library as resources for researching further documentary evidence.

Street Children's Human Rights in Central America

◀ ▶   C   +   🌐 http://www.casa-alianza.org.uk   🔍⌄ casa alia 🔄

📖   **Bookseller**   **Publishing News**   »

> Casa Alianza works with street children and homeless young people and defends children's human rights.

Casa Alianza's Work

Across Central America thousands of children and young people live on the streets. Separated from their families many street children end up sleeping rough in darkened alleys, frozen shop doorways, underground water systems and on rubbish dumps. They are often numb with cold, terrified - some will be beaten, abused and killed. For many street children each day is just another day to endure and survive. That is ... unless they come to Casa Alianza.

For many homeless children we are the only place to go where they can be safe and away from the hostile, dangerous streets that are no place for an adult let alone vulnerable and defenceless children. We offer sanctuary, safety, a clean warm bed to sleep in, hot nutritious food and most important of all ... **hope and an option to leave the streets once and for all and with our help build a future**.

> Street children is a term used to refer to children who live on the streets of a city. They have no family care and protection. Most are between 5 and 18 years old.

... causative factors includes:
- family breakdown
- armed conflict
- poverty
- natural and man-made disasters
- famine
- physical and sexual abuse
- exploitation by adults
- dislocation through migration
- urbanisation and overcrowding
- acculturation.

> _The dangers_
>
> The dangers for street children are great. For example, every month front-line programmes in countries such as Guatemala and Honduras report the murder of around 80–100 children and young people.

> _Surviving_
>
> Street children live in abandoned buildings, cardboard boxes, parks or on the street itself. They range from children who spend some time in the streets and sleep in a house with adults, to those who live entirely in the streets and have no adult supervision or care.

Children on the street are those engaged in some kind of economic activity ranging from begging to vending. Most go home at the end of the day and contribute their earnings to their family. They may be attending school and retain a sense of belonging to a family. Because of the economic fragility of the family, these children may eventually opt for a permanent life on the streets.

Children of the street actually live on the street (or outside a normal family environment). Family ties may exist but are tenuous and are maintained only casually or occasionally.

SECTION 2   CREATING DRAMA AND DEVELOPING SKILLS

183

THE RAGGED SCHOOL.
In West Street (late Chick Lane) Smithfield

This is the Ragged School as seen by the Victorian illustator George Cruikshank, who is best known for illustrating Charles Dickens' work. Like Dickens, he was an acute observer of the values and behaviour of Victorian society.

Street children in literature
Examples from fiction illustrate how common street children were in nineteenth-century Britain and other countries: Fagin's pickpockets in Oliver Twist; the 'Baker Street Irregulars' in Conan Doyle's Sherlock Holmes stories; Kipling's Kim, a street child in colonial India; Gavroche in Victor Hugo's Les Misérables.

Gustave Doré is another famous illustrator of life in Victorian times. This engraving is one of a set of 180 images of London he created over five years in the 1870s. They were published in a book called The Pilgrimage.

A critic complained that in The Pilgrimage "Dore gives us sketches in which the commonest, the vulgarest external features are set down". Not everyone was as willing as Doré to recognise the unwashed face of Victorian London.

Street children have existed throughout history. In 1848 Lord Ashley spoke of more than 30 000 'naked, filthy, roaming lawless and deserted children', in and around London.

Thomas Barnardo came to London in 1866 and found children sleeping in the streets and being forced to beg for food. It was in 1867 that he set up the Ragged School and started helping the abused, vulnerable, forgotten and neglected children of East London, and his work still continues today. His meeting with Jim Jarvis, a street child of the day, set in motion the creation of the Barnardo homes.

The first home for boys was opened in Stepney Causeway in 1871.

Barnardo and his helpers regularly went out at night to find and help destitute boys. One evening an 11-year-old boy, John Somers (nicknamed 'Carrots'), was turned away from the home as it was full. He was found dead two days later – he had died of starvation. From then on the homes bore the sign 'No Destitute Child Ever Refused'. Later, in 1876, a Village Home for Girls was opened in Barkingside, Essex. It was a collection of 70 houses circling a green and providing homes for about 1000 girls.

Dramatic metaphor, analogy and allegory

These dramatic forms all operate by not addressing their theme directly. Working in these ways affects how you shape your drama, how it looks and the way the plot is organised. As with many issues in the arts, things are not always straightforward, there aren't simple right or wrong answers. You could debate whether a play is an allegory or an analogy, whether allegory and analogy actually are the same thing or even whether these formats are genres or styles.

Remember: in this course, debate over definitions is not as important as being able to turn the ideas they spark off in your head into effective drama. Effective drama communicates to an audience, so these concepts are going to be useful only if they help make the dramas you create and interpret more meaningful and engaging for you and an audience. As Shakespeare wrote:

'A rose by any other name would smell as sweet.'

A **metaphor** can be created to give an overall unity to a drama – for example, a character's life story created as a journey with all the various twists and turns (as you saw earlier in this unit, on page 166).

An **analogy** is used to create a similar situation in a different context, which can help understanding of difficult or sensitive issues. Many fairy stories have an underlying theme buried beneath the surface of the basic plot – that is, they have a subtext.

For example, you might work with conflicting groups on a theme that relates to their own conflict. Creating a drama about conflicting claims over land between Native Americans and white pioneers in the 1800s might help a group of present-day Arab and Israeli drama students see some parallels with their contemporary situation. It might create a bridge between them over this very hot issue.

An allegory deals with its theme symbolically. Many fables are allegories – for example, Aesop's Fables. On page 83, you can read about the play *Everyman*, one of the most famous allegorical plays in theatrical history.

Why should playwrights and performers want to work in these ways? Isn't acting out the story in a form that's true to life (Naturalism) going to be the best way of communicating your ideas? The answer to the last question is 'Not necessarily'. Strict Naturalism is not always the best way to expose or reveal the truth of a situation.

Animal Farm by George Orwell is a modern allegory which, taken at face value, is about farm animals taking over from their human masters. But it is also a political allegory of the Soviet Union following the Russian Revolution. Peter Hall's adaptation of *Animal Farm* for the stage would make an excellent text to use in your Controlled Assessment for **Unit 1 From Page to Stage**.

Here are three reasons why you might choose to work in a less naturalistic way:

- By performing the drama in an unusual or novel way you might grab the attention of the audience more effectively.

- The truth of human situations and conflicts is complicated and the reality of the situation may be best created by not making the scene so true to life (naturalistic). For example, flashbacks can emphasise the history of the situation, voice-overs can tell the audience what is going on in a character's mind, sound collage or music can create the emotional state of mind of a character.

- In countries where there is no freedom of speech, criticism of the rulers through allegory may be the only option. The popular story *Gulliver's Travels* was originally a political allegory which attacked powerful people the author couldn't speak out against directly.

Devising a dramatic metaphor, analogy or allegory to create a context for the whole drama has more to it than adding conventions such as flashbacks or voice-overs to a naturalistic plot line. Arthur Miller's play *The Crucible* illustrates this. It is based on the Salem Witch Trials of 1692 but is an allegory of McCarthyism in the United States in the 1950s, when people accused of being Communists were blacklisted. This is another play you could consider using for **Unit 1 From Page to Stage**.

▲ Arthur Miller's play *The Crucible* in a production by the Young Vic

Exploration and performance

Each of the following activities can take from one to three lessons. It depends how much detail you go into and whether you decide to polish them for performance or leave them as improvisations. They are here for you to make your own selection.

■ Take one of Aesop's many allegorical fables and turn it into a naturalistic contemporary drama. The process of tackling such a conversion will really help you understand how allegory works and is a drama challenge. Some suggested fables are: *The Four Oxen and the Lion* (the theme here is 'unity is strength'), *The Farmer and the Stork* (if you keep bad company you will be treated with suspicion however honest you may be), *The Peacock and the Crane* (judge people by what they achieve not by outward appearance).

You must make sure that the original point of the allegory is maintained in the new naturalistic drama, so the first thing to do is to establish what the fable is actually getting at.

■ Fairy stories such as *Little Red Riding Hood* can be seen as analogies – in this case, a story about a girl moving into womanhood and the 'predators' that await her. You could take a fairy story and explore any hidden meaning or subtext within it. Give the new version a title, such as *Red Riding Hood – Uncensored*.

As well as working on analogy, you can extend the plots and themes. For example, a new version of *The Three Little Pigs* could focus on why three youngsters leave home and be titled *Leaving Home*, or *The Pied Piper* could become *The Corrupt Councillors*.

■ Use chairs to create the setting for a lift that will be a metaphor for the different possibilities that life offers the principal character. You could use a character you have created in a previous drama or use a convention such as **role-on-the-wall** to create a new character. Each floor the character alights at offers different possibilities. So each can have a different master of ceremonies or you can have one actor controlling all the floors. The lift, like life, goes up and down.

The metaphor of the lift gives an abstract style to the overall shaping of the drama, but the scenes you create for each floor can be performed in any style you wish: naturalistic, non-naturalistic, abstract or representational. This makes it possible to mix styles and adapt or change the rules. You can find out more about these styles on pages 63–65.

For example, the drama group in the photograph opposite used each floor as a different dream world, exploring the character's aspirations and fears. The metaphor of the lift could be used to create an abstract style for performance.

■ Create a wheel of fortune in a fairground. The barker cries: 'Round and round she goes, where she lands no one knows. Your fate relies on one little spin of the wheel of fortune. Come forward, lady, your destiny awaits.' The pointer is spun to the accompaniment of fairground music. It stops. What is the fate of the subject of the drama? That is up to you to decide. If you choose to work with this dramatic metaphor, the theme of the drama might be the fickleness of fate.

■ Create a hall of mirrors like those often used in old fairgrounds. Some of the mirrors are normal, some elongate, some enlarge,

some widen, some split up the image. Each mirror image sparks off a different drama about the protagonist (main character). This could be a hook for a drama about the image we have of ourselves and how others see us.

The format used for the journey or pathway metaphor on pages 166–169 could also be applied to the lift or wheel-of-fortune metaphors. Working groups could be formed as follows:

The lift	The wheel of fortune
Floor 1: The past	*Spin 1:* Bad luck
Floor 2: Dreams for the future	*Spin 2:* Fame
Floor 3: The present	*Spin 3:* There but for fortune …
Floor 4: A happy or unhappy memory	*Spin 4:* The stranger
Floor 5: The future	*Spin 5:* Through the mist

Stretch your skills

- Think of two issues that might make people in the area where you live feel uncomfortable if you dealt with them head on. Come up with a dramatic analogy, metaphor or allegory that might enable you to explore the issue. Not every situation can be approached through these means, so don't be surprised if you find this hard or can't easily create a parallel. Share your ideas with the rest of the class. If you think the ideas have potential, they could be used to create a piece of drama.

■ Sport is often used in drama as a metaphor, particularly boxing and baseball. Why do you think these sports are used repeatedly while most others rarely feature? The film *The Hustler* takes the game of pool as the background against which the drama unfolds, but it is not essentially a film about pool. The game is a metaphor for the life of its main character, Eddy Felson. If you can, watch some clips from this film featuring the pool games. What do they tell you about Eddy? It is also a good example of method acting.

Two contrasting drama structures

When shaping and structuring a drama, you could also follow the example of the Ancient Greeks and use the unities of time, place and action. Here the action all takes place on one day in the character's life and in one location.

This simple structure has many advantages, besides the obvious fact that you only have to create one set. It concentrates on developing character and the audience is not distracted from the character by changes in location and needing to take in new information. Characters spend longer on stage so the audience can get to know them and their concerns. This is particularly important if the genre is tragedy. You need time to empathise with a character if you are going to take their plight seriously.

Greek theatre had strict rules on structure but rules are there to be broken in drama, so let's look at the opposite of using the Greek unities of time, place and action.

Creating an extended plot can be a very time-consuming and complicated process. In lesson time you won't always be able to create long, well-ordered plots. This is where **montage**, vignettes and **collage** come into their own. They can be used to stitch longer dramas together without having to tie up all the loose ends, as you have to do with a well-constructed plot. Montage, vignettes and collage offer you a way of switching scenes a bit like a film. They reduce the focus on character, but you can make the drama visually exciting and cover great sweeps of content quickly and effectively. This is the way you worked when using dramatic metaphor on pages 166–169.

Review

To review the activities in the second part of this unit:

- list three advantages of working in this way (relate this to any of the specific tasks you have tried)
- think of one drama situation (context) when you might use dramatic metaphor, analogy or allegory and explain why.

2.6 Taking Control in Creating Drama

Your aims

First, you are going to be presented with some stimulus material as a starting point for creating your own drama. It will be up to you to apply what you have learnt and the skills you have gained so far and to decide what type of drama you will create from the stimulus.

Second, you are going to consider a model script extract (the opening scene) devised from the same stimulus material by another group of young people like yourselves.

Rationale: In previous projects there has been a lot of support and advice. In the first part of this one, you will just have the stimulus and some information. This is very much like what you will receive as part of *Unit 3 From Concept to Creation*, and so gives you an opportunity to take control of creating the drama.

By working with material devised by other students in the second part of the project, you can assess how they have structured their material and evaluate the effectiveness of the decisions they made. This part also focuses on the importance of stage directions and technical cues in a script.

Skills and understanding you will develop

- *In creating the drama:* You will be using and applying knowledge and skills already acquired across the six Areas of Study.

- *In working with the model script:* You will be using evaluative skills to assess how other students have applied knowledge and skills across the six Areas of Study in devising a text that draws on documentary evidence. You will also increase your understanding of the use of stage directions and technical cues.

- *Contexts:* In creating your own drama, you will be applying all four of the Contexts – **Performer**, **Deviser**, **Director** and **Designer** – as relevant.

The project will provide ideas and develop devising skills that will prepare you to tackle *Unit 2 Drama in the Making* and the Perfomer (devised) Brief and Deviser Brief for *Unit 3 From Concept to Creation*.

In assessing the script extract, you will be analysing how the Context of **Deviser** has been applied. If you enact the scene, you will work in the Contexts of **Director** and **Performer**.

Record which of the four Contexts – Performer, Director, Deviser or Designer – you focused on. List the skills you are developing, your level of competence and what you need to improve.

■ *Evaluation:* If you are doing this project as an assessed unit, remember that you will need to create a **Working Record**.

Source material for creating your own drama

The stimulus material on Matoaka (Pocahontas) in this section could be developed for *Unit 2 Drama in the Making*. From the work you have already done, you should be well capable of researching and structuring this material for yourself, making it your own drama.

It is a rich story for drama, with wider (macro) issues linked to the colonisation of North America and the decimation of the indigenous peoples. In the hundred years after Columbus landed in the Americas in 1492, the native population of North America fell from 7 million to 700 000.

◀ The 'Pocahontas' story. Do Europeans use it to justify their colonisation of North America?

Matoaka, now
Rebecca Rolfe, in
London in 1616

On the personal (micro) level there is the story of Matoaka (Pocahontas) herself: how she married the English settler John Rolfe. How they travelled together to London as ambassadors for the Jamestown settlement, to encourage more people to make their home in Virginia. Presenting Matoaka, the baptised Native American wife of an Englishman, was not only a marketing ploy but a symbol of the old world imposing its will on the new.

Rolfe and his wife may have visited the court of James I. It has even been suggested that she saw a production of Shakespeare's *The Tempest* at court. This play has undertones of colonisation, with the so-called 'primitive monster' Caliban, who has been taught by Prospero to speak a 'civilised' tongue and abandon his 'primitive' native tongue. If Matoaka, or Rebecca as she had by then been baptised, was indeed present at a performance of *The Tempest*, how ironic that was, a case of art imitating life. Then of course there is the fact of her tragic death at Gravesend on the return journey, leaving her young child orphaned.

The story of Matoaka that has been handed down to us is not without controversy. The version of the story used by Disney is regarded as myth by the Powhatan Nation. This is what inspired the epilogue below. Enjoy creating your version of this continuing saga.

 ## Epilogue

The story of Pocahontas has been colonised by the white man. We have a different story.

'Pocahontas' was a nickname. Her real name was Matoaka. Did she save the 'heroic' John Smith from being clubbed to death by her father in 1607?

This epilogue was used for a student version of a play about Matoaka (Pocahontas). It was based on a statement issued by the modern-day Powhatan Nation which the students found on the Internet.

'Pocahontas' is remembered because she became the hero of Euro-Americans as the 'good Indian', one who saved the life of a white man.

In an account Smith wrote after his winter stay with Powhatan's people, he never mentioned such an incident. In fact, the starving adventurer reported he had been kept comfortable and treated in a friendly fashion, an honoured guest of Powhatan.

The first time John Smith told the story about this rescue was 17 years after it happened.

Smith's fibbing has been elevated to the status of a national myth. Euro-Americans must ask themselves why.

The true Pocahontas story has a sad ending. In 1612, at the age of 17, Pocahontas was treacherously taken prisoner by the English while she was on a social visit and was held hostage at Jamestown for over a year.

During her captivity, a 28-year-old widower named John Rolfe took a 'special interest' in the attractive young prisoner. As a condition of her release she agreed to marry Rolfe. In April 1614, Matoaka, also known as 'Pocahontas', daughter of Chief Powhatan, became 'Rebecca Rolfe'. Shortly after they had a son whom they named Thomas Rolfe.

Two years later, in the spring of 1616, Rolfe took his wife to England, where the Virginia Company of London used her in their propaganda campaign to support the colony. She was wined and dined and taken to theatres. It was only after her untimely death and her growing fame in London society that Smith found it convenient to invent the yarn that she had rescued him.

History tells the rest. The white men turned upon the Natives who had shared their resources with them and had shown them friendship. During Pocahontas' generation, Powhatan's people were decimated and dispersed and their lands were taken over. The pattern had been set which would soon spread across the American continent.

Model script extract based on Matoaka

The scene presented here was written by a group of drama students. Their script *Pocahontas – A North American Myth* is one response to the story of Matoaka.

The script has been divided into three small chunks providing a model for rehearsing text in small bites. This will also make sure that considering stage directions and technical cues is not missed out in your eagerness to speak the characters' lines.

Here is the opening to the scene.

"

Pocahontas – A North American Myth
Section 1

Note: LX = lighting cue; SD = sound cue.

(Cast enter in darkness.)

LX 1:   *(Wide expanse of the ocean. Cast all upstage centre.)*
SD 1:   *(The sea.)*

(Cast stare into blankness.)

LX 2:   *(Slow change of lighting state. The harbour. As the lighting changes, cast slowly move to create the illusion of standing around the harbour. Still upstage centre.)*
SD 2:   *(Sounds of harbour.)*

(Mime to show cast are the 'dregs of England' and getting ready to depart for the New World. Add snatches of half-heard dialogue, the cast develop these lines by improvisation.)

Stage 1

Exploration and performance

Read through the first section from the script above. You are going to direct and perform this opening to the play.

As it is unlikely that you will be able realise quickly full lighting or sound effects, talk through what lighting and sound effects you would like to create. Then, when you perform, one of you can narrate what should be happening with the lights. You may be able to make the sound effects with your voices or, again, narrate what you would like.

You have three dramatic problems to solve:

- Moving into a visual image of being on the dockside. Here, adding the sound effects will help both actors and audience to understand what is happening.

- Creating the 'dregs of England'. You should attempt to be quite realistic, and this is hard to do authentically. There is a danger of doing too much. For example, to show that the 'dregs' drink a lot, a determined swig from a flagon might be more effective than rolling about as a cartoon drunk. Violence might be shown by a look or one strong gesture, grabbing a throat, for example, rather than a full-scale scrap. You might choreograph the mime so that you are all working in unison – all give a violent look at the same time, all swig at the same time. Sometimes this works brilliantly, rapidly capturing the atmosphere needed, sometimes it is too false.

  This is a real drama challenge, making this small stage direction work authentically, a stage direction that could have easily got lost as you moved on to the spoken words in the script. Working in detail on moments like this can make all the difference in terms of the quality of a performance. It's the detail that counts.

- Creating improvised dialogue to match the status of the 'dregs' and the situation – boarding ship for the New World. This was a very dangerous journey then. You need to use lines that are going to sum up quickly for the audience what is happening. Here are some ideas to get you started.

  Lines from ship masters:
  - All aboard now, my hearties.
  - The New World beckons.
  - Clear those lines.
  - Visitors ashore.

  Lines from crew:
  - Fortune or bust.
  - Let's drink to success.
  - Who sails on the *Constant* with me?
  - I'll take this rather than a hangman's noose.

  Try fragmenting the lines (using only part of a line) to see what effect you get.

How to excel

When you narrate lighting and sound effects don't do it mechanically, in a matter-of-fact way. Create the atmosphere as much as you can by the way you perform the words: 'The lights dim. *(Pause.)* All is silent. *(Pause.)* Gra-a-a-a-dually....'

Now you have the opening of the scene in place, move on to the second section of script below. This includes narration and physical theatre.

Pocahontas – A North American Myth Section 2

Narration 1: All England's colonial ambitions ride with the Virginia Company's flagship, the 100 ton *Susan Constant*.

(A group of the cast takes the shape of the first ship, the Susan Constant, *upstage centre.)*

Narration 2: The 40 ton *Godspeed*.

(Second group takes shape of the Godspeed, *upstage right.)*

Narration 3: And the 20 ton *Discovery*.

(Third group takes shape of the Discovery, *upstage left.)*

Narration 1: And the 105 men who sail them.
Narration 4: The Virginia Company is a joint stock company seeking profits for its investors. Its Royal Charter of 1606 stated that it should –
Priest: We must propagate the Christian Religion to such people as yet live in darkness. All the rich endowments of Virginia are wages for all this Godly work. God in wisdom having enriched the Savage Countries, that those riches might be attractive to we Christian suitors.

(Improvised lines of casting off: 'Pull up the anchor'/ 'Unfurl the sails', etc. This is done in sequence, one boat at a time.)

Stage 2

You will need to form the three groups to make the boats and allocate the narration and priest roles. The narrators speak and then step aboard their respective boats, joining the crew. The ships then cast off.

The dramatic problems to solve are:

- How will you create the illusion of a boat? The script uses **physical theatre** to solve this, so you need to follow that approach.

- How will you speak the narration? It needs to be heightened speech. Can you use the location, the docks, to almost call out across the open space? Will there be an edge in the tone you use – for example, a pompous tone when speaking of the Virginia Company or a cynical businessman's tone? You could take time out and all have a go at the narration together to encourage each other to be bold.

- How will you time and order the sequence? The speaking of each narration, the forming of the boat and the narrator boarding the boat will need to be co-ordinated.

- How will you deliver the Priest's speech? This came directly from the historical documents researched and is quite a shocking speech for a modern audience. How will you tackle this and what action will go with it? Is he going with them or wishing them *bon voyage*? Again you could take time out and all have a go at this.

- How will you devise the improvised lines for casting off? These need to be highly exaggerated, shouted loudly, slowly and clearly as if shouting across large spaces. A few lines said in a fixed sequence will do this job very effectively. The same sequence could be repeated for each boat, as if the sailors are all following the same routine for casting off.

In the last part of the scene (on the next page), the three boats have to travel towards the audience creating the illusion of ships on the ocean. Half way to the audience the motion pauses and we are introduced to two of the key historical figures in this part of the story.

CREATING DRAMA AND DEVELOPING SKILLS

SECTION 2

199

Pocahontas – A North American Myth
Section 3

(The ships cast off. It is a staggered start for the three ships, they set sail one at a time.)

LX 3: *(The open ocean, full expanse of stage lit, bright daylight effect.)*

SD 3: *(The ocean.)*

(Boats move across the stage, pause half way across stage.)

LX 4: *(Localised on* Susan Constant, *centre stage for following duologue.)*

Narrator 1: There is a history of dislike between Smith and Wingfield. There was precious little Christian harmony on the Journey to the New World.

Wingfield: I've had a hatred for you since the day we set sail from England.

Smith: I cannot but deny that the feeling is mutual, Captain Wingfield.

Wingfield: Captain Smith, it is well you remember you are a yeoman. And may I remind you a yeoman is not the same as being of genteel birth. We are all aware of the stories of you begging in Ireland like a rogue. To such a man as you I would not my name should be a Companion.

Smith: If your name carried as much weight among the men as mine then perhaps this expedition would not be the fiasco it is becoming.

Wingfield: Does your insolence know no bounds!

Smith: I speak as I find, sirrah, and judge a man on his deeds not his birth.

Wingfield: You don't belong in this company, you common rogue, you'll never be one of us.

Smith: Sir, I would rather cut my own throat before I took my model from you.

Wingfield: You overstep the mark, you rogue. I take your comments as an incitement to mutiny. Guards, put this mutineer in chains.

Narration: And in chains Captain Smith would remain, until his practical skills led to a change of heart once they reached the New World.

LX 5: *(10 second lighting change. Approaching land.)*

SD 4: *(The shoreline, sound of gulls. Possibly a subtle drum to indicate the Natives are signalling the arrival of strangers to those inland.)*

Narration: It was an April morning in 1607 when they sailed into the bay of Chesapeake. What a sight for the Natives to behold / the three ships from beyond the seas / pennants – the red cross of St George on a white foreground – fluttering at the mastheads / the topsides of the ships brightly painted / the royal arms – strange beasts, the unicorn and the lion – on the painted shields that bedecked the forecastle / the mariners' costumes – bright red and blue shirts, caps, long trousers / the men scurrying about the decks / clambering up and down the rope ladders into the rigging.

(First ship Susan Constant *lands on the beach of the New World, downstage. Improvised lines 'Lower the anchor,' etc.)*

*(*Godspeed *and* Discovery *continue across sea.* Godspeed *lands. Improvised lines 'Lower the anchor,' etc. Crew enjoys being on land.)*

*(*Discovery *lands. Improvised lines 'Lower the anchor,' etc. Unloading of cargo, building of fort.)*

(The action eventually covers the whole stage and narrators speak downstage centre.)

Narration: These Founding Fathers of Virginia, or as some would have it, 'the refuse of the English Nation' dumped into Virginia. They were soldiers of fortune / mercenaries / vagabonds / desperadoes / convicts / and debtors. 'The scum of people' according to Sir Francis Bacon. / You remember I said Smith would be released when his practical skills were needed. *(Nods to Smith and gaoler.)*

(Smith released, shackles taken from his wrists.)

LX 6:   *(Bright daylight.)*
(The sails used for the boats are used to make the tents of the 'fort', upstage centre. Light focus on the fort.)

Narration: Unloading the ships and with no fortifications we were at our most vulnerable. / Least able to resist assault by the Savages. / Our 140 men against their who knows how many. / We constructed our settlement. / James Fort.

The background

The duologue between Smith and Wingfield was adapted from historical records. It seems such arguments and petty jealousies were a feature of this whole ill-fated expedition. The historical language is quite strange, but this makes it fun to perform. The class attitudes that come across give both actors a lot of scope for parody. You could split into pairs and all have a go at this duologue, to get a feel for how this documentary material plays.

▲ Rehearsing with the sails

The building of the fortifications is a design problem. The design for the original performance was very clever. Each of the three ships had sails, a main and minor sail, plus sides with shields. Some of the actors creating the ships held these as they travelled across the 'ocean'. When the ships landed, these prop sails and side pieces became the tents and fencing of the fort. (See the designer's sketch for this on page 42.) Luckily they had a very good designer who made this work for them. There was an organised system of poles, ropes and weights and the cast turned the sails 'magically' into the settlement. All this was done while the narrators spoke their lines.

Stage 3

Exploration

You are going to create the arrival in the New World and the setting up of the fort, which has to be upstage, leaving room for subsequent scenes. It acts almost like a backdrop.

The dramatic problems to solve for this last part of the scene are:

- Creating sound effects or a soundscape to help the illusion of the ships' progress.
- Delivering the duologue between Smith and Wingfield.
- Devising the action that goes with 'Crew enjoys being on land.'

The same kind of detailed work as you did on the stage direction '*dregs of England*' is required.

- Landing in the new land and setting up the fort. Do they hear the drum beat? Do they post guards?

- Making the narration engaging, using your voices as storytellers so that the audience enjoys listening to you.

It might help you to know that the full script was originally produced as a dance drama for one youth theatre group and three youth dance groups.

Review

This unit was designed to:

- provide stimulating theatrical material from a historical source and use it in a performance style you may not often use

- consider the approach to devising taken by another group of drama students and compare it with your way of working

- examine small sections of their script and tackle specific drama problems.

Discuss with your teacher your views on:

- the structure used for the opening scene of the play
- the dramatic resonance of the material
- the use of historical documentary material in some of the dialogue and script
- alternative solutions to some of the design problems created by the script, such as the movement of the ships, the building of the fort.

2.7 Working with the Design Concept

Your aims

You will learn what a **design concept** is and how it can be used in your practical work.

Rationale: This is an opportunity to show, using examples from professional theatre, how the Contexts of **Performer**, **Deviser**, **Director** and **Designer** all interrelate and contribute to one another.

Skills and understanding you will develop

- *In rehearsal:* You will expand and deepen your understanding of dealing with audience and **performance space** (Area of Study 3) and of the semiotics of drama (Area of Study 6).

- *Contexts:* Your main focus will be the **Designer Brief**. List the skills you are developing within this brief, your level of competence and what you need to improve.

- As you work through this project, consider whether you might like to select the Designer Brief for *Unit 3 From Concept to Creation*.

The design concept

One of the key aspects of the theatrical designer's work is creating the **design concept** for the play or drama being produced. Your Drama course emphasises this rather than individual design elements, such as costume or make-up. The course details say, *'Design is seen as something that covers all aspects of a piece of Drama'*, and go on to encourage you to look at all elements of a performance as a unified whole. This is why you need an overall design concept for a production which is linked to the director's overall concept for the play, the genre, the performance style and the general ideology (or politics) of the performance.

The design concept in this course covers:

- period the performance is set in
- performance style
- colour scheme
- any social, cultural or historical connections.

The design concept will be your focus if you select the Designer Brief in *Unit 3 From Concept to Creation.*

In earlier projects, you have taken on tasks with design aspects and got into the mindset of a designer (thinking from the viewpoint of a designer). These tasks have always been appropriate and practical for a GCSE Drama course, asking you to make rough and ready mock-ups rather than full-blown sets, costumes or lighting plots. Much of a designer's work is very specialist and requires very specialist skills. These skills take a lot of time to acquire – time that is simply not available on a GCSE Drama course. Remember: the Context of Designer is only one of four to be applied in this course. However, in this project you will be given more information and approaches to add to your knowledge and involve you further in thinking like a designer.

For your information

You are going to look at part of a design concept written by professional playwrights. The drama is a trilogy (three plays) called *The Island of the Mighty* by John Arden and Margaretta D'Arcy. These writers were unhappy about how their plays were being interpreted by some directors so they wrote quite detailed notes on their design concept. This illustrates how devisers, or directors or even performers can have a strong vision about how a play should be staged and designed. In such cases, the designer uses specialist skills to help the playwright (or director) realise their design concept.

The Island of the Mighty is based on the defeat of King Arthur and the destruction of the army in Britain during the troubled times after the Romans left. With the Romans gone, there is a power vacuum, with no single group in control, and tribal, religious and family loyalties cause constant conflict. But in such times of social change, economic and political upheaval, people still have to live. The plot draws on ancient Irish and Welsh versions of the story of Arthur. Characters like Arthur, Merlin and Gwenhwyvar and other 'familiar' figures are not as they are usually portrayed in the legend. Perhaps that is why the writers wanted to be clear about the design – they had not written a 'Knights of the Round Table' play!

Here are their notes on how the action should be staged:

> ## ❝Staging
>
> Whether the play is done on an open or a proscenium stage, a light platform should be erected in the middle of the acting area, large enough for all the scenes to be acted upon it (with the possible exception of some of the crowd episodes). The platform is to be backed by a frame holding a number of backcloths, which are drawn across to indicate the various sequences of the play. The drawing of the backcloths can be done either by one of the actors on stage, or by a stagehand, whichever is most convenient on each occasion.
>
> The convention to be established is that the 'stage-upon-the-stage' is the precise point at which the significant action takes place; actors seen approaching it, or waiting beside it for their cues, can be in or out of character according to circumstances. ...❞

This approach has been influenced by the ideas of Bertolt Brecht and designers, like Caspar Neher, who worked with him. If you have worked on *The Threepenny Opera* project on pages 140–155 you will be familiar with some of Brecht's techniques already.

Stretch your skills

Research images on the Internet of Caspar Neher's work to get a visual flavour of it. Other influential stage designers you could google are Edward Gordon Craig, Ralph Koltai, Richard Hudson, Maria Bjornson, Ming Cho Lee and Ernst Stern. A helpful website is The Theatre Design Website at <u>www.scenography.co.uk</u>

The playwrights' notes continue:

> 66 The audience will thus be confronted with a group of actors and musicians, moving on and off the 'normal' stage area, who one after another climb onto the 'stage-upon-the-stage' in order to present three narratives in as athletic and rapid and light a style as possible. The backcloths are not to be taken as realistic scenery, they are emblems of the kind of environment, emotional and temporal as well as geographic, required for each scene. No other properties (other than the hand props, such as swords etc., the dragon-standard, and maybe the odd stool) will be needed. 99

The playwrights drew and described eight backcloths required in the script. Two examples are shown below and on the next page.

▲ Backcloth 1 for *The Island of the Mighty*: 'Camp.' A number of tents with soldiers and their equipment crowded all about.

MORS
CRUDELITAS
BARBARITAS
HIC EST

▶ Backcloth 2 for *The Island of the Mighty*: 'Raid.' Some savage-looking soldiers and their equipment crowded all about.

Here are the playwrights' descriptions for the other six backcloths:

> **Backcloth 3** 'Fort.' A rectangular, symmetrical Roman establishment, in somewhat disrepair.
>
> **Backcloth 4** 'Woodland.' Bare trees clustered darkly and thickly together, with animals among them.
>
> **Backcloth 5** 'Ruins.' The remains of a Roman imperial building, all broken down by bad weather and neglect. An indication that people live among the ruins.
>
> **Backcloth 6** 'Seascape.' Murky water inhabited by strange and perilous creatures.
>
> **Backcloth 7** 'Mill.' A working water wheel adjacent to a dilapidated wooden house.
>
> **Backcloth 8** 'Snowscape.' A dark sky full of snowflakes, with some indeterminate footprints on the ground beneath it.

> These cloths should be painted in bold colours and clear lines; no perspective or naturalistic chiaroscuro [monochrome picture made by using several different shades of the same colour].

Preparation

1 Choose one of Backcloths 3–8 and create a design that follows the playwrights' description. Quickly sketch your design first and then draw it on a large sheet of paper (A1 or A0). You have a maximum of 15 minutes.

2 In role as theatre designers for the production, share your backcloth design with one of the other design groups and discuss together whether you think it fulfils Arden and D'Arcy's brief. Do the same for their design.

3 Now all take your designs to your teacher (in role as D'Arcy or Arden) and present your ideas to them.

The playwrights were also upset by the costume designs used in a production of the play and say this about costume:

> It is necessary that the characters be shown to be alive at a time of considerable material scarcity, when clothes would on the whole be made out of wool and linen. The early British were very fond of jewellery, and of bright colours. They were a vain people, but not necessarily very well-washed. The weather in Britain is not very hot, and much of the action of the play takes place in winter and in the north. The science of tailoring was not common – the normal costumes for both sexes was a loose woollen tunic of varying length: men would wear trousers and women too on some occasions. There would be a very clear and observable difference between the dresses of the rich and poor.

The playwrights go on to give not only more advice on producing the play, but also advice about the social, cultural and historical context. This includes the music. Having done a mass of research to write the play, they are likely to have more insight into the social, cultural and historical context than the director, designer or actors.

How to excel

Many playwrights make such notes in the introductions to their plays. If they do so, read them – they are often a goldmine of insights into the text.

What Arden and D'Arcy were doing was giving any director a very clear design concept. When you are working on your assessed units you should use this approach to design. So, for example, in **Unit 2 Drama in the Making** one of your items could be creating a design concept for an improvision you have devised, or describing or drawing backcloths as above. The same approach could be used in **Unit 3 From Concept to Creation** if you tackle the Designer Brief.

Creating impact via design

Try this piece of hands-on costume design. You can use the same approach with many other plays and drama.

Exploration

1 This activity is based on Shakespeare's *Macbeth*. Your teacher will supply some visual references and materials to make the costumes. You may want to refer to the banquet in Act 3, Scene 4, where Macbeth describes how Banquo's ghost looks:

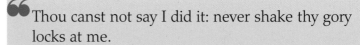

> Thou canst not say I did it: never shake thy gory locks at me.
>
> Ay, and a bold one, that dare look on that which might appal the devil.

In groups of three or four you are going to mock up a costume for Banquo's ghost that works with these text references. Work as a team of designers dressing one member of your group. You have 10–15 minutes to use pens, fabric and masks to create your design.

2 Once finished, invite each Banquo to parade up and down. Each design team should explain their design ideas to the class and your teacher.

3 Ask each Banquo to go into role and point an accusing finger at Macbeth. They can develop this by performing some of the following lines as they point:

> "Murderer
> Lesser than Macbeth, and greater.
> Not so happy, yet much happier
> Thou shalt get kings, though thou be none.
> Fly, good Fleance, fly, fly, fly!"

▾ The designers explain their costuming ideas.

Performance

Try creating the banquet scene as a whole class, using all the Banquo ghosts you have created. Wherever Macbeth looks, there is a Banquo. Those of you who were the designers should take on the roles of Macbeth, Lady Macbeth and all the Lords and Ladies at the banquet.

Through activities like this you are integrating design into the practical process of creating a drama.

Review

This unit was designed to:

- consider different aspects of design that are all part of the design concept
- offer practical design activities that lead to the creation or enrichment of the drama
- recognise that devisers often have strong views on the design concept for their plays.

Discuss with your teacher your views on:

- how the design activities helped your understanding of the text
- how the design activities brought your performance to life
- what types of design work can be achieved in your GCSE class.

For more on working on the Designer Brief, see **Unit 3.4** on page 227.

SECTION 3
Preparing for Assessment

■ What's Expected and How to Do Well

This section is full of practical tips and suggestions about each of the three assessed units in the course. You will find ideas about:

- how to decide what goes into your Working Record
- preparing and undertaking the two Controlled Assessments
- preparing and undertaking the Examined Unit
- resources you might use to help you.

Your Working Record

You will have to produce a Working Record for each of the three assessed units. This can contain work in a variety of formats: notes, diagrams, CD or DVD, continuous writing, storyboards, scenarios, photographs, drawings, short extracts from dialogue, designs, character notes, your own views and ideas and those of others.

You may use and draw on the ideas of others in your Working Record. It is positive to make use of other people's ideas – Shakespeare did it all the time. But you must be sure to acknowledge where the ideas first came from. Where you are using someone else's script or quoting them, indicate this by putting those words in quotes. If you are using a general idea or approach suggested to you or something you read or saw, identify the original source. This demonstrates good practice and you will be credited for it, as you will be using knowledge acquired as a result of your research.

Research hints

Never include complete downloaded pages from the Internet or pages of photocopies. This will not impress an examiner or moderator. They are interested in what you select from any information you have researched, your reason for selecting it and how you are going to use it.

The Working Record has a slightly different format for each of the three assessed units. You will find more detail in the sections on each unit which follow.

3.1 Unit 1 From Page to Stage – Controlled Assessment

Suggested structure for Unit 1 Working Record

1 Background, Context, Genre and Performance Style
2 Creating the Performance
3 Evaluation – What did we achieve as Performers, Directors and Designers?

Unit 1 is about exploring the possibilities offered by a **published text**, with the emphasis on working to the intentions of the playwright. This means you don't have to do any devising – the plot and structure are already there in the text. Also the genre and performance style are most likely to be fixed or heavily hinted at. By exploring the text you should be able to work out the playwright's intentions. This is the prime job of any director. Together with the designer and the performers, the director works to bring the text to life on the stage. This is why this unit has been titled *From Page to Stage*.

You will be assessed on what you put on the stage plus your Working Record. The Working Record in this unit needs to be a combined set of director's, performer's and designer's notes.

You do not have to give each of the three Contexts of Designer, Director and **Performer** equal weight. You may choose to concentrate on two of the Contexts rather than all three because of the time you have available. If this is your decision, make sure you note it in your Working Record so that your examiners know that you have excluded one of the Contexts.

In *Unit 1* you will need to demonstrate your ability to:

- apply performance and production skills
- examine and evaluate the text and decide how it should be performed to match the playwright's intentions
- work as a team collaboratively and creatively to perform an extract from the text.

Before you start work on the extract, you will take part in a series of lessons and workshops with your teacher. This will help you to understand the requirements of the text and to select the extract you wish to perform. The lessons/workshops will follow a format similar to the one below. But you and your teacher can vary this to suit the way your particular group works on a text.

Preparation

You will need to discuss and establish:

- the intentions of the playwright
- the social, cultural and historical context of the text
- the key features of the genre and any implied performance style
- the design elements suggested by the text plus any others you think should be added
- the parts of the text that it would be fun to act, direct or design.

Working Record hints

Make a 1–2 page collection of notes, snippets from the text, diagrams and relevant photographs/images you have collected from research. This **mood board** should capture the essence of what you think the text is about (see example on next page). Remember to be selective! Everything you select should be something that is going to help you or inspire your performance of this text. The notes can be referred to later when you complete the first section of your Working Record, *Background, Context, Genre and Performance Style*.

Upper Class house

photos of streets in 1950, still signs of wardamage.

A painting of Rye Station early 1950's

1950's

sketch of a kitchen in 1950. Usually Brown and cream or green and cream walls.

MENS FASHION

the household telephone

white socks (everyday)

Bobbed hair and fringes

washing mangle

NEWSPAPER ARTICLES/ADVERTS

WOMENS FASHION

Boussant skirts (lots of puff)

CHILDRENS TOMS

71 DEAD IN NURSING HOME FIRE; LICENSE FOR PLACE HAD BEEN HELD UP BY STATE

Raging Fire Draws On-Lookers to Scene

ROSIE. GASTON 10 NC

▶ A student's mood board

Exploration

This may vary according to the text your teacher has chosen for you to work on. Whatever the text, make your exploration practical. Even though the script has already been written for you, improvisation is an important rehearsal and exploratory technique. Here are some novel, interesting ways you could start working on the text:

1 Look at the opening stage direction of the play (if there isn't one, create one). Focus on this and not the dialogue. Create the

start of the play. For this exercise, effects such as lighting and sound can be narrated – for example: 'Lights dim on the audience, bring up a single spotlight centre stage. The sound of a heartbeat gradually fades in, reaches crescendo then stops.'

You must work out the entrance of the first actor(s) in precise detail. This takes you up to the point of the opening lines of the play. If your stage direction differs in any way from the original, justify why.

Spend 20 minutes on this.

2 Select five or six other stage directions in the text. Split into groups, take one stage direction each and repeat what you did in the opening exercise. Share your ideas with each other. If you are adding to the original stage direction in the text, justify why.

Spend 10 minutes on each stage direction.

3 Create a 'rough and ready' setting for the play or one of the scenes. Do this as a whole class. Decide together what is needed and then split the jobs between you. Create the setting in your working space in 20 minutes. Use whatever you have in your working space. Effective rehearsal settings can be created with fabric, sugar paper, sellotape, gaffer tape and scissors.

4 Use the setting you created in the previous exercise as a location to rehearse a short section of the text. You can do this as a whole class, sharing ideas for this section with one group as the performers while the rest of you collectively direct. Or you can take it in turns to use the setting.

Spend 10–20 minutes exploring the possibilities the setting offers directors and performers.

5 Select a section of the text and rehearse it. Turn to page 153 for approaches to rehearsing a text.

Spend 20–30 minutes on this.

Working Record stage 1: During your final exploration lesson, complete the first section of your Working Record, *Background, Context, Genre and Performance Style*. Refer to the notes you created in the preparation work. This section needs to identify the possibilities and challenges you think the text offers the director, designer and performer. It should also identify the extract you are going to work on and why it has been selected. You can work with other students collectively to complete this section of your Working Record, but all other sections must be entirely your own work without any collaboration with other candidates or your teacher.

Rehearsal

This is the 10 hour Rehearsal Period of the Controlled Assessment.

Rehearse your selected section of the text. This will involve both directing and performing. It can also include some design, depending on resources and time.

Working Record stage 2: As rehearsals progress, complete the second section of your Working Record, *Creating the Performance.* Here you need to identify the key performance, directing and design decisions you are making.

Working Record hints

Once again, be selective. It is not necessary or helpful to record everything you do like a personal diary. Include only the key points you have decided on as Performer, Director or Designer. These are the points that are going to impact on the actual performance the audience sees. As well as your own work, you may include key elements introduced by your fellow performers. You are expected to reflect on and analyse your own work and that of others.

Presentation

1 Perform the extract to your teacher and other students.
2 Take feedback from the audience.

Working Record stage 3: Now that you have presented your extract to an audience, you can complete the third and last section of your Working Record, *Evaluation – What did we achieve as Performers, Directors and Designers?* You will have a maximum of 1 hour to do this. Note: this is an additional 1 hour of Controlled Assessment, not part of the 10 hour Rehearsal Period of the Controlled Assessment (see page 218).

This section will be your final reflection on the potential of the text and what you did with the extract. You will have had feedback from your audience, so take their views into consideration. You may like to give your audience a feedback questionnaire to help you analyse their views.

How the marking works: Your teacher will mark your Controlled Assessment. Your final performance will be filmed on DVD and sent together with your Working Record and your teacher's marks to the OCR moderator. This will be the evidence of the standard of work you have achieved.

3.2 Unit 2 Drama in the Making – Controlled Assessment

> Suggested structure for Unit 2 Working Record
> 1 Potential for Drama
> 2 The Application for:
>   ▪ Item 1
>   ▪ Item 2
>   ▪ Item 3
> 3 Evaluation – Is this the right material for an engaging drama?

Unit 2 is about exploring the possibilities offered by a stimulus. You are not expected by the end of the unit to have devised a complete drama or even the template for a complete drama. What you will have to do is identify **three items** that could contribute to a drama based on the stimulus. This will enable you to make a decision about the potential of the stimulus to create a good drama. So this unit focuses on the process of creating drama rather than the final product. This is why it has been titled *Drama in the Making*.

You may well take the view that you would not develop a full drama from this stimulus material. In this case, you will have tested the material and if you were a playwright you would now look for something else to base your new play on. On the other hand, the stimulus material may have real dramatic possibilities so that you definitely would be interested in using it to develop a full drama. Or your view may lie somewhere between these two points.

You will be assessed on the three Workshop Presentations you make, one for each item, and your Working Record. Your Workshop Presentations and your Working Record need to demonstrate your ability to trial and assess the potential of the stimulus material to make an engaging drama.

Remember: In this unit none of the presentations will be fully realised or rehearsed outcomes. The key factor is the potential you can identify and communicate during your Workshop Presentations.

Your Working Record for this unit will be mainly from the viewpoint of the Deviser. But considering the Contexts of Director, Performer and Designer may be important too, as their skills can add something extra to any performance based on the stimulus material.

In *Unit 2* you will need to demonstrate your ability to:

- use improvisation skills to explore and generate drama stimulus material
- select, synthesise and use ideas and skills to create drama
- reflect on and evaluate the potential of the stimulus material being trialled
- apply performance and production skills
- work as a team collaboratively to create and evaluate the stimulus material.

Before you start work on preparing your three items for presentation, you will take part in a series of lessons and workshops with your teacher. This will help you to consider:

- how a drama can be structured and plotted

- how genre and performance style impact on devising
- how improvisation can be central to devising character, context and plot
- the target audience, the staging and how that may impact on the devising of the drama.

The lessons/workshops will follow a format similar to the one below. But you and your teacher can vary this to suit the way your particular group works when creating drama.

Preparation

During your preparation sessions:

1 Look for the dramatic possibilities within the material. Make a 1–2 page collection of notes, pictures, cuttings and extracts that could complement or support the stimulus and help you create a drama. Remember to be selective, and include only the material you really would like to use. Refer to this later when you come to plan your group improvisation and complete the first section of your Working Record.

2 Suggest two possible scenarios that could be acted out.

3 Identify what genre and performance style might suit the material best.

4 Consider how design might support the drama and any eventual performance.

Exploration

1 Test out ideas for the rehearsed improvised scene (Item 1 of your three assessed items for this unit). Check out how the ideas work in practice. This means you will have to decide on a structure, plot, genre and performance style, as well as creating some characters. All these elements will help establish a well-defined context.

2 Test or consider ideas for your other two assessed items, e.g. design ideas, songs, additional script work.

3 Consider an appropriate audience and performance space.

4 Towards the end of the exploration, identify the first item, the group improvisation, you are going to work on for your presentation and who you will be working with.

Working Record stage 1: During your final exploration lesson, complete the first section of your Working Record, *Potential for Drama*. Refer to the material you collected in the preparation work. This section should identify the possibilities you think the stimulus has for creating a good drama. Don't list every idea you have had – include only those you would select if you were writing or directing a play on this material. You can work with other students collectively to complete this section of your Working Record, but all other sections must be entirely your own work without any collaboration with other candidates or your teacher.

Rehearsal

This is the 10 hour Rehearsal Period of the Controlled Assessment. Note: the time for your Workshop Presentations is not included in this period. This time might work best if broken into three chunks, one per item, to give you time between each to organise what you are going to do for the next item.

This is the process of creating your three items for presentation to your teacher.

Working Record stage 2: As you develop each item, complete the second section of your Working Record, *The Application* (one entry for each the three items). Identify the key decisions, good drama ideas and ongoing evaluation.

Working Record hints

This section needs to be a selective and concise record. Include only those decisions or insights which are relevant to devising a good drama. Think about what is going to help or hinder the creation of a good script/design for performance. Remember: good scripts often include notes on direction and staging. As well as your own work, you may include key elements introduced by other students. You will need to reflect on and analyse your own work and that of others.

Preparation

Follow this format for your Workshop Presentations:

- You will make three mini presentations.
- The first item you present will be the rehearsed improvisation.
- Once Item 1 has been presented you will prepare Item 2, then present it.
- Once Item 2 has been presented you will prepare Item 3, then present it.

Working Record stage 3: Now that you have presented your items to an audience, you can complete the third and last section of your Working Record, *Evaluation – Is this the right material for an engaging drama?* You will have a maximum of 1 hour to do this.

You will have had feedback from your audience, so take their views into consideration. You may like to give your audience a feedback questionnaire to help you analyse their views.

The big question you need to answer in your evaluation is: 'Is this a drama you would like to develop fully and perform to an audience?' Record your decision, giving your reasons.

How the marking works: Your teacher will mark your Controlled Assessment. Your presentations will be filmed on DVD and sent together with your Working Record and your teacher's marks to the OCR moderator. This will be the evidence of the standard of work you have achieved.

3.3 Unit 3 From Concept to Creation – Examined Unit

> **Suggested structure for Unit 3 Working Record**
> 1 Inspiration and Intention
> 2 Creating My/Our Response
> 3 Final Evaluation.

Unit 3 gives you an opportunity to play to your strengths and concentrate on a Context you enjoy working in. There are options to work from text, or stimulus or both in the Pre-Released Exam Material. You can work in a group or individually, choosing to be assessed either as Performer, or Deviser or Designer. It is a chance to demonstrate your enthusiasm and skill in your chosen Context to the examiner.

Elements of the Pre-Released Exam Material
Your starting point will be the Pre-Released Exam Material set by OCR. This will contain:

- a text extract and stimulus item(s)
- the Performer (devised) Brief – this requires you to devise and perform your own drama using the text extract and/or stimulus as your initial inspiration
- the Performer (text extract) Brief – this requires you to perform a section of the text extract
- the Deviser Brief – this requires you to write either an additional scene for the text extract or a script that uses the stimulus item(s) for inspiration
- the Designer Brief – this requires you to prepare designs for the text extract covering any **three** from set, costume, lighting, stage and personal properties, make-up or sound
- administrative instructions, marks available and time limits.

Special features of the Examined Unit
You will get to see the Exam Paper, which contains the Pre-Released Exam Material (the text extract, stimulus item and the

You can view a Specimen Paper on the OCR website (www.ocr.org.uk) or your teacher will show you an example. This will enable you to see exactly what is on the paper and how it is laid out and worded.

Performer, Deviser and Designer Briefs), **10 weeks** before you start the Examined Unit, so there will be no surprises.

During the 10 weeks your teacher will work with you in a series of lessons and workshops. These will involve preparation and exploration exercises – the same process as you followed for *Unit 1* and *Unit 2* for Controlled Assessment.

By the end of the 10 weeks you will have chosen the brief you are going to tackle, and who you will be working with, if working in a group. Select the brief which will allow you to demonstrate your drama knowledge, understanding and skills to best effect.

Working Record stage 1: You will have 1 hour to prepare the first section of your Working Record, *Inspiration and Intention,* during the last lesson before you start your work on the brief. This first section needs to outline what you are intending to do and any ideas or sources of inspiration you intend to draw on. Your ideas and intention will come from the preparation and exploration work you have already done. If you are working in a group you can complete this section of your Working Record collectively. All other sections must be entirely your own work without any collaboration with other candidates or your teacher.

Tackling your brief: You will have 10 hours to create and rehearse your piece and complete the second section of your Working Record. These 10 hours can be organised in normal lesson time or your teacher may choose to block some or all of the time together. This could mean having a whole day to work on the brief.

Time management hints

Before you start this unit, discuss the lesson planning possibilities with your teacher so that together you select the best option for the whole group. The option chosen will have to be practical in terms of the school's overall examination timetable. There will obviously have to be some compromises as you won't all get exactly what you want.

Working Record stage 2: In the second section of your Working Record, *Creating My/Our Response,* you need to cover any relevant planning, any specific applications from the Areas of Study, your

individual responses to the brief and any ongoing evaluation.

Dress rehearsal: Once the 10 hour rehearsal period has been completed, conduct a dress rehearsal in preparation for the examiner's visit. The dress rehearsal will allow you to get feedback from your audience – other candidates and your teacher.

Working Record stage 3: You will have a maximum of 1 hour to complete the last section of your Working Record, *Final Evaluation*. Here you need to take into account any relevant feedback you received after the dress rehearsal.

The examiner's visit

As soon as possible after you have held the dress rehearsal and completed your Working Record, the examiner will visit your school and you will perform/present your piece to them. They will award marks based on this performance/presentation and your Working Record, which they will take away with them to mark.

Working Record hints

When you complete your Working Record, make sure you cover all of the following:

1   *Inspiration and Intention*
    - The link to the starting point
    - Your intention for the drama/script/designs
    - The decisions you have made relating to audience, performance space, genre and performance style.

2   *Creating My/Our Response*
    - Your contribution to the Contexts of Deviser, Designer, Director and Performer
    - Significant contributions by other members of your group
    - Information from outside your group that had an impact, e.g. from teachers, other students, books, theatre performances, films.

3 *Final Evaluation*

- How well did the final drama or script or designs match your intention?
- How effective were the genre, performance style, structure and plot used?
- How successful was the final performance or script or designs in engaging the audience?

3.4 Focus on the Designer Brief

Choosing the Designer Brief

If you decide to tackle the Designer Brief in *Unit 3 From Concept to Creation* (the Examined Unit), you will be preparing designs for the text extract set for this unit. You will need to cover **three** aspects selected from this list:

- set
- costume
- lighting
- stage and personal properties
- make-up
- sound.

You are asked not to treat these as separate items but to design all within an overall design concept, so that they all work together to support a clear interpretation of the play.

So the first thing you need to consider before you start work on any actual designs is your overall design concept. For the course, the **design concept** is defined as:

- period the play is set in
- performance style
- colour scheme
- any social, cultural and historical connections.

These factors should influence your thinking and focus your research. When working on set and costume designs, it's a good idea to start collecting images, ideas from books, magazines and newspapers, etc. Images will provide you with visual stimuli, while articles and stories that connect with the play may provide social, cultural and historical connections.

Look at the illustration below. This student has made a collection of images and thoughts for the play they are working on – it could be called a 'mood board'. This has started the creative process, helping the student to create the designs for the production. A mood board can also be useful for the actors – for instance, to help them visualise the historical context the play is set in.

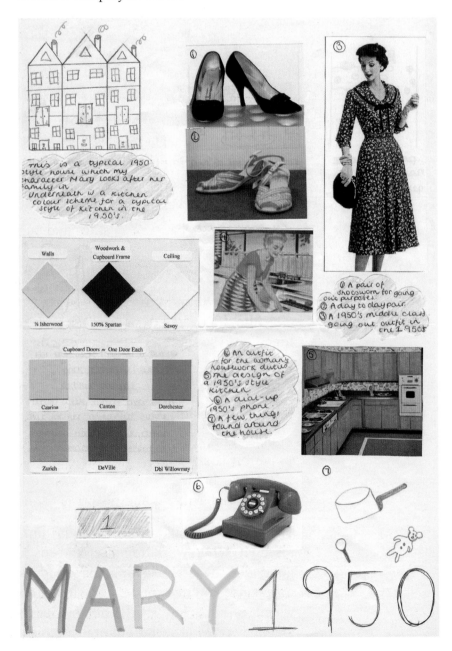

▶ A student's mood board showing initial research for their design concept

▲ An African setting for *Macbeth* by the Highfield Action Theatre

This process will also apply if you are working on the technical areas of lighting and sound. Both lighting and sound designers need to work within an overall design concept. They might have specific technical cues within the text, but their designs will be influenced by the director's approach to that text. For example, a production of *Macbeth* set in medieval times in Scotland will have very different light and sound design to one where the director transposes the action to Africa and tribal conflicts. If you choose the Designer Brief for **Unit 3**, you will not be working with a director, so will have to decide these issues and create the design concept.

Lighting and sound can be used as an alternative to creating a set, either for the whole play or for specific scenes. At a simple level, a sound cue of traffic noise can immediately establish a street location. Lighting focused on a defined area with **straw-coloured filters** can establish a candlelit interior or a window **gobo** can be used to create the effect of daylight streaming into a room. Full stage coverage with no colour filters or **steel-blue filters** creates a wide-open exterior location.

A design-concept case study

Let's look at an example that illustrates practical and artistic points to consider when working to an overall design concept.

Context for the design concept

Charles Dickens' story *A Christmas Carol* is set in Victorian times. It tells how Scrooge, a mean-spirited miser obsessed with money, is shown the error of his ways by four ghosts who visit him on Christmas Eve. He comes to realise that true happiness is found in fellowship and humanity.

The following notes appear at the start of Neil Duffield's adaptation of *A Christmas Carol* and relate to a professional performance of the play at the Octagon Theatre, Bolton:

> **SET:** The set has two levels, upper and lower, linked by a huge chaotic heap of various items – safes, strong boxes, chains, locks, bolts, hinges, ledgers, files, cash-boxes, bundles of keys, furniture, plates, cutlery, bells, etc. And a piano. It's as if the whole story and everything belonging to it has been tipped in a random pile.
>
> It should be possible to use the pile as a staircase from the lower level to the upper. On the upper level stands Scrooge's bed – a four poster with curtains. The lower level is used for all other locations. Somewhere there is a fireplace which provides the focus for various rooms.

A youth theatre chose to perform the play, so what did their director and designer do with these set ideas? They were going to perform the play in a theatre space very similar to a school hall and there would be a cast of fifty. This created these problems for the designer:

- Backstage space was limited with very restricted space stage left.
- They needed to create a backstage space that allowed the large cast to exit and enter efficiently. (The acting area was not large enough for the whole cast to stay on stage throughout the performance.)
- If two levels had been created, as suggested in the script, this would have reduced the options for creating wide enough exits and entrances.

The practical considerations about exits and entrances were crucial with such a big cast. The efficient flow of groups entering and leaving the acting area was vital to give the production the appropriate pace.

The designer's sketches

The director of the play liked the original set outlined in the
script, as it illustrated where Scrooge's life had taken him at
the start of the story. But it couldn't be directly recreated for
their performance. So the designer, in consultation with the
director, took some practical and artistic decisions and created
the designer's sketches and ground plan shown below and on
the next two pages.

▶ Designer's sketch
for the backdrop

▶ Designer's sketch
for the Cratchitt
family's hearth

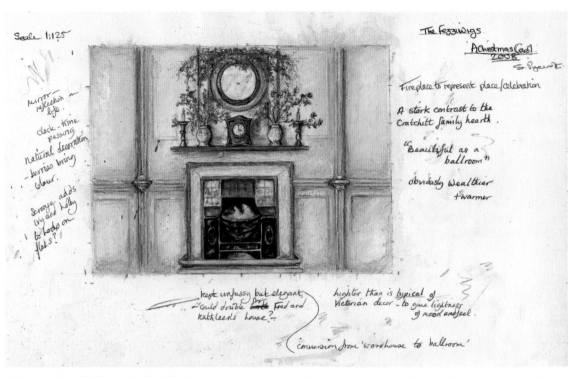

Scale 1:125

The Fezziwigs.
A Christmas Carol
2008
S. Pycroft

mirror reflection on
life.

clock - time
passing

natural decoration
- berries bring
colour.

Scrooge adds
ivy and holly
to looks on
flats?

kept unfussy but elegant
"could double as Fred and
kathleen's house?

lighter than is typical of
Victorian decor - to give lightness
of mood and feel.

(conversion from 'warehouse' to 'ballroom')

Fireplace to represent place/celebration

A stark contrast to the
Cratchitt family hearth.

"Beautiful as a
ballroom"

obviously wealthier
+ warmer

▲ Designer's sketch for the Fezziwigs' hearth

Scale 1:125

inside/outside

paving stones
becoming less
distinct -
cold colours
to work with
back cloth.

Practical decisions

■ To use flats (screens) centre stage left
and centre stage right to create a
backstage and provide entrances
upstage left and upstage right.

■ To pull back and tie up of the curtain-
track drapes behind the flats so that
they did not restrict entry into the
backstage area created behind the
flats.

■ To put the bed on castors so that it
could be wheeled forward when
needed, and back when not.

■ To put Cratchitt's desk on castors so
that it could be wheeled into place.

◀ Section from designer's sketch for
the floor cloth

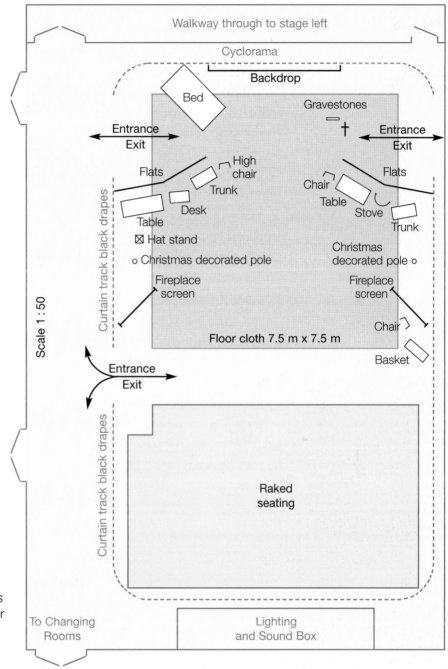

Walkway through to stage left

Cyclorama

Backdrop

Bed

Gravestones

Entrance Exit

Entrance Exit

Flats

High chair

Chair

Flats

Trunk

Table

Desk

Stove

Table

Trunk

⊠ Hat stand

o Christmas decorated pole

Christmas decorated pole o

Fireplace screen

Fireplace screen

Chair

Floor cloth 7.5 m x 7.5 m

Basket

Entrance Exit

Scale 1 : 50

Curtain track black drapes

Curtain track black drapes

Raked seating

To Changing Rooms

Lighting and Sound Box

▸ Designer's ground plan. The scale marked on the plan is the scale the designer used on their (larger) original drawing.

■ To create two screens on castors with the poor Cratchitt family's fireplace painted on one side and the wealthier families' fireplace on the reverse side. These two screens were pushed together to create the hearth images.

■ To have a floor cloth to define the acting area.

Artistic decisions

- To create a composite set (as suggested in the script) – that is, one set useable for all the various locations without having to be changed.
- To create a medium-sized backdrop to hang upstage. This backdrop was not to be a realistic scene, but a collage of themes from the play.
- To decorate the flats with drapes of material and chains. (Chains are a key motif in the story – Marley's ghost drags chains with money boxes attached.)
- To arrange all the **stage properties** and most of the **personal properties** in front of the screens, so that the actors could collect them as needed.
- To have the two painted fireplace screens as part of the general jumble, downstage left and downstage right.
- To try and find suitably old and period-looking stage properties that matched the overall colour scheme.
- To create a paving-stone effect for the floor cloth, not totally realistic as it would be used for outdoor and indoor scenes.
- Not to use bright primary colours for the overall colour scheme, but rather create a dark, morose atmosphere. Colours selected to do this were purples through to dark blue, cream to vanilla, edged with black to add definition. The floor cloth was painted in cold colours to complement the backcloth.

Exploration

Discuss how far you think this set design captures what was suggested in the set notes (on page 230) provided at the start of the script. Look at the backdrop (on page 231 and opposite). What does it suggest about the themes of the play?

Design hints

If you choose the Designer Brief for *Unit 3*, design for a specific space, one that you know well. For most students it will be most practical to design for a space at your school. Whatever space you design for and even if it is for a touring performance, having a specific theatre space to work to will fix actual practical parameters – shapes and sizes – giving a framework for your design.

These photographs show the realisation of the set design as it looked on stage: the backdrop and properties, the flats wheeled into position to signal the hearth of the poor Cratchitt family.

▲ Scrooge's wheel-on bed to signal his room, and portable graveyard properties

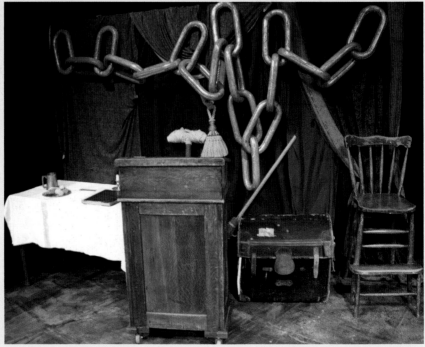

The costumes

Look at the initial costume sheets below and on the next page. The designer has gone to an edition of *A Christmas Carol* first published in 1911 that is famous for its illustrations by Arthur Rackham. His images were in colour but the designer has coloured over black-and-white copies to get an idea of what the colours they have chosen might look like. The pictures also helped the designer to identify the shape and cut of clothes in this Victorian historical period.

The photographs below and on the next page show some of the costumes created for the production.

▾ Scrooge's costume and (below right) the designer's notes around the Rackham sketch

top hats made from card/ buckrum + covered in gnee felt with contrasting band of ribbon for the period

dressing gown patterns still available. green pattern with purple fabric contrast round neck.

◄ Mr and Mrs Fezziwig's costumes and (below) the designer's notes around the Rackham sketch

Pale lilac bonnet with possible darker purple ribbon + trim

white ruff (any collar, tied white fabric + bow)

dress in purple silk /satin with darker purple bows.

Basic Victorian shape — skirt, blouse with long frill sleeves and leg of mutton shoulders.

Design hints

Don't think that you always have to draw your own original sketches. Like the designer above, you can use illustrations by artists who have worked from the text/script before to support your work and speed up the design process.

Exploration

See if you can create your own design concept for *A Christmas Carol* without having read the play or seen it performed, but just using the designs and notes on pages 230–238. Make sure you cover each of the four bullet points on page 227 that define the design concept. You can draw intelligent conclusions about the performance style from the evidence on pages 230–238.

A stage-properties case study

Stage properties feature as one of the aspects of design you can cover in the Designer Brief. Here is another example to help you think about this aspect of the design. It is based on a youth-theatre production of *Beowulf*, the Anglo-Saxon epic poem.

The monster Grendel is terrorising Hrothgar and his thanes. They have built a feasting hall named Heorot after the hart (a deer). Grendel hears the songs and senses the good fellowship that fills Heorot each night. Grendel breaks this contentment, bringing death and slaughter night after night until no one dares to stay in Heorot.

Beowulf, the hero of the Geats, hears of this and journeys with his followers to assist Hrothgar. Beowulf battles with and kills Grendel, but Grendel's ferocious mother comes to Heorot to wreak bloody revenge. Beowulf now has to slay the mother too, first hunting her down in her underwater lair. Beowulf, of course, eventually triumphs and returns home to Geatland a hero. He is made king. Later he fights an unnamed dragon and is fatally wounded in the final battle. He is buried with all honour.

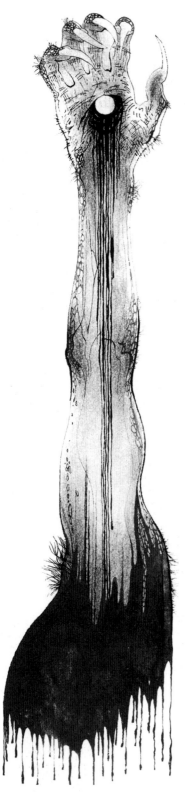

▲ The severed arm of Grendel
as visualised by Charles Keeping

The youth-theatre production was devised from a children's version of *Beowulf* by Kevin Crossley-Holland with illustrations by Charles Keeping (see **Resources** list, page 258). The production took the story as far as the triumph of slaying Grendel's mother.

There were to be eight episodes matching sections of the story (these are listed on page 244). It would be an ensemble production with none of the cast leaving the stage. There would be no set and costumes would be simple basic tunics and trousers, russet coloured. The performance would rely on simple storytelling techniques with much of the action described rather than attempting to enact every element of this all-action story.

So it was decided to have three key props placed downstage on a wooden stand:

- An elaborate drinking horn – there is much feasting and celebrating in the story, so this communal horn could be passed around to symbolise the feast rather than having lots of plates, food, drinking vessels.
- Deer's horns – in the story, the thanes place deer's horns above Heorot after they have built their great feasting hall. The horns would be positioned on the stand at the appropriate point in the story.
- The severed arm of the monster Grendel – in the story, Beowulf rips off the arm and it is nailed to a tree. Grendel's mother is enraged and pulls it down.

These three key stage properties, plus the basic costumes and a lighting plot, made up the complete design for the play. Sound effects were created vocally by the cast, in keeping with the storytelling performance style. The three properties helped to signal a historical context and provided a visual stimulus (like pictures in a storybook). They also helped the actors and audience focus on three key elements in the story: the naming of Heorot, the feasting scenes and the death of Grendel.

Like much property making, creating these props involved experimenting with all sorts of odds and ends of materials. Property making gives you a chance to demonstrate your artistic creativity.

▶ This elaborate drinking horn was made with withies (long bendy sticks very good for sculpting with and used a lot for making giant carnival puppets), silver paper, gaffer tape and black paint for shading.

▶ These deer antlers were foam piping with mod-roc layers built up around them.

▶ This severed arm of Grendel was sculpted around a wooden base using plaster of Paris, then painted. Plaster of Paris did not turn out to be the best choice as it was easily damaged.

Review

This unit was designed to:

- develop your knowledge and confidence in designing for the stage
- help you work to an overall design concept when creating your designs
- look for visual stimuli and cultural and historical background material to inform your designs
- explore your potential as a designer.

Discuss with your teacher:

- the key pointers you have taken from the unit regarding design
- what you might use in any future drama work
- your potential as a designer.

3.5 Focus on the Deviser Brief

Choosing the Deviser Brief

If you decide to tackle the Deviser Brief in *Unit 3 From Concept to Creation* (the Examined Unit), you can choose **one** of two options:

- write an additional scene for the text extract set for this unit
- write a script that uses the stimulus item set for this unit as your inspiration.

Whichever option you choose, you must follow the conventions of scriptwriting, using **stage directions** and any relevant **staging** or **set notes**. Plays are written using many different approaches, at one pole realistic and true to life, at the other as a jumble of ideas almost like a stream of consciousness. So using the conventions of scriptwriting gives you lots of options. But your scene must have some form of closure or appropriate ending.

Additional scene for the text extract

If you are using the set text extract, the genre and overall context you work with will have already been established by its author. You will either be set a context for a new scene to write or be asked to think of a new context for a scene yourself. In either case, you will be operating as many professional scriptwriters do – for example, a writer joining the script team for an established drama such as *EastEnders* or *Coronation Street*. In these dramas the characters and plot lines already exist. A new writer might introduce fresh characters, but they will work with what is already there and add to it. Alternatively, they may be commissioned to create a storyline on a given issue.

Script inspired by the stimulus

If you choose to devise a scene from the set stimulus item, then you are free to create whatever takes your interest or inspires you. You do not have to devise a complete play, but you must devise a fully developed scene. It could be the opening; it might be the ending along with a brief outline of what has happened in the rest of the play. The dead-warrior structure in **Unit 2.5**, pages 157–163, starts with the end of the story and then works backwards. If you get your ending sorted out, it can be easier to work out what happened previously.

If you choose to write a short sketch, then you can create a drama that is complete in itself. Try looking at some of the short sketches that acclaimed playwright Harold Pinter wrote in his early career: *Trouble in the Works*, *The Black and White*, *Request Stop*, *Last to Go*, *Applicant* or the short plays in *A Slight Ache and Other Plays*.

Context

Whichever of the two options you decide on, you must produce a page that explains the context you have chosen. This needs to cover:

- period it is set in
- genre
- suggested performance style
- any social, cultural or historical connections.

If you are working with the text extract, the context will already be set, but you will need to note any deviations or additions you have chosen to include and why.

Your script should draw on the practical work, knowledge and understanding you have been developing throughout the course. You will find the different structures in **Unit 2.5** on pages 157–191 particularly useful when devising your drama.

Devising hints

Remember the importance of the magic 'T' – tension – in any script (see page 119). Make sure your stage directions and set notes will help the director and performers visualise how your drama is going to work on stage.

Preparation

Practise your scriptwriting during the course.

- In the youth-theatre production based on the story of *Beowulf* outlined on pages 239–241, there were eight episodes:

  1 The building of Heorot
  2 The coming of Grendel
  3 Beowulf comes to Heorot
  4 Grendel is slain
  5 Into the deep
  6 Grendel's mother
  7 Fight to the death
  8 Beowulf returns.

  Using the children's version of *Beowulf* by Kevin Crossley-Holland with illustrations by Charles Keeping (see page 258), or another version, take one of these episodes and write a script for it.

- For a longer project, you could split the eight episodes between your Drama group and create a whole play. You could then rehearse it and perform it to Year 7s or a local primary school.

Review

This unit was designed to:
- consider the requirements for writing your own script
- practise your scriptwriting.

Discuss with your teacher:
- the key pointers you have taken from the unit regarding scriptwriting
- what you might use in any future drama work
- your potential as a scriptwriter.

3.6 Tips on Material for Your Working Record

Working on a mood board

The outlines for the three assessed units on pages 214–227 offer advice to help you prepare for creating your Working Record. This advice suggests that early on in the exploration stage in each unit you spend some time creating sketches, notes, a mood board or ideas on your intended focus for the rehearsal phase.

Below is an example of a mood board created by a student for *Unit 2 Drama in the Making*. The stimulus was a photograph titled 'Gorbal Boys' taken by Bert Hardy in 1948, which you can see on page 170 in **Unit 2.5**. The student was asked to research Bert Hardy, the Gorbals and Britain in 1948. She responded by presenting a selection of Bert Hardy's photographs taken in the Gorbals around 1948.

Alicia Martino 11P
GCSE Drama

Gorbals, Glasgow
The Gorbals was originally a single-street village, it began around the river Clyde's most westerly crossing point-a bridge completed in 1935 by Bishop Rae of Glasgow.

Bert Hardy
Hardy was born in London, in 1913. He started his own agency, shortly after, he brought a cheap small plate camera and started getting his photographs published. When he was twenty five he became one of the first photographers to use a Leica 35mm camera. Hardy started to become famous for his photographs in 1948 when he worked on 'Blitz' which was drafted into an army photographic unit. He worked on this alongside Tom Hopkinson (editor of 'Picture Post') who recruited him not long after he started working as a freelance. After working on projects such as photographs of concentration camp victims, he then went back to 'Picture Post' with Tom Hopkinson where he covered the Korean War and Vietnam War for the magazine. After the magazine closed in 1957 Hardy worked in advertising until he retired in 1995. At the age of 52 Bert Hardy Died.

(Above Shows some images of Hardy's Work)

▶ A student's 'Gorbal Boys' mood board

Let's consider how this student might have made her mood board more explicit and so a more useful aid for developing her drama. She could have considered these points:

- *Why did Bert Hardy choose to take pictures in the Gorbals?* If you can find this out, it will give you clues as to the viewpoint of the artist who created the photo (if you can't, deduce what you can from the photo itself). Remember: all artists work from a viewpoint or an ideology (a set of beliefs that shape how they see the world, especially their political stance). You become the artist when you create drama.

- *What was the Gorbals?* It was a working-class area of Glasgow, the very name at one time being a byword for tough, poor, uncompromising urban environments – perhaps the equivalent of the Bronx in New York.

- *What was Britain like in 1948?* It was only three years after the end of the Second World War. The country was still recovering from the devastating economic and social consequences of that massive conflict. There were great social changes being made by the government, the start of the National Health Service, nationalisation of the railways and coal mines. Independence for India and Pakistan was starting the process of dismantling the British Empire. The ship *Windrush* had brought West Indian immigrants to help fill the labour shortage. Britain had started to become a very different nation from that which existed before the war.

Theatre of the time featured the gentle escapism of Noel Coward and Ivor Novello; the giant theatrical presences of Laurence Olivier, John Gielgud, Donald Wolfitt, Peggy Ashcroft and Ralph Richardson; and music hall, which was entering its death throes. John Osborne's *Look Back in Anger* (1956), the visit to England of Brecht's Berliner Ensemble (also 1956), and the Edinburgh Fringe Festival review *Beyond the Fringe* (1960) had yet to change the whole theatrical landscape.

Questions like these should lead you to consider the social, cultural and historical context, which is so important to the process of creating strong dramas. Of course, you will be selecting information for your mood board which resonates with you and which could influence or inspire you to create an engaging piece of drama.

Preparation

By considering the three questions posed opposite and any others you think relevant, expand the student's 'Gorbal Boys' mood board. You might add to your version an additional sheet noting potential scenarios that come to mind from your research. Make it a springboard for dramatic action.

Remember: A question is as useful as an answer at this stage in your work. Some of the best dramas derive from the posing of a question. For example, enacting a murder scene is not as engaging as a drama that answers or explores a question such as why a particular person might be driven to commit a murder.

Producing original designs

The design-concept work on *A Christmas Carol* on pages 237–239 shows how you can use illustrations from books as a basis for costume design. However, you may wish to create your own original designs, especially if you have a flair for this type of work. Pages 248–249 show some designs by one GCSE student.

Below and continued on page 250 is an excerpt from her group's planning notes. The names are all of characters in *Blood Brothers*.

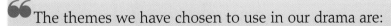

"The themes we have chosen to use in our drama are:

- **Love** – this is taken from when Mickey is in love with Linda.
- **Deceit** – when Eddie and Linda have a romantic fling and Mickey finds out.
- **Revenge** – death, when Mickey shoots Edward in revenge for being with Linda. This theme is also taken from *Macbeth*, when Macduff kills Macbeth in revenge for him killing his wife and son.
- **Guilt** – this is when Mrs Johnston feels guilty for giving away one of the twins she had given birth to.

Costume Design Scene 1 "LOVE"
This scene is when Rose falls in love with Danny.

Her hair is tied back because she is nervous and isn't confident enough to let her hair out

It is quite tight, complementing her figure, this is so the dress makes her look sexy resulting in her seducing Danny.

There are also Hints of grey in this dress representing her nervousness

It is a long dress; this shows her nervousness as she is trying to cover herself up. This also shows how she is trying to cover the truth.

This dress is black to show how she is masking her true feelings as she doesn't want to admit that she has fallen in love with Danny

Roshny presented these sketches as part of her Working Record. They were for a devised drama that drew on texts she had studied during her course: *Blood Brothers* and *Macbeth*.

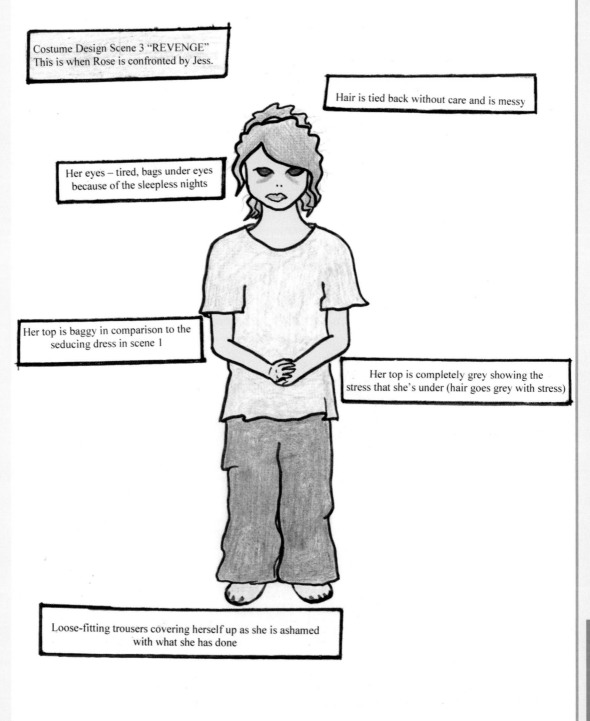

Costume Design Scene 3 "REVENGE"
This is when Rose is confronted by Jess.

Hair is tied back without care and is messy

Her eyes – tired, bags under eyes because of the sleepless nights

Her top is baggy in comparison to the seducing dress in scene 1

Her top is completely grey showing the stress that she's under (hair goes grey with stress)

Loose-fitting trousers covering herself up as she is ashamed with what she has done

We have greed in our drama. This is from *Macbeth* as he becomes greedy for power and also when Lady Macbeth is greedy for wealth and convinces Macbeth to kill Duncan. We also have the idea of 'fate' in our concept. This is taken from Macbeth because the witches were almost like fate. This is shown by the way they told Macbeth what was going to happen in the future, then it occurs (they played the catalyst by speeding the story along). This idea of fate also comes from *Blood Brothers* as there is a certain character playing Fate and showing the consequences of superstition and destiny.

Our overall intention was to show that fate has a part in all of our lives. We show this by having a Fate character intervene in all the scenes, almost forcing the characters to do what he wants them to do …

"

Roshny and her group also planned a drama starting with the stimulus 'The people who walked in darkness have seen a great light'. They decided to create a drama based on death row. Roshny produced a character study and acting notes (shown opposite), and a costume design (below).

MESSY HAIR COVERING FACE
This is to cover her feelings (this is because people think she is over her baby). It is also to cover her eyes to avoid eye contact with Tony.

DULL COLOURED CLOTHES
It reflects her mood and emotions

BAGGY DULL TROUSERS

PALE SKIN
She has lost her healthy glow with her depression.

BLACK JUMPER
The colour black represents how she has detached herself from Tony.

CLUTCHING TEDDY TIGHTLY
To show she is in fear of letting go of her family and also it symbolises her baby.

My Character:

The main character I play is Gina; she is the wife of Tony and is in her late 20's. She is sensitive and loves her family no matter what. She is very optimistic and tries to put the fun into everything as we see this when we first encounter her at the beginning of the play.

We can see that she is sensitive by the way she reacts to the social services when they try to take her baby away. Also, by the way she can't let go of the thoughts of her child though out the years gone by.

She can also be tempered quite easily when something is harming her family, for instance when Tony tells her about The Don, that he is released and after him, she is angry and frustrated that he still gets into trouble. She forced Tony to drop the drug business to protect the family but it didn't help as her son was still taken away.

Tony is the reason for her son being taken away by social services, and even though he is her husband, inside she has never forgiven him about it. We can see this by her attitude towards Tony in the two scenes. Firstly she is in high spirits; nevertheless, over the years she has detached herself from Tony, keeping her feelings inward.

The first scene I'm in as Gina is when I am seen with Sammy and look lively and happy and my body language is bouncy and enthusiastic. On the other hand, when the social services come and try to take Sammy I become very defensive and back away as much as I can. My body is wrapped around the baby like a shield in which I'm trying to protect him. When the social services take the baby out of my arms I turn to Tony for some comfort but as he does nothing I gaze at him helplessly and run off.

In my scene transition I'm pacing up and down. My body language and tone of voice is quite panicky and edgy. I fidget with the teddy in my hand and I try not to take my eyes off it as if I think will disappear just as the baby did if I were to take my eyes off it. I slow my pace down when I turn a corner to show how I have calmed down over the years. I still clutch on to the teddy and talk dreamily about Sammy and wonder. After a few turns I stop and repeat the line "13 years" I look regretful, then turn away to change role into a gangster.

My body language as a gangster is quite relaxed. I wipe my nose roughly and push the other guys (as a joke). When I am talking I keep my chin up as if to look down on the other people around (as we feel that our gang is superior), we think we are better than the rest and we show it.

When I meet Sammy after 13 years I feel overjoyed yet I feel overcome by many emotions as I'm still worried about The Don and what he might do. I'm also scared if someone might try and take Sammy away from me again. So in this scene I am emotionally confused. As I try to comfort Sammy's he is crying a lot I talk about Tony and how where going to get away from that place. When Sammy tells me something's burning I suddenly loose all the emotions I was feeling before and become very curious. My body language then changes as I walk slowly towards the kitchen (like I'm afraid of what I'm going to see). After I see the fire I become panicky and do everything I can to get Sammy out safely. At the same time I feel helpless and quite fragile as I'm not in a position I have been in before and that I know what I'm doing.

Showing the structure

It is vital that you explain in your Working Record how your drama will work or be structured. The examples here show how one student, Krupa Thakrar, based her devised drama around the themes of *Blood Brothers*.

The chart excerpt below records her plan for the structuring and devising of the drama. It might be a way of working that suits you.

The chart opposite is used to review and evaluate the drama. You might use a similar format in the evaluation sections (stage 3) of your Working Record.

Devising

We now were able to gather a deeper understanding of the play and thus we began to consider conventions and the semiotics of drama.

Structure	Brief note of content	Any conventions used? Explanation	Any use of semiotics?
Scene 1	Mrs Johnston takes Dina and David to unfold their prophecy at the church.	We decided for the monks to perform a ritual ceremony to present the sin. We thought that if performed successfully the audience would be put in a position of unease as they may be alarmed by the misfortune.	During the ritual ceremony the monks attempt to join two sticks together to form a cross yet they fail, highlighting the fact that the twins' destiny is beyond natural and certainly is contradicting religious beliefs.
Scene 2	A gang beat up Dina harshly. David as a passer by calls for help and supports her.	We choreographed a dance to display the gang beating up Dina. We felt that this would be more engaging rather than acting it out. We also presented a soundscape of a market scene so that the background action was appealing (we decided to perform as an ensemble so we thought that this would be effective).	This of course is a sign of destiny unfolding right before the audience's sight and so this scene must be strong.

Review and Evaluation

Structure	Use of conventions	Effect	Use of semiotics	Effect
Scene 1	Ritual ceremony	We felt that the actions were effective yet the kind of humming supporting the action weakened the arousing tension. This simply needed polishing through a few more rehearsals.	Attempting to join the sticks in the ceremony	Although the overall effect of the ritual ceremony was not as strong as we had anticipated, the actions were effective as they clearly symbolised the contradiction between evil sin and religious beliefs.
Scene 2	Choreographed fight	The beginning of this scene was especially effective as we feel as though we had set the scene well (see proxemics of drama). The choreographed fight looked much more appealing than an ordinary acted out fight scene.	Sign of destiny unfolding right before the audience's sight	I do not feel that we focused on this enough as we assumed it to be stronger, allowing the audience to see this for themselves, but after performing we realised that we should have made this more apparent.

Review

The purpose of the Working Record is to help you create strong practical drama/theatre. This unit has encouraged you to use the Working Record as part of your practical working process. It was designed to encourage you to:

- be selective
- be analytical
- have a clear intention in all your work
- make your drama/designs support your intention.

Useful working processes were outlined and examples given of how professional artists work on creating theatre.

Resources

■ Possible Texts for *Unit 1 From Page to Stage*

Here are some texts you might consider using for **Unit 1 From Page to Stage**. These texts will also help you to develop knowledge and understanding in the six Areas of Study and when you are working in the four Contexts of Deviser, Director, Designer and Performer.

Texts containing short scenes/narratives

The short scenes/narratives within these texts will make them ideal for your Controlled Assessment.

A Christmas Carol adapted by Neil Duffield from the novel by Charles Dickens. Published by Aurora Metro Publications, ISBN 978-0-9551566-8-7
Excellent version of this classic story, suitable for performance as an ensemble or in a more traditional fashion.

Arabian Nights adapted by Dominic Cooke. Published by Nick Hern Books, ISBN 1-85659-432-X
Although quite wordy, the storytelling element is strong, with scope for imaginative staging. Each Arabian Nights story in this collection can stand on its own.

Coram Boy adapted by Helen Edmundsen from the novel by Jamila Gavin. Published by Heinemann, ISBN 978-0-435233-42-6
Set in eighteenth-century England, this play tells the story of two orphans, with villains, loyal friends, cruelty and hope. It is structured into lots of short scenes to cope with the great panorama of the story. It was produced at the National Theatre in 2006 to great acclaim. There are some good resources, including rehearsal and performance video clips, on their website: www.nationaltheatre.org.uk The National Theatre has also published a resource pack.

The script includes teaching resources, so you'll find useful ideas to try out, rather like the drama activities in Section 2 of this book.

If you would like to research the background to the play, try to persuade your teacher to organise a drama-group trip to The Foundling Museum at 40 Brunswick Square, London (entry free for schools). The museum tells the story of the Foundling Hospital, London's first home for abandoned children, and of three major figures in British history associated with it: its campaigning founder, the philanthropist Thomas Coram, the artist William Hogarth and the composer George Frederick Handel.

This text is a good example of how historical material can be developed into an imaginative play. It could be useful if you are interested in doing a documentary play or using historical material as a stimulus for **Unit 2 Drama in the Making**.

Trojans by Simon Adorian, with additional resource material by Sue Cottam. Published by Collins Educational, ISBN 0-00-330311-X
Modern adaptation of the classic Greek story of the Trojan War, specially written for use by schools. There are ten short scenes, staging notes and teaching materials. This is a good resource for all units of the course, with examples of ideas that will be useful if you decide to tackle the Designer Brief for **Unit 3 From Concept to Creation**.

The Seven Basic Plots – Why We Tell Stories by Christopher Booker. Published by Continuum, ISBN 0-8264-8037-3.

For more about the seven basic narrative plots listed on page 174.

Texts for exploring different genres

These texts will help you develop your knowledge and understanding of genre.

The Golden Masque of Agamemnon by John Wiles. Published by Samuel French, ISBN 0-573-1-5008-7

Commissioned by the Cockpit Theatre in 1977 as a youth-theatre production. As a play written for young actors, it is a good starting point for tackling Greek theatre and introduces one of the classic narratives of this genre.

The Greeks adapted by John Barton and Kenneth Cavander. Published by Heinemann, ISBN 0-435-23068-9

Cycle of ten short plays telling the full story of Agamemnon and Orestes, originally performed as a trilogy by the RSC (Royal Shakespeare Company). The ten sections each have terrific narrative power and can stand on their own. They can also be cut and adapted. Very suitable as the text for your Controlled Assessment.

The Mysteries by Tony Harrison. Published by Faber and Faber. ISBN 0-571-19707-8

This trilogy draws on the classic mystery cycles of York, Wakefield, Chester and Coventry, weaving them into three plays. Mystery plays were religious morality dramas with traditional set storylines performed by ordinary working people. These texts celebrate theatre as simple, direct storytelling very much as it would have been done by the original performers. The language is rich and these texts may be seen as challenging, but rather like Shakespeare, they reward those willing to work at them. The original National Theatre productions ran to great acclaim. The plays are episodic so you can select the bits you want to tackle. You could use one of them as the text for your Controlled Assessment or as a stimulus to create your own modern mystery play as part of your work for **Unit 2 Drama in the Making**.

Sweeney Todd – The Demon Barber of Fleet Street by C.G. Bond. Published by Samuel French, ISBN 0-573-01547-3

This is melodrama in its 'gritty' form, as opposed to the comic parody you may have worked on in **Unit 2.3**, pages 129–139. A production of this play inspired Stephen Sondheim to pen his classic musical *Sweeney Todd*. Although it has elements of parody, the script contains dark and sinister moments and shows how revenge ultimately destroys the perpetrator. Quite a demanding script so you may want to adapt it if you use it for your Controlled Assessment.

Living with Lady Macbeth by Rob John. Published by Cambridge University Press, ISBN 978-052145207-0

A contemporary play written for young people to perform to young people. Deals with a school performance of *Macbeth*, very accessible. An ideal play as the text for your Controlled Assessment.

Dracula adapted by Jan Needle from the novel by Bram Stoker. Published by Collins Educational, ISBN 0-00-330224-5

The classic horror story adapted as 12 short scenes for use by schools, with staging notes and teaching materials. A good resource for all units of the course, with examples of ideas that will be useful if you decide to tackle the Designer Brief for **Unit 3 From Concept to Creation**. (For another, fuller version of the story, see *Dracula* adapted by Jane Thornton and John Godber, published by Josef Weinberger, ISBN 0-85676-216-4.)

Four Plays for Coarse Actors/More Plays for Coarse Actors by Michael Green. Published by Samuel French, ISBN 978-0573-00008-9 and ISBN 978-0573-10005-5

Short scripts which send up genres and the theatre generally.

Happy End by Bertolt Brecht, Dorothy Lane and Kurt Weill. Published by Methuen, ISBN 0-413-51020-4

Brecht continued his successful collaboration with Kurt Weill with this musical play. The plot is strikingly like *Guys and Dolls* but, as you'd expect from Brecht, it has greater edge. The tongue-in-cheek gangster style makes this a fun play. The scenes are relatively short and snappy.

The Woman in Black – A Ghost Play, adapted by Stephen Mallatratt from the novel by Susan Hill. Published by Samuel French, ISBN 0-573-04019-2 Although written for only three actors, this play can be adapted for more performers and has lots of potential for creating atmosphere, creating technical effects and working with stage directions. A good play for helping you develop your technical theatre design skills, it will give you useful practice if you decide to tackle the Designer Brief for **Unit 3 From Concept to Creation**.

Texts based on other cultures
The Ramayana by Peter Oswald. Published by Oberon Books, ISBN 1-84002-201-9 Contains 24 short scenes based on the great Hindu epic poem. Great for developing storytelling techniques, working on physical theatre and using elements of the fantasy genre. This is a good resource for all units of the course and will pose some interesting design challenges.

The Mahabharata adapted by Jean-Claude Carrière and Peter Brook. Published by Harpercollins, ISBN 978-00-6039079-2 Divides the great Hindu epic into a series of shorter self-contained episodes. Like *The Ramayana*, it poses interesting design challenges. There is also a DVD available of Peter Brook's production.

Plays written for use by schools
These plays are based on documentary material and/or novels and come with drama activities like those in Section 2 of this book.

Carrie's War adapted by Robert Staunton from the novel by Nina Bawden. Published by Oxford University Press, ISBN 0-19-831295-4 Based on evacuees in the Second World War.

The Burston School Strike by Roy Nevitt. Published by Oxford University Press, ISBN 0-19-831274-1 Based on a famous school strike which became a cause célèbre for the Trade Union movement and was the longest strike in Britain's history. You can visit the museum in the old school room, in Burston, Suffolk. (There is another, musical play on this story: *The Burston Drum*, book by Ellen Dryden, lyrics by Don Taylor, published by Samuel French, ISBN 0-573-08082-8.)

The Rebels of Gas Street by Jan Needle, Vivien Gardner and Stephen Cockett. Published by Collins Educational, ISBN 0-00-330232-6 Fictional account based on spontaneous action taken against the oppressive school regime by many schoolchildren in different parts of Britain just before the First World War.

Anthologies
New Connections: New Plays for Young People. Published by Faber and Faber, ISBN 0-571-19148-7 Twelve short plays for young people commissioned by the National Theatre for the NT Connections project. NT Connections is an annual celebration of youth theatre which has been running for over a decade now. Each year's new plays are published in an anthology by Faber and Faber, so there are a number of volumes to choose from, some easier to track down than others, containing dozens of plays between them.

Beasts and Beauties: Eight Tales from Europe adapted by Carol Ann Duffy, dramatised by Melly Still and Tim Supple. Published by Faber and Faber, ISBN 0-571-22669-8 Eight short classic self-contained dramas based on such traditional classics as *Beauty and the Beast*, *The Emperor's New Clothes*. As you might expect from Carol Ann Duffy, these are not sugar-and-spice children's versions of these stories.

Stimulus Items for Use in *Unit 2 Drama in the Making*

> These resources will also help you to develop knowledge and understanding in the six Areas of Study and when you are working in the four Contexts of Deviser, Director, Designer and Performer.

Photographs

Photographs can be a good way to start off the devising process, e.g. the picture of the Gorbals Boys on page 170. As well as using photos in standard textbooks, you can seek out your own through Google Image. Here is a photo archive and some photographers you could research:

The Hulton Archive: A rich collection of material, regarded as the greatest archive of photojournalism.

Bert Hardy (1913–1995): Famous for his social realism and photographs of firefighters in the London Blitz.

Dorothea Lange (1895–1965): Documentary photographer particularly famous for her photographs of the Great Depression in the USA.

Don McCullin (born 1935): British photojournalist, especially noted for his war photography and pictures of urban strife. He specialised in examining the underside of society, the unemployed, downtrodden and impoverished.

Terry Fincher (1931–1978): British photojournalist, particularly noted for his war photography.

Robert Capa (1913–1954): Hungarian photojournalist, famous for his work on the Spanish Civil War, Second World War and 1948 Arab–Israeli War.

Gerda Taro: Jewish German war photographer, the companion and professional partner of Robert Capa. Taro is often regarded as the first female photojournalist to cover the front line in a war and to die while doing so.

Annie Leibowitz (born 1949): Portrait photographer.

Ray Lowry: Cartoonist and illustrator working on magazines from the 1960s. He accompanied the Clash on tour and created an illustrated record of the tour.

Paintings

Like photographs, paintings will provide you with good starting points. Here are some examples:

The Scream by Edvard Munch
Guernica by Pablo Picasso
Self-Portrait with Bandaged Ear by Vincent Van Gogh
The Death of Marat by Jacques-Louis David
The Raft of Medusa by Théodore Géricault
The Disasters of War by Francisco Goya
Intrigue by James Ensor

Pictures in books

The high-quality images in many modern books provide a rich source of material for devising. Here are some examples:

Rose Blanche text by Ian McEwan, illustrated by Roberto Innocenti. Published by Red Fox, ISBN 0-09-943950-6
Story of a young German girl in the Second World War who stumbles upon the death camps. The illustrations are full of dramatic resonance.

The Arrival by Shaun Tan. Published by Hodder, ISBN 978-0-340-96993-9
This mixture of realistic and fantastic illustrations explores the situation and experiences of people arriving in a new country.

Anne Frank text by Josephine Poole, illustrated by Angela Barrett. Published by Red Fox, ISBN 978-009-940976-2
The classic story succinctly told with the supporting images.

RESOURCES

These picture books have some good text that can be adapted for drama work:

Beowulf by Kevin Crossley-Holland, illustrated by Charles Keeping. Published by Oxford University Press, ISBN 0-19-272369-3
Adapts very well into episodes, using simple storytelling techniques. Its very rich use of language provides an alternative way of scripting. This will help you concentrate on crafting language for speaking on stage – very useful if you are considering tackling the Deviser Brief in **Unit 3 From Concept to Creation**.

There is also a more graphic-novel/superhero version: *Beowulf* by Gareth Hinds, published by Candlewick Press, ISBN 978-076363023-2. This could make for a very different approach using pastiche and mimicking Superman-type stories.

Pinocchio by Carlo Collodi, illustrated by Roberto Innocenti. Published by Jonathan Cape, ISBN 0-224-07056-8
This famous story lends itself to varied interpretations, some very dark. The illustrations in this book are very evocative and resonate with implied drama. It could be used alongside the play *Pinocchio* by Brian Way, now out of print but often available in libraries.

The Lion and the Unicorn by Shirley Hughes. Published by Red Fox, ISBN 0-09-925608-8
Story of evacuees which is rich material for devising. The book gives a narrative that can easily be adapted for drama work.

The Snow Queen by Hans Christian Andersen, illustrated by P.J. Lynch. Published by Andersen Press, ISBN 978-184270901-6
The evocative illustrations make this a good starting point if you wish to work on children's theatre and take a performance to the local primary school.

Historical documentary material
Here are some specific events and broad historical themes you might use as the basis for devising a documentary play:

The match-girls' strike at Bryant & May's factory (1888): An Internet search will give rich material, evocative photographs and engaging historical characters, e.g. Annie Besant.

Tutankhamun's tomb: Accounts of the opening by Howard Carter and the subsequent fate of those involved make good material for devising. There is scope for drama pursuing the 'curse of the tomb' in a mystery/horror genre, for going back to the time of the pharaohs and the original burial (e.g. how did Tutankhamun die?) and scope for parody, pastiche or thriller.

The Titanic disaster: Lots of documentary accounts and information on the Internet make this a good topic for a documentary or a fictionalised drama.

Evacuees: Children evacuated in the Second World War.

The history of the youth service or of teenagers: Linking documentary legislation/world events with changing fashions and social attitudes. This can mix the light hearted with the serious. You can have a lot of fun with music, fashion and creating a composite collage style setting.

Life stories: Famous or infamous people from a wide variety of walks of life, e.g. Nelson Mandela, Judy Garland, Paul Robeson, Mary Seacole, Emily Pankhurst, Galileo.

Miscellaneous stimulus items
Adapting parts of classic stories or novels, e.g. *Dr Jekyll and Mr Hyde* by Robert Louis Stevenson, *The Tell Tale Heart* by Edgar Alan Poe, *The Hunchback of Notre Dame* by Victor Hugo.

Adapting song lyrics, e.g. *Celebrity, Another Brick in the Wall, She's Leaving Home*, or poems.

Websites
Playwright Neil Duffield's website http://homepage.ntlworld.com/n.duffield1/childrens.htm lists a wide variety of engaging texts suitable for young actors.

The major theatre companies all have very good websites with educational resources with video clips that provide good material for drama activities.

On the Globe Theatre site www.shakespeares-globe.org/globeeducation the Much Ado resource has a very helpful section on the language which will help you understand such elements as iambic pentameters.

The National Theatre website www.nationaltheatre.org.uk is a very rich source. The education section www.nationaltheatre.org.uk/discover has some excellent general support material. For material on specific texts, e.g. *The Crucible, His Dark Materials, The Caucasian Chalk Circle, Women of Troy, Henry V, War Horse*, see www.stagework.org/stageworks/productions.html

The Royal Shakespeare Company site www.rsc.org.uk/learning focuses on all things to do with the Bard.

Barnardo's site www.barnardos.org.uk has good resource material on its history including an excellent photo archive. It also has resources on contemporary issues relating to young people.

The National Archives Learning Curve site provides a rich wide-ranging history archive, including authentic testimony, case histories, documents and pictures. It is ideal for adding personal life stories to historical research or for creating a documentary drama. Visit www.learningcurve.gov.uk/index/keystage4.htm – other key stages may also be useful.

The website www.getintotheatre.org has lots of useful information on technical aspects of theatre as well as on careers in the arts.

Websites such as www.nasa.gov/home are very high quality and useful for drama work specifically related to space exploration.

Stagecraft Books and Websites

Books

The Stagecraft Handbook by Daniel A. Ionazzi, published by Betterway Books, Cincinnati, Ohio, 1996, ISBN 978-155870404-6

Improvisation for the Theater by Viola Spolin, 3rd edition, published by Northwestern University Press, USA, 1999, ISBN 978-081014008-0

Theatre of the Oppressed by Augusto Boal, new revised edition, published by Pluto Press, 2008, ISBN 978-074532838-6

Theatres of the Left: 1880–1935: Workers' Theatre Movement in Britain and America (History Workshop) by Raphael Samuel, MacColl, Cosgrove. Out of print but available in reference libraries.

Caspar Neher – Brecht's Designer by John Willett, published by Methuen in association with the Arts Council of Great Britain, London, 1986, ISBN 0-413-41240-7

Websites

Performance space
www.sceno.org/theatre-design-101/ and www.bbc.co.uk/schools/gcsebitesize/drama/performing/stagerev1.shtml

Early stage designer's sketches
www2.arts.ubc.ca/TheatreDesign/crslib/drw09/skch1.htm

Physical theatre
www.4dr.co.uk and www.dv8.co.uk

Glossary

In this section, you will find definitions of terms used in the **language of drama** (see pages 3–4) including all the terms highlighted in blue in the text of this book.

Some words refer to conventions, forms, strategies and techniques for exploring and expressing meaning through drama. Many of these explorative strategies can be used both as exercises to help you develop your drama and in performance work (e.g. still images or marking the moment).

These definitions are designed to help you in your GCSE Drama work. There may be times when you come across some terms being used in a slightly different way.

Absurd theatre – The writer Martin Esslin invented this description. He used it to describe the plays of some post-1945 writers in Europe and the USA who felt that the values of society had disintegrated and no longer existed. Playwrights often included under this heading are Samuel Beckett, Eugene Ionesco, Harold Pinter and Jean Genet, although they never described their own work using this term. Also known as **theatre of the absurd**.

Accepting – In improvisation, 'accepting' the role, situation or circumstances which another player suggests. For example, if Player A says, 'Will they ever let us out of this place?' then Player B would accept the implication that the characters are being held captive. (See also **Blocking**)

Acting – The art of mimicking, imitating, representing or portraying another personality or role. It is what actors do when they are performing a role to an audience or on film. **Acting out** refers to more process-based work where situations and roles are acted out

in order to understand and experience a particular set of circumstances. It is acting without the need to be concerned with the 'trappings' of a performance.

Action – The events that happen in a drama or play and that an audience witnesses taking place on stage.

Action narration – A technique where a narrative is read out and performers react to the actions being described.

Actions – What a character does in a play. Actions may be physical or psychological but will usually impact on the plot and on other characters as well as on the individual who initiates the action.

Agitprop – From the Russian phrase *agitatsiya-propaganda*, theatre which has political agitation and propaganda as its main purpose.

Alienation – See **Making strange**

Allegory – A story, picture or drama in which the meaning is represented through symbols.

Alter ego – Latin term meaning 'other self' – a second self, or opposite character. Alter ego is a technique sometimes referred to as **devil and angel** or **good angel/bad angel**. Its most common form is where as someone acts out a character, another person speaks their thoughts out loud. The purpose of the technique is to demonstrate how a character can be saying something quite different to what they are thinking. It is a useful exercise for exploring subtext.

Anagnorisis – Originally used by Aristotle to describe the way in which a character comes to recognise their true identity. Its broader meaning relates to any moment in a play where something about the characters or the situation is revealed.

Analogy – Recreating a situation in a different context. This can help understanding of difficult or sensitive issues.

Anti-climax – A climax is where everything comes together as a conclusion. An anti-climax, conversely, is incomplete so can be disappointing or unsatisfying.

Arena staging – A form of theatre in-the-round where the audience surrounds the stage. Ancient Greek theatres had arena stages and the term suggests performances on a large scale.

Artefact – An object which might be used as a starting point in a drama activity. Artefacts (which on stage become props) can signify context, actions and meaning.

Aside – A dramatic convention when an actor addresses the audience but the other characters are unaware that they are doing so.

Audience – For this course audience is defined as *those for whom the performance or outcome is intended*. The nature of the relationship between performers and an audience is the cause of much debate. Argument centres around the relative passivity of the audience in relation to the action on stage. In your drama work the audience may be fellow participants, whereas in a theatrical performance the audience may take a more observational stance. Some types of performance (e.g. street theatre) call for greater audience involvement. (See also **Fourth wall** and **Spect-actor**)

Auditorium – The area within a theatre that accommodates the audience.

Back story – Providing a history to a character or plot before the events in the play, scene or drama being enacted.

Blocking – In improvisation work, the opposite of accepting. The role, situation or circumstances which other players suggest is blocked by an individual through deliberate contradiction. For example, if Player A says, 'Will this bus ever get us to the airport?' then Player B might block the idea by saying, 'I'm glad we decided to catch the train.' In experienced hands this might have surreal possibilities, but will generally inhibit the flow of the improvisation.

Caption making – Looking at an image or a freeze frame and deciding on a simple, short statement that represents what is happening. This strategy can also be used to look at sections of scenes to help you understand the structure of a scene.

Caricature – Exaggerating the nature of a character, usually for comic effect. This can involve emphasising a particular vocal or physical mannerism.

Catharsis – Where matters in a drama come to a head and there is a moment of emotional release.

Centring – A technique to focus the actor, sometimes referred to as 'grounding'.

Character – The person/persona that an actor wishes to convey. The term is used interchangeably with role, but character tends to have a more specific meaning, and refer to an actual person. A character, for example, can play a number of roles in a play such as parent, employer and friend, as individuals do in real life. Also an actor can play a number of differing roles in a play, each of which can be a different character. (See also **Role**)

Character transfer/Role transfer – When one person begins acting out a character or role then passes it on to another person to develop, imitate or alter.

Choreography – Used in dance to describe the creative process of putting a series of movements together to create a piece. Choreographed work in drama is movement that follows a prescribed plan that has been carefully worked through and thought out. Stage fights, for example, are usually highly choreographed.

Chorus/chorus work – A group of people working collectively using vocal and movement skills to communicate thoughts, feelings and ideas. The group may act homogeneously, as one whole, or be broken down into subgroups. Like a classical Greek chorus, they may narrate a story, comment on the action or express an opinion.

Climax – The moment when the threads of the plot or events in a play come together and are satisfactorily resolved. There is a sense in most plays or drama of a build-up in tension towards a climactic point, followed by some kind of resolution. (See also **Anti-climax**)

Collage – Putting together a 'patchwork' of dialogue, sounds and visual images from different contexts to provide an impressionistic presentation – where what is seen and experienced may be more important than what is heard in dialogue. For example, fragments of scenes from *Romeo and Juliet* could be selected and linked together and presented as a 'collage version'. The way in which the material is juxtaposed, organised and presented can shed new meaning on the characters, their situation, the playwright's intentions and the language of the play.

Collective character/role – Similar to chorus work, but each individual plays the same character. A character can be played in unison by the group so that each movement, gesture and spoken word is replicated by everyone. Alternatively, each person can demonstrate different aspects of the character.

Commedia dell'arte – Developed in Italy in the sixteenth century and spread across Europe. Mainly improvised drama, it has stock characters, uses masks, tumbling and other skills of a physical nature. Some modern playwrights claim to be influenced by its form, including Berkoff.

Communal voice – A variation on chorus work where a group of performers speaks with 'one voice'. Here the voice of the chorus has a shared understanding and views about a situation or character.

Composite setting – A stage setting where several locations are represented in the same space and isolated or highlighted by lighting each area separately.

Conscience corridor/Conscience alley/ Thought tunnel – Two straight lines are formed and the individuals in each group face each other with a gap (the corridor, alley or tunnel) of about 1 metre between them. A person in a role which the whole group knows about in advance walks through the corridor. As they move from one end to the other, they hear thoughts or questions from each person either side of them. This exercise is useful for character building and development.

Context – The situation or circumstances in which a piece of drama is set or devised, including historical, cultural or social influences. Context may be explored using the 'W' questions: What? Who? Why? Where? When?

Convention – **Stage conventions** or **theatrical conventions** are practices that have become accepted over time or that can be established within a performance piece. For example, it is a convention in pantomime that the Dame is played by a male performer and the Principal Boy by a female performer.

'Convention' may also be used to describe drama activities such as conscience corridor.

Costuming games – Using costume to drive forward an improvisation, usually spontaneous. The costume may be a full one, or an accessory such as a hat, handbag or walking stick.

Cross-cutting – A term which comes from film editing. This involves changing back and forth between scenes or episodes of action. The first scene runs up to a selected point and the action freezes or the lights fade out on it. As this happens, the second scene starts and runs up to another 'cutting point'. The action reverts (cuts) to a section of the first scene. The process of switching between scenes continues.

Dance drama – A type of performance that is a crossover between dance and drama, using movement to music to express an idea or communicate a narrative.

Denouement – The point in the plot near the end where everything is explained.

Designer – Set, costume, lighting, sound, make-up, properties, furniture and mixed media will all be considered by a designer as part of the design concept. Taken together these support the drama by developing atmosphere, using symbol or by creating an appropriate environment for the work.

Deviser – Creator of drama, whether it is improvised or in the form of a script. Devised drama covers work created by you and work created by others, including published plays. See page 4 for more about the Context of Deviser.

Director – The function of the director is to guide the development of the drama, structuring it in a way that will maximise the impact upon an audience.

Documentary theatre – A form of theatre which examines an event or issue by presenting evidence, filling in lack of knowledge with educated guesses. The focus of documentary theatre may be something that is about to happen in a community. Here the drama may attempt to demonstrate that this would be a mistake, by drawing on research and resources to show a picture based on evidence. Other examples may look at historical events and ask questions about the decisions that were made.

Doubling/Doubling up – When the same performer plays more than one role/part in a play or when more than one player portrays the same role.

Dramatic irony – Where the audience knows more about a situation on stage than one of the characters in the drama.

Dramatic resonance – When specific dramatic ideas or scenarios are engaging for both the actors to work with and an audience to watch. The potential to create theatrical meaning or tension.

Dramatic tension – Moments in a drama where the audience feels a heightened sense of anticipation about what is going to happen next.

Dramatic theatre – Aristotle's model of drama that has an exposition, followed by development, building in tension towards a cathartic climax and ending in resolution.

End-on staging – When a space is divided in two with the performance space in one section and the audience in the other, facing the performance space.

Ensemble – This term can refer to performers working together as a group or to the cast of a production other than the protagonists or leading players.

Epic Theatre – A reaction to dramatic theatre which is manifest in Brecht's later work. Features of Epic Theatre include episodic scenes, a lack of tension, breaking the theatrical illusion through devices such as direct audience address, use of songs, projections and narration. Elements of Epic Theatre can be found in earlier plays such as the use of the chorus in Greek drama and short episodic scenes in Shakespeare.

Epilogue – Speech or scene that closes a play or presentation and comments on the drama.

Explorative strategy – Term used to describe many of the activities listed here. For example, still image and conscience alley are strategies that help to explore situations and characters.

Exposition – Giving the audience necessary information, usually but not always near the beginning of a drama or story.

Flashback – The enacting of a moment from a character's past. This can also be used as a strategy to explore a character's behaviour, emotions and attitude. Flashbacks are often found in drama structure where the meat of the plot is contained in events that occurred before the starting point of the play, and the action moves between the past and the present, often in a series of mini scenes. (See also **Back story**)

Form – The shape and structure of a drama. In theatre, form is determined by the content of the drama (e.g. the way the playwright has constructed the narrative elements) and by the way it is presented (the choices made by actors, designers and directors in interpreting the material for performance). Form is closely associated with genre and these terms are often confused but they do not have the same meaning. For example, a play classified as in a naturalistic genre will be recognised by the audience as naturalistic by the form it takes on stage. (See also **Genre** and **Style**)

Forum theatre – A way of working developed by Augusto Boal. Participants sit or stand in a large circle to observe an improvisation usually started by two of them. The improvisation is based on a given situation or set of circumstances agreed by the group at the outset. At any point, the performers can stop the action and ask the rest of the group (the forum) for help or advice about what to do or say next. The improvisation may continue from the point of interruption or start again. Anyone from the forum can also stop the action if they think what is happening is inappropriate or believe that the drama should be taken in a different direction. They can either offer advice, decide to take over from one of the performers or join in by taking on another role.

Fourth wall – The idea that the stage is like a room with four walls with the audience looking in 'through' one of the walls. Associated with Naturalism, where there is a convention that the performers act as though the audience is not there.

Frame distancing – A device developed by Dorothy Heathcote to explore issues at one remove from the original incident. For example, rather than depicting the scene of an accident at the school gates, the action might be frame distanced by playing a scene at the gates the next day with bouquets of flowers placed where the accident happened. Or the same content might be approached through different frames, e.g. you could also be framed as council employees tasked to draw up road-safety guidelines that arise from the incident.

Framing – A technique similar to storyboarding in film. Framing uses sheets of paper each containing a blank frame. In each frame, an image is drawn to represent a moment or scene from the drama being developed. The image may be given a title or a caption or key lines of dialogue may be used as speech bubbles. The frames are each given a number and can then be ordered into any sequence. So instead of playing the events of the drama in the order 1, 2, 3, 4, the sequence can run 4, 2, 3, 1. (See also **Storyboard**)

Freeze frame – During an improvisation or the playing of a scene, the instruction 'Freeze' is called out and the performers hold their positions at that moment. This has the same effect as holding down the pause button on a DVD player. 'Freeze frame' is often misused to describe a still image or tableau – these are not freeze frames but techniques used to consciously set up a stage picture. (See also **Still image** and **Tableau**)

Genre – A category of drama identifiable by common elements, usually characterised by the nature of its subject matter or its form of performance. A genre may be linked to a historical period, or to a particular company or group of practitioners. Genres such as comedy, tragedy, musicals, melodrama and pantomime have easily identifiable features and everyone involved in a performance, including the audience, will understand the conventions and codes used. Other genres, such as Naturalism, Expressionism and Epic Theatre, are more difficult to pin down but can often be identified from their form or elements of their style). (See also **Form** and **Style**)

Gestus – A term associated with the use of gesture. Brecht uses it to refer to the attitude or stance of one character in relation to another, communicated through behaviour, movement, expression and intonation. Relationships between characters are determined by social conditions and conventions. So, if two characters are separated by being rich and poor, this will predetermine the attitude of one to the other. This attitude will come across through gesture irrespective of what is being said.

Given circumstances – According to Stanislavski, this refers to all of the available information that an actor uses in creating a role.

Giving witness – Giving factual and eyewitness evidence about what has happened in the same way as a witness in a trial. This can be used as a technique to reflect on performance and in the development of a character. It may also be used as an element of performance to 'break the fourth wall' and help an audience retain objectivity and avoid empathy.

Good angel/bad angel – See **Alter ego**

Guided tour – An exercise to develop the use of the imagination. Someone acts as a tour guide and shows people around an imaginary place.

Hot seating – A technique used to gain a deeper understanding of a character or role. An individual sits in a chair designated as the 'hot seat'. The rest of the group asks the person in the hot seat relevant questions about their feelings, thoughts, actions or circumstances. The person in the hot seat answers the questions in role or as they think the character they are playing would answer.

Improvisation – Performing quickly in response to something or acting without previous planning. **Spontaneous improvisation** refers to making up a role as you go along. **Prepared/planned improvisation** refers to working and reworking within a structure of ideas and roles agreed in advance.

Irony – Using language that is the opposite of what is happening in a form of sarcasm. **Dramatic irony** refers to the audience knowing something that the characters do not.

Kitchen-sink drama – A type of drama that developed as a reaction to the middle-class, drawing-room, polite settings that provided most of the contexts for plays in the 1940s and 1950s. Kitchen-sink drama can be set anywhere, including the kitchen, uses realistic language, involves the working class, and can take anything at all for its content.

Making strange – Brecht's expression *Verfremdungseffekt* is often misleadingly translated from the German as **alienation**, but 'making strange' is more accurate. It refers to the devices and acting style used in Epic Theatre to distance the audience from having any sense that the theatrical experience is real. Brecht used the word to describe how it makes something ordinary and everyday fresh and exciting, so that the audience sees it in a new light.

Mantle of the expert – A technique developed by Dorothy Heathcote that places a whole group in the role of experts. For example, the task might be to design a museum exhibition about life in Shakespeare's England. Each member of the group is assigned a role and has to carry out research and tasks related to that role. Different information is fed into the drama, usually linked to problems that will need solving. For example, the teacher might enter in role as the Health and Safety Officer and question the way the exhibition is being planned.

Marking the moment – A convention used to highlight a significant point in a drama. It can be achieved through techniques such as freeze frame, spotlighting, narrated announcements, projected captions, sound effects, musical underscoring or changing the lighting.

Melodrama – Although music gave melodrama its name – literally 'play accompanied by music' – it is its content and style that has given it a distinctive quality as a genre in Britain. At its height during the 1800s, it had a number of recognisable features. Religion, morals and the law were upheld and there had to be a happy ending so that it could be seen that wrong did not win, and that the villain was dealt with. Usually, the villain would confess their guilt and express remorse. Today, melodrama is often considered as comedy where the actors overact and shout and declaim, and no one really takes it seriously.

Metaphor – Using the imagination to describe something by saying it is something else. For example, a journey might be used in a drama as a metaphor for someone's life, with a crossroads representing a particular moment in their life.

Method acting – A system where actors rely on their own emotional memory (as advocated by Stanislavski) and/or detailed observation/ research to create a role. The emphasis is on the sensory, psychological and emotional rather than the more external techniques of more 'classical' acting. Lee Strasberg's New York Actors Studio in the 1950s popularised the 'method' and actors associated with it include Marlon Brando, James Dean and Robert de Niro.

Mime – Communicating emotion, meaning or an idea without words, using only gesture, expression and movement.

Modelled reading/performance – An actor or teacher with developed expertise delivers some text or written words. In their reading they model commitment, focus with artistic use of voice and gesture.

Monologue – Literally 'one person speaking'. Monologue is a genre in its own right (e.g. the film *Shirley Valentine*), but in other genres it can also be a speech enacted by one character alone on stage. Dialogue spoken by a narrator can take the form of a monologue. A soliloquy is a particular type of monologue where a character speaks their inner thoughts out loud to the audience.

Montage – A term from film production referring to a dramatic sequence made up of a series of connected but different images edited together. (See also **Collage**)

Morality play – An allegory where the characters represent an idea or moral stance.

Motif – A distinctive feature or dominant idea in dance, drama, music and creative writing or in art, decorative designs and patterns.

Mystery play – Drama, from medieval times, on religious topics, such as retelling stories from the Bible. These plays were often one of a cycle. They were staged on pageant wagons and prepared/supported by trade guilds.

Narration – Dialogue designed to tell the story or provide accompanying information. Narration can accompany on-stage action or be presented in its own right.

Narrator – A role that functions like a storyteller. A narrator can be used to describe the action, provide a commentary or give additional information. A narrator can be present on stage or be an off-stage or prerecorded voice.

Naturalism/Naturalistic – A genre that attempts to replicate nature and present events and characters on stage as in real life. Not always distinguishable from Realism, Naturalism attempts to hold up a mirror to nature and give the illusion of characters as actual people in real-life situations using everyday language. As an artistic movement, Naturalism originated in the late nineteenth century, later than Realism. Naturalism is said to be less concerned with authenticity than Realism. (See also **Realism**)

Noises off – Sounds that come from offstage that represent something that is happening.

For example, a crash from another room, the sound of breaking glass, or a shout by another character. Usually these sounds are provided live but can be recorded as a sound effect. The sound can start off an improvisation or can change the direction of a scene.

Obligatory moments – Those moments in a drama that the audience anticipate. The audience will feel cheated if they do not occur.

Open stage – A performance space that thrusts out into the audience. Shakespeare's Globe Theatre was an example of this. (See also **Thrust staging**)

Performance style – See **Style**

Peripeteia – A twist in the plot that normally occurs towards the end of the play. The audience has been led in one direction and suddenly finds that the ending is different to what they have been led to expect.

Physical theatre – A theatre form and a performance style that emphasises and exaggerates the movement and gestures used in performance. It is a form very close to contemporary dance and requires performers to be fit and agile. It can also extend to mask work, mime and use elements of circus skills. Companies like DV8, Trestle and Complicite are major practitioners of this type of work.

Plot – The outline of what happens in a literary work, story or the action of a play. The way a character responds to the situation and how other characters, in turn, respond.

Planned improvisation – See **Improvisation**

Pressure circle – A character in a drama who has reached a crisis point or dilemma is circled by other actors. These actors speak lines or gesture in a way that emphasises the problematic situation that character finds him/herself in.

Prologue – Speech or scene introducing a play or presentation. It often sets the scene or introduces the action.

Promenade staging – When the audience moves around to different areas or stages in a performance space. Medieval mystery plays performed on carts and wagons are an early example of this.

Proscenium staging – A type of staging sometimes described as the 'picture-frame stage'. The term 'proscenium arch' refers to pillars and a crosspiece that make up a division between audience and acting space, framing the action on stage.

Proxemics – A term borrowed from studies of the organisation of human space. When applied to the theatre, it describes how spatial relationships between one performer and other performers and between the performers and their stage environment work and create meaning.

Ranking – An exercise used to explore the status of roles or character. Each performer ranks their role according to a quality such as social standing or economic prosperity and assigns a number between one and, say, ten. The exercise can be repeated at any time to find out if the status of the role has altered during the course of the drama.

Realism – A genre that sets out to portray everyday life as faithfully as possible. It originated in the visual arts during the early part of the nineteenth century. In drama, it requires an approach to acting that depicts natural behaviour and speech and is anti-illusory in character. The terms 'Realism' and 'Naturalism' are used interchangeably, but Realism is said to be more concerned with detail and aims to be closer to real life than Naturalism. (See also **Naturalism**)

Repertoire – A collection of regularly performed pieces or techniques, usually attributed to a particular performer or playwright.

Representation/Representational – In this style characters represent an idea. Setting and props may also be used as symbols.

Rising action – The events that build up the pace and perhaps the excitement in a plot/drama.

Ritual ceremony – Repeated activity that has special meaning. It may be related to a religion or to simple contemporary rituals such as the way teams march out at a football match, or chants the crowd may shout.

Role – Used generally to refer to any part portrayed by an actor in a play. It may be used rather than 'character' to refer to more representational figures in a drama such as Death, Devil, First Man, First Woman or non-human representations such as War, Peace, Dog, Fidelity.

Role-on-the-wall – A life-sized outline of a figure is drawn on the wall to represent a character or role being developed or explored. Members of the group take it in turns to write facts and information about the character/role within the outline. Physical details might all be written in the head area, for example, whereas things the character likes might be written in the right leg. Opinions and views from other people or characters can be added around the outside of the figure.

Role play – Pretending to be someone (or something) else. Role play is generally confined to taking on a clearly defined role such as a doctor, a bus driver or teacher without any attempt at in-depth psychological analysis or understanding. What distinguishes it from acting is that role play is not intended for performance to an audience.

Role reversal/Role transfer – When, during an improvisation or rehearsal for a scene, the actors swap the roles/characters they are portraying to gain a different view or understanding of their own role.

Satire – A form using ridicule and irony to expose foolishness, often of higher-ranking or hypocritical characters or events.

Sculpting – A technique used in conjunction with still-image work developed by Augusto Boal into image theatre. A group is divided into sculptors and sculptees. There are normally only one or two sculptors, who create a sculpture by moving the sculptees into different positions and stances in response to a stimulus or idea.

Semiotics – How meaning is created and communicated through systems of encodable and decodable signs and symbols of drama. The way meaning is signalled to an audience.

Shaping – The way a section of a drama, which may be very small, is moulded to deliver the meaning intended by the deviser or by the director. Ideas are developed into a form that will achieve an effect or impact. Shaping exists within structure. (See also **Structure**)

Signs and symbols – These relate to semiotics, but all of the elements that make up a theatrical presentation have meaning and an audience 'reads' or interprets the whole experience as a series of signs and symbols. There is a subtle but important distinction between signs and symbols: signs suggest or 'signal' meaning but a symbol is a sign in itself that represents something else. For example, a clenched fist can be interpreted as a sign of aggression but it can also be a symbol for power or solidarity.

Simulations – These are designed to imitate or represent real events, enacting what might actually happen. For example, the emergency services may run a simulation of a disaster such as a train crash for training purposes.

Social drama – Plays with strong, everyday content, reflecting social situations and based on reality. Often very down-to-earth in their content.

Soundscape – Using sounds to create an aural environment for a scene. A director or designer might develop a soundscape to create an atmosphere appropriate to the drama. Each individual might create a sound appropriate to accompany or introduce the scene. For example, one person might make sea sounds vocally while another imitates the cry of a seagull to suggest the seaside. Repeated words and phrases overlapping each other can also be used to suggest a location or to portray sounds in a character's head from a nightmare or series of flashbacks.

Spect-actor – A term from the work of Augusto Boal that describes participants in a drama that are both observing it and taking part in it, as in forum theatre.

Split screen – A technique where two or more scenes take place in a performance space simultaneously or alternate with each other.

Spontaneous improvisation – See **Improvisation**

Spotlighting – Replaying an improvisation or scene with the action redefined by focusing attention on a selected area of the performance space. This can be done by using lighting or marking the floor area, so that in the replaying, any action that previously happened outside this area no longer takes place. (See also **Marking the moment**)

Stereotype – A role that has set characteristics, easily recognisable and sometimes exaggerated, and that follows consistently a generally agreed form.

Stichomythia – Dialogue first used in classical Greek drama where characters alternate lines of dialogue, usually to build up dramatic tension. It is typically found in scenes that involve two characters arguing, with one trying to outdo the other.

Still image – Creating a picture to represent a frozen moment or to sum up what is happening in a drama. It is a useful technique for exploring the effects of positioning characters in relation to one another in terms of levels and proximity and to demonstrate non-verbal communication. It is often used with sculpting and thoughts in the head. (See also **Tableau**)

Stock character – A role with set characteristics that may be used frequently in certain types of drama, e.g. melodrama.

Storyboarding – A series of images and/or text showing the sequence of the action planned for a play. (See also **Framing**)

Strategies – A term used synonymously with 'techniques', 'forms' and 'conventions' to describe the kind of drama activities listed here.

Stream of consciousness – Where there is no structure except to follow the flow.

Structure – The way a piece of drama is put together; the connections between episodes, scenes or acts; the framework. (See also **Shaping**)

Style – How a drama might be performed. Style is often indistinguishable from genre and form. For a drama to be recognised as being in a particular genre, it has to be presented in a way which has the hallmarks of that genre. Style refers to the way the actors perform, the visual characteristics of the setting and costumes, and the choice of conventions used. Confusingly, a drama belonging to one genre (e.g. Naturalism) can be presented in different styles. For example, the acting may be in a naturalistic style but the stage design in an abstract style.

Stylisation/Stylised – The process of selecting elements of a character, situation or setting to present on stage. In one sense, all drama is about simplifying reality and making artistic decisions about what to show and how to represent it on stage. Stylisation is the conscious process of emphasising and often exaggerating elements of the design or characteristics of a role.

Subtext – In narratives, this term refers to a secondary plot or storyline. In acting and character analysis, it refers to the idea that there are other meanings below the surface of what is actually said and done.

Suspension of disbelief – The idea that an audience watching a drama is willing to accept that what is happening on stage (or on film) is real.

Symbols – See **Signs and symbols**

Tableau(x) – A dramatic grouping of characters. A tableau may not necessarily be a still or frozen image. It can be a general 'stage picture' during a sequence in a scene where dialogue may be spoken and gestures used. In tableau vivant, the performers are positioned to represent a picture or 'fresco', and props and costumes are often used as an integral part of the stage picture. 'Tableau' can also be used to describe a pause on stage where all performers briefly freeze in position. This can typically be found at the end of scenes in Victorian melodramas. (See also **Still image**)

Teacher-in-role – When a class or group of participants in a drama accepts that the teacher (or leader) is going to play a role to which they are going to react and respond. The participants may or may not be in role.

Technique – Used here to refer to drama forms, exercises, strategies and conventions that are widely used to develop understanding and explore meaning through the drama process. In a broader context, techniques encompass the whole range of physical and psychological processes and exercises that an actor might use to develop their skills as a performer.

Tension – See **Dramatic tension**

Theatre-in-education (TIE) – A movement that developed in the 1960s whose principal purpose is to use theatre in educational settings to teach an audience about a particular issue, idea or theme. It often involves the audience as participants in the drama.

Theatre-in-the-round – A type of performance space where the audience surrounds the acting space on all sides.

Theatre of the absurd – See **Absurd theatre**

Thought tunnel – See **Conscience corridor**

Thoughts in the head/Thought tracking – An exercise that allows the inner thoughts of a character or role to be heard out loud. It is often used with freeze frame or still image, where a participant is asked to say what they are thinking at that point in time.

Thrust staging – Where the audience is on three sides of the performance space.

Transporting a character – Technique used to explore how a character or person in role might react or behave in a different situation,

location or time. For example, an intimate bedroom scene between two lovers might be transported to a crowded supermarket.

Traverse staging – Where the audience is on either side of the performance space.

Unities (of time, place and action) – Aristotle's analysis of classical drama identifies a certain consistency about timescale, location and action. Plays that conform to these unities contain events that take place within one day, in the same place and have action that is limited to what can be expected to be seen in the one place. For example, extraordinary events like murder happen off stage and are reported on by a messenger.

Verfremdungseffekt – See **Making strange**

Vignette – A short, evocative episode, bringing to mind strong images, memories or feelings, that may focus on a character or event.

Warm-ups – Exercises or games designed to warm up the body or voice in preparation for performance or drama work. Warm-ups can include icebreakers, to help a group of people to work together and get to know each other, or exercises to stimulate the imagination and the creative thinking process.

Workshop – Has developed to mean a type of performance that is less formal. 'To workshop' a play means to present it to an invited audience in order to receive some kind of feedback before developing the work further. 'Workshop' can refer to any practical drama session and it is quite common for professional theatre companies to offer workshops to schools and colleges that are linked to a performance. It may also refer to an area where sets, costumes and props are made.

Writing in role – An exercise where, for example, a letter, a diary or journal is written as if by the character or role being portrayed. It is a useful technique in work on building character.

Index

Acknowledgements

The Publishers would like to thank the following for permission to reproduce copyright material:

Photography and other imagery
p. iv: © Sheila Burnett/ArenaPAL; p. vi: © Johann Persson/ArenaPAL; pp. 3, 4, 5 & 7: © Gareth Price; p. 12: photo © Nobby Clark from *Snake in the Grass*, a Stephen Joseph Theatre production; p. 15: photo © Nobby Clark from *The Lion, The Witch and The Wardrobe*, a Birmingham Rep production; p. 17: © Donald Cooper/ Photostage; p. 24: © Keith Thomson; p. 28: © Roger-Viollet/ Topfoto; p. 30: © Keith Thomson; p. 32: © The Granger Collection/Topfoto; p. 35: © Andrew Billington, courtesy of the New Vic Theatre; p. 37 (both): courtesy of the Stephen Joseph Theatre, Scarborough; p. 39t: courtesy of the Natural Theatre Company; p. 39b: courtesy of the Minack Theatre, Porthcurno; p. 40: photo © Nobby Clark from *The Lion, The Witch and The Wardrobe*, a Birmingham Rep production; p. 41: © Keith Thomson; p. 42: courtesy of Leicestershire Arts in Education; p. 48t: photo © Robert Day from *Dangerous Corner*, a New Vic production; p. 48b: photo © Nobby Clark from *Haunting Julia*, a Stephen Joseph Theatre production; p. 51: © Keith Thomson; pp. 57, 58, 60 & 62: © Donald Cooper/ Photostage; p. 65: © Eric Bornstein/Behind the Mask Theatre; p. 66: © Manuel Harlan, used with the permission of Frantic Assembly; p. 67: © Dave Gatward, used with the permission of Woodhouse Players; p. 75: © Dan Whitmarsh, used with the permission of Suffolk Youth Theatre; p. 79: photo © Nobby Clark from *Snake in the Grass*, a Stephen Joseph Theatre production; pp. 101 & 102: © Gareth Price; p. 109: © The Granger Collection/Topfoto; p. 111: © R. M. Fryer, used with the permission of Exeter School; pp. 117 & 120: © Gareth Price; p. 122: © Donald Cooper/Photostage; p. 126: © Gareth Price; p. 130: © John Kobal Foundation/Getty Images; p. 131: © Courtesy Everett Foundation/Getty Images; pp. 133 (all) & 135: © Gareth Price; p. 142: © bpk/Willi Saeger; p. 145: © Gareth Price; p. 150: © akg-images; p. 153 © bpk/Kunstbibliothek, SMB/Deitmar Katz; pp. 157 & 158: © Gareth Price; p. 159: Reg Wilson © RSC; p. 163: photo © Spencer Arnold/Getty Images; p. 164: © Crispin Rodwell/ Alamy; p. 166: © studiomode/Alamy; p. 168 © Gareth Price; p. 170: © Bert Hardy/Getty Images; p. 183 © Corbis. All rights reserved; p. 184 (both): © Bridgeman Art Library; p. 187: © Donald Cooper/Photostage; p. 189: © Gareth Price; p. 193: © Time Life Pictures/Mansell/Getty Images; p. 194: © MPI/ Getty Images; p. 202: © Gareth Price; pp. 207 & 208: © John Arden and Margaretta D'Arcy, used with permission; pp. 211, 218, 222 & 226: © Gareth Price; p. 229: © Keith Thomson; pp. 231 (both) & 232 (both): set designs © Sue Pyecroft; pp. 235 (both) & 236 (all): photos © John Tillotson, set design © Sue Pyecroft; p. 237l: photo © John Tillotson, costume design © Sue Pyecroft; p. 237r: costume design © Sue Pyecroft; p. 238t: photo © John Tillotson, costume design © Sue Pyecroft; p. 238r: costume design © Sue Pyecroft; p. 240: © the estate of Charles Keeping; p. 241 (all): © John Tillotson.

Text extracts
pp. 112–113: the song for *Julius Caesar* was devised by David Cross and members of the Leicestershire Arts in Education Youth Theatre; pp. 148–149: from Bertolt Brecht, *The Threepenny Opera*, trans. Ralph Manheim and John Willett, reprinted with the permission of Methuen Drama, an imprint of A&C Black Publishers; p. 183t: text from the website of Casa Alianza is used with permission; pp. 196, 198, 200–201: from *Pocohontas – A North American Myth* devised by David Cross and members of the Leicestershire Arts in Education Youth Theatre; pp.206–209: from the Production Notes for *Island of the Mighty* © John Arden and Margaretta D'Arcy, reprinted with permission; p. 230: from the Set Notes to *A Christmas Carol* © Neil Duffield.

Earlier versions/parts of the 'theatre detectives' activity on pp. 144–147 and the 'Dead Warrior' activities on pp. 157–163 first appeared in articles written by David Cross for *Teaching Drama* (Rhinegold Publishing Ltd, www.rhinegold.co.uk).

Every effort has been made to trace all copyright holders, but if any have been inadvertently overlooked the Publishers will be pleased to make the necessary arrangements at the first opportunity.

The Authors and Publishers would also like to thank the following: the students whose written work appears in this book – Rosie Gaston, Alicia Martino, Roshny Patel, Hannah Roberts and Krupa Thakrar; the students whose drama practical work features in photographs in this book: Matthew Bateman, Felicity Bolger, Peter Byrne, Natasha Cartwright, Joanne Finnegan, Anne-Marie Heeley, Kane Jackson, Thomas Kaye, Natasha Kondrashova, Isabel Lamb, Aisling Lammond, Monika Lorek, Larnie Mallion, Jordan Muggleton, Susan Mullen, Emma Mycroft, Stephanie Newsome, Allan Rafferty, Megan Smith, Emily Turner, Kyle Walker, Nikita Watson-Paley, Brandon Watts; the design team for *A Christmas Carol* at Leicestershire Arts in Education: Linda Burton, Annie Kinchington, Jane Towers and scenic artist Eddy Gadd; St Benedict's Catholic School and Performing Arts College, Derby, for hosting some of the photography of student work specially commissioned for the book.